"Long Years
of Neglect"

PORTRAIT OF WILLIAM GILMORE SIMMS BY WILLIAM WEST
COURTESY OF MARY C. SIMMS OLIPHANT FURNAM

"Long Years of Neglect"

The Work and Reputation of
William Gilmore Simms

Edited by John Caldwell Guilds

Essays in Honor of
Thomas Cary Duncan Eaves

The University of Arkansas Press
Fayetteville • London
1988

Designer: Francile Otto
Typeface: Linotron 202 Century Schoolbook
Typesetter: G & S Typesetters, Inc.
Printer: Thomson-Shore, Inc.
Binder: John H. Dekker & Sons, Inc.

The paper used in this publication meets the minimum
requirements of the American National Standard for
Permanence of Paper for Printed Library Materials
Z39.48-1984. ∞

Library of Congress Cataloging-in-Publication Data

Long years of neglect.
    "Essays in honor of Thomas Cary Duncan Eaves."
    1. Simms, William Gilmore, 1806–1870—Criticism
and interpretation. 2. Eaves, T. C. Duncan (Thomas
Cary Duncan), 1918– . I. Simms, William Gilmore,
1806–1870. II. Guilds, John Caldwell, 1924–.
III. Eaves, T. C. Duncan (Thomas Cary Duncan),
1918–.
PS2853.L66 1988   818'.309   87-34297
ISBN 1-55728-028-2

Charleston owes it to herself to do what she can to atone for the long years of neglect which were all the reward she gave to her devoted son during his lifetime.

—*William Peterfield Trent*

Acknowledgments

I am deeply indebted to the twelve scholars who have generously contributed to the making of this book, most of all for sharing so freely their vast knowledge and wise counsel. Particular thanks are owed to my research assistant, Caroline Carvill, and especially to Suzanne Maberry for her help beyond the call of duty, and to Juliet Caruana Eaves and Mary Simms Furman for their special assistance.

Contents

CONTENTS

Preface

It is highly appropriate that the first published collection of essays on William Gilmore Simms be dedicated to the memory of T. C. Duncan Eaves. As this book demonstrates, the literary fortunes of William Gilmore Simms have risen and fallen periodically, sometimes dramatically, since his advent on the American literary scene in the 1830s and in the more than century since his death. But the high-water mark in Simms scholarship does not fluctuate: *The Letters of William Gilmore Simms,* a six volume work (1952–82), stands alone, towering above other scholarly efforts like Grand Teton over the surrounding plains. The product of painstaking labor, love of learning, and unrelenting research, *Letters* is a working monument to its editors, particularly to T. C. Duncan Eaves. In an unsolicited tribute written on April 10, 1986, when he was unaware of Eaves's death six days earlier, Louis Rubin spoke tellingly for all scholars of Southern literature and culture:

> . . . those who write about ante-bellum Southern literature have available to them that treasure-trove of letters, essential not only for matters involving Simms but almost anything having to do with Southern literature, intellectual and political life during those key years when fateful identity of the region was being established. Nobody who writes about the period in any depth can do it without consulting those letters. . . . They constitute the most important single document in the study of ante-bellum Southern cultural life. For this we are perhaps more indebted to Duncan Eaves than anyone else. . . .
>
> (Letter to John C. Guilds)

In this volume Simms scholars, making frequent use of *Letters,* thereby honor Eaves in contributing to our understanding of Simms.

Discipulus sapiens est gloria summa magistri,
  Istius laus est illius utilitas.

        —Abelard, *Monitum ad Astralabium*

"Long Years
of Neglect"

"Long Years of Neglect": Atonement at Last?

JOHN C. GUILDS

I

The intellectual and social history of the United States has not been kind to William Gilmore Simms. A widely read and nationally respected man-of-letters prior to the advent of the Civil War, Simms suffered in loss of reputation in the post-bellum era even more than most of his Southern literary contemporaries for several significant reasons. First, since Simms was recognized in both North and South as an uncompromising yet highly articulate and influential spokesman for his region, the Reconstruction backlash of opinion against the South had a particularly adverse effect on the North's concept of the ebullient novelist from "hotspur South Carolina." He and his once popular works were now denigrated or—even worse to Simms's posterity—forgotten or neglected by the Northern press, which ten years earlier had praised them for their imaginative sweep and verve. Second, when the first full-length biography of Simms was contracted for in the American Men-of-Letters Series more than two decades after the close of Civil War hostilities, what appeared was a carefully researched but badly biased book. Its author, William Peterfield Trent, did Simms irreparable harm in helping to create the myth that the prodigious Southern writer, a man of extraordinary talent, drive, and courage, was wasted, corrupted, and sacrificed by the moral and cultural evils of a benighted, self-centered society incapable of aesthetic nurturing or appreciation. Put bluntly, Trent argued that if Simms had lived somewhere other than the South, he would have amounted to something. Despite the fact that Trent's target was Charleston and the Old South rather than Simms, the myth has damaged Simms, not Charleston. That Trent was himself a Southerner, and presumably favorably disposed toward Simms in castigating the society that produced them both, lent credibility to his objectivity in the eyes of most readers. To its discredit, American literary scholarship (with a few notable exceptions) bought Trent's thesis without seriously examining its validity or questioning its price to Simms's reputation. If Simms is ever to receive thorough and impartial consideration, scholars must not beg the question of his worth by accepting the theory that his mediocrity can be attributed to his environment.

But perhaps the chief deterrent to a sympathetic reappraisal of the man and his work is that, measured by present-day standards, Simms is a racist. In his letters and treatises, and sometimes in his fiction, Simms clearly voices racial views unacceptable to readers attuned to the historical injustice of racism in any form. In attempting in the late twentieth century to evaluate an early nineteenth-century man-of-letters who believed the white race to be morally and intellectually superior to the black, the scholar must communicate with a reading public understandably reluctant to isolate racial issues from literary judgment. The idea of racial equality is so central in our consciousness that even a semblance of racial prejudice effectively undercuts our appreciation of other values in a racial bigot who, when not blinded by that bigotry, is a compassionate human being with clear moral and ethical insight. It appears necessary to confront the race issue in this introductory essay in the hope that readers will accept Simms's racial views as one thing, however unfortunate or misguided, and look upon his accomplishments, including the literary, as quite another. For the most part Simms was not a racial propagandist in his fiction or poetry; his best work mirrors the society that he portrays, and that it is a slave society is an unavoidable fact. The purpose here is not to argue for Simms's literary greatness, but rather to suggest that his accuracy as a reflector of the mores and manners of the Old South should not *per se* weigh against his literary significance. Perhaps one reason historians have shown more interest in Simms than have literary scholars is that the historian values the authenticity of Simms's picture of the slave-holding South, whereas the literary critic is put off by the authenticity of his racism. Whatever the reason, there is a paucity of serious scholarship dealing with the writer and his contributions to the literature of the nation. On the credit side, the question of the character of the intellectual life of the Old South is being reassessed by historians like Drew Faust and Michael O'Brien, but even this valuable scholarship is in a state of flux and needs input from literary scholars that it is not now receiving.

There are reasons for the confused condition of Simms scholarship other than the Reconstruction backlash, the dominance of the Trent biography, and the slavery issue. In the excellent introduction to *William Gilmore Simms: A Reference Guide,* James E. Kibler, Jr., contends that Simms "is one of the truly controversial figures in American literary criticism," partly because critics have never been able to agree upon his classification (romanticist or pioneer realist?), his forte (novel, short story, poetry, criticism, letter writing?), or his best works. His reputation has fluctuated like the stock market, hitting its peaks in ten-year cycles beginning in 1835, rising again about 1845, and once again about 1855–59; thereafter to plummet until a very gradual ascension set in the twentieth century, beginning most noticeably in the 1930s, with a major flurry coming in the thirty years after 1950, followed by some stagnation and perhaps even retrogression in the past decade. The major publication event in Simms scholarship is unquestionably the superbly edited *Letters of William Gilmore Simms* (five volumes, 1952–1956, with a supplementary volume in 1982). This valuable collection of letters firmly established Simms's central position in the literature, politics, and publishing of the era; but it as yet has failed to elicit the major reappraisals of Simms the man-of-letters predicted in the early reviews.

An important reason for the shortcomings of Simms literary scholarship is the sheer bulk of his writings and their relative inaccessibility. All too many books and articles on Simms seem

5

to rely upon Trent rather than upon fresh, independent reading of his seemingly endless array of texts. The collection of studies in this volume, it is hoped, will cast light upon dark areas of Simms's life and work in a manner that will present this fascinating, versatile man without apology or pleading as a step towards enlightened recognition of his accomplishment.

Within the covers of *"Long Years of Neglect"* are perceptive essays convincingly demonstrating Simms's artistic prowess in two major (but little studied) novels; in his poetry; in his backwoods humor; in the newly recognized genre of "fictional history." Earlier scholarly treatises have maintained that Simms at his best excelled in the short story; in literary criticism; and in journalism, especially the editing of magazines. Indeed, in his time Simms's literary versatility was unmatched in the United States; of America's *litterateurs* in the 1850s, for instance, only Simms performed competitively in every genre, although he dominated none. Moreover, his role as mid-nineteenth-century American man-of-letters *par excellence* is enhanced by his stature as an accomplished, knowledgeable, prolific letter writer.

If American critics recognized letter writing as a legitimate genre—as, say, the British and French do—it is one literary form in which Gilmore Simms might emerge as best among his contemporaries. Simms's letters, meticulously edited by Odell, Oliphant, and Eaves, reveal a warm, witty, verbose, profound, emotional, persuasive, courageous, strongly prejudiced but high-minded raconteur with an amazing gift for writing facile, seemingly inexhaustible English prose. These letters not only delineate the multi-faceted development of American literature and publishing from 1830 to 1870, but are also highly sensitive to—and provide rich insight into—the social, cultural, political, and economic pressures that fanned the fires of sectionalism into secession and rebellion. Awareness of the rhythms tormenting Simms, author and statesman, as revealed in these letters, aids comprehension of one of the most complex periods in American history. Simms's correspondence, to Northerners and Southerners alike, to literary people and political people, to friends and foes, offers a remarkable record of forty prime years of Americana. Like Samuel Johnson to eighteenth-century England, Simms to nineteenth-century America played the role of central man-of-letters who corresponded with important people on subjects ranging from poetry and prejudice to morality and war. Simms in his letters was advocate, motivator, and critic of political, social, economic, agricultural, cultural, and moral causes; but his advocacy of literary America comes through strongest. Simms's penchant for correspondence lends support to Michael O'Brien's thesis that intellectual discourse in the Old South was at a much higher level than has been previously recognized. Indeed, Professor O'Brien quietly (if audaciously) hints that Charleston, not Boston, was the intellectual center of colonial America—a suggestion that leads to exploration of another reason for Simms's relative obscurity.

Whereas Nathaniel Hawthorne has profited from his close identity with New England ("New England is quite as large a lump of earth as my heart can really take in"), Gilmore Simms has suffered from his close identity with the Old South ("I am a Southron"). Hawthorne's New England background has, of course, long been a subject for fruitful study; our increasing knowledge of the history of his region and of the author's relationship with it has provided illumination for the whole corpus of his work. Perry Miller, in his penetrating study entitled *The Raven and the Whale* (1956), puts it best:

> Scholars diligently hunt out the earliest scrawls of Emerson, Hawthorne, Thoreau; the slightest stirrings of intelligence in New England became part of the national record, for here, the assumption runs, began the problem of the mind in America. The reason is, of course, that New England, by its peculiar coherence, not only presents to the country a body of literature which even those who resent the hegemony have to salute, but that New England scholars have taken care of their own.

Since their original publication in pre-Civil War years, Simms's works, too, have been viewed in light of their author's pronounced regional characteristics—but with an important difference. As Perry Miller points out, Hawthorne's New England has, almost without challenge, been considered as the fountain of the *American* tradition and the literary productions of its "flowering" period as the true mainstream of a native American literature. Simms's Old South, on the other hand, has, until recently, too frequently been looked upon as a curiously separate land of sentimentality, chauvinism, and racial bigotry—its people devoid of, and incapable of, serious intellectual and artistic accomplishment. Perhaps the most damning statement against the intellectual pretensions of the Old South appears in Wilbur Cash's influential *The Mind of the South* (1941):

> One almost blushes to set down the score of the Old South here. If Charleston had its St. Cecilia and its public library, there is no record that it ever added a single idea of any notable importance to the sum total of man's stock. If it imported Mrs. Radcliffe, Scott, Byron, wet from the press, it left its only novelist, William Gilmore Simms, to find his reputation in England, and all his life snubbed him because he had no proper pedigree . . .
>
> And Charleston is the peak. Leaving Mr. Jefferson aside, the whole South produced, not only no original philosopher but no derivative one to set beside Emerson and Thoreau; no novelist but poor Simms to measure against the Northern galaxy headed by Hawthorne and Melville and Cooper; no painter but Allston to stand in the company of Ryder and a dozen Yankees; no poet deserving the name save Poe—only half a Southerner. . . . In general, the intellectual and aesthetic culture of the Old South was a superficial and jejune thing, borrowed from without and worn as a political armor and a badge of rank; and hence . . . not a true culture at all.

In brief, whereas New England scholars generally led other American scholars in "tak[ing] care of their own," Southern writers like Cash too frequently joined others throughout the land in deprecating things Southern, particularly if intellectual, literary, or artistic. Cash's voice was perhaps the dominant cry, but it was almost drowned out in the chorus of scholars who condescendingly apologized for the intellectual life of the Old South. Though the derisive chorus was loudest perhaps in the 1940s, it had slackened only slightly by 1982, when Michael O'Brien opened *All Clever Men, Who Make Their Way; Critical Discourse in the Old South,* one of the first books seriously to question the Cash thesis, with the following assessment:

Very few are disposed to grant any vitality to the mind of the
Old South. That it was superficial, unintellectual, obsessed with
race and slavery, enfeebled by polemic is a ruling assumption of
American scholarship.

A result of this "ruling assumption" has been an almost inevitably patronizing view of the writings of William Gilmore
Simms. At best, the critic simply "apologizes" for Simms's
Southern background; at worst he blames Simms's "failure" directly upon the South and intimates that a potentially great
artist was ruined by a perverse love for the benighted institutions of his native region. The fountainhead for most of these
tributaries of untruth about Simms and his environment is
Trent's ideological biography (which ironically may in turn
have sprung from observations on Simms made after his death
by his friend and protégé, Paul Hamilton Hayne. See Rayburn S. Moore's essay in this volume.) What is basically wrong
with Trent's volume is that he was precisely the wrong man to
write it. Trent, a banner-carrier for the New South of his own
day, had as his subject a man who throughout his career championed an ideal of Southern society that stood belligerently opposed to Trent's. It is no wonder, then, that Trent appraised
Simms and his work against the background of a "primitive
and unprogressive Old South, lacking in imagination and orig-
inality, deprecating the efforts of its own writers."
   If Simms had loved his native region, that admiration was
not reciprocated, according to Trent, by his fellow Charlestonians. "Charleston owes it to herself," Trent wrote in the
closing pages of his biography, "to do what she can to atone for
the long years of neglect which were all the reward she gave
to her devoted son during his lifetime." These lines and more
like them sprinkled generously throughout the book, are an
anathema to every serious Simms scholar. They helped to give
birth to the myth, not yet totally refuted, that Charleston neither understood nor approved of, much less appreciated and
honored, the writings and person of William Gilmore Simms.
Because of the pervasiveness of this point of view, and because
its acceptance prevents dispassionate appraisal of Simms and
his accomplishment, it is important that the record of his re-

9

ception in Charleston (and elsewhere in the state, region, and nation) be accurate and unequivocal. Only by challenging the Charleston-rejects-Simms myth can disinterested scholarship begin the long, arduous process of reevaluating Simms and his standing in the world of letters. The purpose in the segment that follows is to establish, as accurately as possible, the reputation Simms held in city, state, region, and country shortly before and after his death, as one means of refuting the concept that Simms died unappreciated by his native city—a belief, it is abundantly clear, that underlies much of the existing scholarship.

Several articles appearing in regional and national publications reflect the esteem in which Simms was held in the years just prior to his death. In an essay on Simms for a series on "The Southern Poets" appearing in the Baltimore *Southern Society* (November 23, 1867), J. Parish Stelle praised not only Simms the poet but also Simms the novelist. Simms, according to Stelle, possessed the qualities of a novelist admired most by Americans: imaginative plot conception, artistic skill "of the Sir Walter Scott stamp" in story development, and the realistic portrayal of characters and scenes. Realism, in Stelle's opinion, was also the most outstanding of Simms's many qualities as a poet. In testimony to the wide reputation and high regard enjoyed by Simms at the time, Stelle did not include examples of Simms's poetry in his essay because "with one so universally read as he is, . . . it would be simply a waste of space." Because "the reader always expects something new," he even hesitated to provide "a biographical sketch of him at all." But he could not leave Simms out of his series on southern poets, Stelle concluded, "simply because the whole world knew [him], and therefore might not be interested in a thrice-told tale."

Fourteen months later, a New York weekly, the *Illuminated Western World* (January 9, 1869), affirmed Simms's natural reputation in announcing its good fortune in acquiring his romance "Voltmeier." The weekly dismissed descriptions of Simms as the "Cooper of the South," insisting he was "no imitator of Cooper, nor, for that matter, of anybody else." As far as the *Western World* was concerned, Simms had "won a distinguished and distinctive position in American literature as poet, historian, journalist, and novelist."

Perhaps the best indication of Simms's "official" reputation shortly before his death is found in James Wood Davidson's encyclopedia, *The Living Writers of the South,* published in New York and London in 1869. Davidson's sympathetic critical treatment of Simms the novelist has him occupying "a position not held in the same degree by any other writer of fiction, North, South, or British." In comparing Simms to Cooper, Davidson declared that while the latter excelled at "characterization and in polish," Simms "clearly" surpassed him in "energy of action, variety of situations, and perhaps in literal truthfulness of delineation." "In general," Davidson concluded, "it may be reasonably questioned whether Mr. Simms has an equal in America." He believed not, asserting that "in general value to his sphere of literature he is *facile princeps* both North and South."

While these publications establish Simms's reputation in the upper-South and the nation as a whole, Charleston's respect for Simms is best symbolized by the invitation he received to deliver the main address at the inaugural meeting of the Agricultural and Immigration Convention held in Charleston in May, 1870. All events of this state-wide convention, with delegates also from North Carolina and Georgia, were prominently covered by the press, and the Charleston *Daily Courier* of May 4 published in its entirety Simms's excellent address, "The Sense of the Beautiful," which "was listened to with marked attention by the large crowd in attendance, and at the conclusion . . . was warmly applauded." Could a city pay more fitting tribute to a distinguished son than to choose him as its chief spokesman for "the most important Convention ever assembled in this State since the close of the war"? Obviously Simms's local reputation was at a pinnacle in the month before his death.

When Simms died on July 11, 1870, the country reacted with a chorus of grief and praise, almost as if recognition of his life of solid accomplishment was a mandate, both locally and nationally. Two days after his death both the Charleston *Courier* and the Charleston *News* carried long, laudatory accounts of

Simms's life and achievements—but with differences in tone
and fervor. The *News* carried a largely straightforward, five-
column obituary with only one emotional outpouring in the
opening paragraph:

> The bells of St. Michael's tolled yesterday—the solemn notes
> conveying to the whole city the mournful tidings of the death of
> him who was the ornament and the pride of the State he loved
> so well.

Less restrained, the *Courier,* in a black-bordered editorial, be-
moaned the loss of so loyal a native son and asked who "with the
loving tenderness of son for mother, had with more pious zeal,
more unremitting devotedness, delved in the rich archives of
that mother's honored past, and made glow with the burnish of
his pen, the wealth and glories of her storied long ago?" The
Courier was impressed not just by the reputation Simms had
earned as the author of history, poetry, fiction, and criticism,
but by the fact that he had achieved so much "without any of
those important aids which spring from wealth [and] family
connexion."

Simms's death elicited similar responses from the rest of the
state as well as the South as a whole. In South Carolina the
Columbia *Phoenix,* of which Simms had been the first editor,
lamented the loss of the "Nestor of literature in the South,"
while the Georgetown *Times* admired Simms especially as historian and poet. Not only had Simms perpetuated the history of
South Carolina, the *Times* asserted, but he also had earned "a
prominent place among our American poets." Outside of South
Carolina, the New Orleans *Times,* the Mobile *Register,* the Atlanta *Constitution,* the Savannah *Advertiser,* the Montgomery
Advertiser, the South *Alabamian* and the *Southern Farm Journal* were among the many Southern newspapers and magazines
carrying highly favorable notices of the region's acknowledged
literary leader and spokesman. This outpouring was noted by
the Atlanta *Constitution* in its tribute to Simms. Pointing out
that writers, unlike generals and politicians, were rarely rewarded with affection and praise, the *Constitution* suggested
that occasionally, as in the case with Simms, "the popular heart

throbs in sorrow at the announcement of the death of a great literary man."

Outside the South, the press response to Simms's death was understandably less effusive, but nevertheless widespread and generally commendatory. The New York *World* considered Simms second only to Cooper as an American historical novelist and described him as a "genial, refined, and pleasant gentleman, frank and courteous in his manners, and blameless in his personal life." Maintaining that Simms was better known and esteemed in the South than in the North, the Pittsburgh *Commercial* suggested that a traveler to the South on the eve of the Civil War would have "noticed how extensively his works were diffused" throughout the region and would have heard Simms depicted as "an American Walter Scott in prose and verse." The *Commercial* observed that Simms's works were also read in the North, "though with less enthusiasm," and admitted that he was known in England and "even praised by critics of renown." As far west as Ohio, the Cincinnati *Enquirer* regretted the passing of Simms, "the more so as we have no romance writer to take his place."

While the nation's press was generally laudatory in its obituaries and editorials on Simms, unsolicited actions taken by South Carolina and Charleston citizens themselves reveal the extent of their appreciation of both the man and his work. For example, the widely publicized, statewide Union Reform Convention assembled in Columbia on June 15, 1870, responded by adopting a set of resolutions offered by Robert Aldrich. In the preamble the delegates noted that not only the state but the entire nation had received news of Simms's death with "profound sorrow." Declaring that South Carolina had sustained an "irreparable loss," they resolved that in Simms's "life-long works and labors which have so distinguished this great man, and which have reflected as much honor on his beloved state as on himself, he has merited the love and gratitude of his fellow citizens." The delegates requested the president of the Convention to express their sympathy to the children of the "illustrious dead," and asked newspapers throughout the state to publish their resolutions.

In Charleston, friends of William Gilmore Simms conceived the idea of erecting a monument in his honor. On June 15, 1870, the Charleston *Courier* reported the suggestion of such a memorial and gave its full approval of the project: "Let the high appreciation of our state be expressed for his genius and noble contributions to her letters . . . in a structure worthy alike of herself and her illustrious son whom she would honor." Charlestonians responded favorably and quickly to the suggestion. On June 30, 1870, less than three weeks after the death of Simms, both the *Courier* and the Charleston *Daily News* headlined a meeting in which Charleston's "most prominent citizens" decided that "a suitable monument . . . be erected to the late Wm. Gilmore Simms." That monument, a bronze bust resting on a pedestal of South Carolina granite, stands today in the center of Charleston's White Point Gardens as testimony to the city's esteem for its native son.

In summary, Simms's death brought forth a nation-wide expression of grief: the longest, most laudatory, and most warmly personal tributes emanated, in descending order, from Charleston, the rest of South Carolina, and the rest of the South; those from north of the Mason-Dixon line were noticeably less eulogistic and fervent, but nevertheless complimentary. This reaction to the demise of a distinguished Southern man-of-letters only five years after the Civil War is precisely what one would have anticipated; any other result would have been surprising indeed. But surely this brief survey points up the absurdity of the contention that Simms was not appreciated by his native city, state, and region—especially his native city.

Small though it seems on the surface, removal of this detriment to an impartial understanding of Simms has symbolic significance beyond its extrinsic worth. More than any comparable writer of his time, Simms, in relationship to his environment, has suffered from lightly questioned, deceptively damaging stereotyping that, if unchallenged, practically excludes serious artistic consideration. To crack at any point the theory that falsely has placed Simms outside the American intellectual mainstream may help to invalidate the "great man-poor writer because of environment" generalization with which he has been saddled since Trent. It is conceivable that replacing myth with fact will become fashionable in Simms scholarship; and, even more important, that reading the works—instead of reading the reasons why they should be avoided—will become the standard for Simms as it is for other authors of his caliber. Certainly, until the latter occurs, the major questions about Simms's worth will remain unanswered.

II

In the essays that follow, certain works and aspects of Simms are studied in depth for the first time; for this reason, "*Long Years of Neglect*" should prove valuable in helping to establish Simms's place in American intellectual history. Though each contributing scholar selected his or her own aspect of Simms to examine, and no editorial effort has been made to achieve consistency of tone or judgment, the pieces fit surprisingly well into a unified whole. The essays may be divided into four categories, ranging from the specific to the general: (1) those closely studying individual works by Simms; (2) those dealing with broader aspects or genres of Simms's writings; (3) those centering upon Simms's literary or political relationships; and (4) those putting Simms in the perspective of his times.

In the lead essay in the first grouping, James B. Meriwether offers a brilliant appreciative analysis of *Woodcraft*, perhaps the best of Simms's novels. Indeed the first "full scholarly and critical treatment" of this major American novel, Meriwether's "The Theme of Freedom in Simms's *Woodcraft*," demonstrates convincingly that misreadings of *Woodcraft* have obscured its main theme and purpose and thus have dimmed recognition of its accomplishment. Simms, Meriwether points out, has significant things to say in *Woodcraft* about what might be "the single most important theme of his work as a whole: the process of the evolution, growth, and progress of a society and a culture from their crude beginnings." And to give vitality and substance to his theme of freedom and responsibility, Simms creates two of his most memorable characters, Captain Porgy and Widow Eveleigh, the subtleties and complexities of whose characterization come alive in Meriwether's sophisticated treatment.

15

In her study of an even more neglected masterpiece of Simms's, Anne M. Blythe first traces the history of the composition and publication of *The Cassique of Kiawah*, a lifelong personal favorite of its author. She then forges into a perceptive analysis of the book's powers of description, narration, and characterizaton, finding its "best characters and scenes . . . painted in colors so vivid" that the result is perhaps Simms's finest, most resplendent achievement. Since *The Cassique of Kiawah* has never before been fully and closely reviewed in print, Blythe's article stands alone in its sensitivity to the novel's strength of dramatization and pictorial imagery. Above all, Blythe contends, the complex, multi-cultural character of Zulieme Calvert "lies at the heart" of Simms's accomplishment, and this sensuous, charming, believable but symbolic female creation is "perhaps the chief reason" for *Cassique's* hold on the reader's imagination.

Linda E. McDaniel, in "American Gods and Devils in *Paddy McGann*," scrutinizes the short novel published by Simms in 1863 and reveals his skillful technique in using gods and devils to portray (sometimes with raucous humor) various stages of American experience, moving "from the age of the hunter step-by-step to the Civil War." It is interesting to note how well McDaniel's essay explicates, in particular examination of *Paddy McGann*, Mary Ann Wimsatt's general thesis of the evolution of backwoods humor in Simms. The last of the articles focusing upon individual books, Nicholas G. Meriwether's "Simms's *The Lily and the Totem:* 'History for the Purposes of Art'" evaluates the author's perhaps unique achievement in a field which Meriwether defines as "fictional history." This previously unstudied "blending of fiction and history" is indeed a *rara avis,* and, after demonstrating Simms's adroitness in weaving factual characters and events into a continuity of fiction, Nicholas Meriwether persuasively concludes that *The Lily and the Totem* "shows a mature author using all of his powers of creativity and scholarship in a first-rate work of fictional history."

This volume's second category of essays, those concerned with Simms's collected efforts and achievements in a single broad critical, historical, or philosophical context, is headed by the extraordinarily useful exegesis of Simms's poetry by James E. Kibler, Jr. "Perceiver and Perceived: External Landscape as Mirror and Metaphor in Simms's Poetry" is unquestionably the most substantial evaluation yet attempted of Simms as a poet; and although Kibler acknowledges that much work on the prolific Charlestonian's poetry remains to be done, his thoughtful and judicious study greatly advances our understanding and appreciation of Simms's underrated and largely unknown contribution to a genre that the author himself prized and to which he committed unflagging energy and thought.

In his precisely stated "Ordered Progress: The Historical Philosophy of William Gilmore Simms," David Moltke-Hansen explores the effect of Simms's "whig philosophy of history" upon his writings, actions, and world view. An understanding of Simms's philosophy of history helps, Moltke-Hansen maintains, to explain his interest in tracing in his novels and stories the *mouvement* of American civilization under frontier conditions: the westward expansion, in the Border Romances; the clash between European antecedents and native American cultures, in the Colonial Series; and the "wrenching shift" from colonialism to independence, in the Revolutionary War Series.

Mary Ann Wimsatt picks up on Simms's abiding passion for depicting the Southwestern frontier in her study of "The Evolution of Simms's Backwoods Humor." Her thesis—that Simms by inheritance, by inclination, by experience, and by linguistic ability was drawn to the comic and the humorous—reinforces her modestly stated conclusion that Simms's talent in Southern backwoods humor is undervalued and that a closer look at "th[e] energetic and inventive strain of humor" in his work would be fruitful. Once again a groundbreaking of Simmsian literary turf has found fertile soil.

In the third category of essays in *"Long Years of Neglect,"* Rayburn S. Moore, the biographer of Paul Hamilton Hayne, contributes an impressive study of the close and complex relationship between Hayne and Simms; and Miriam J. Shillingsburg offers a penetrating analysis of Simms's controversial lecture tour of 1856 based on her discerning examination of unpublished manuscript materials. In "Paul Hamilton Hayne and William Gilmore Simms: Friends, Colleagues, and Mem-

17

bers of the Guild," Moore carefully records the friendly relationship between Charleston's two dominant literary figures of
the nineteenth century and reveals a fascinating alliance of
minds and hearts despite the strong natural rivalry and the occasional resentments or misunderstandings that flashed between them. Hayne, it is interesting to note, perhaps inadver-
tently contributed to Trent's thesis that Simms, a better man
than writer, sacrificed his talents in the sterile ethos of the
South and went unappreciated in the city of his birth; though
Moore, to be sure, points out that Hayne was loyal to Simms
and would have been shocked and offended by Trent's basic interpretation. In her essay on "Simms's Failed Lecture Tour of
1856: The Mind of the North," Shillingsburg, making extensive
use of Simms's unpublished lecture "Antagonisms of the Social
Moral. North and South," traces the tragedy of the aborted lecture tour which, ironically, Simms had planned in order to im-
prove North-South relations, but which exploded with devas-
tating effect on the good will of both sides. Her valuable essay
reveals in stark detail the intensity of rising sectional ani-
mosities after the Brooks-Sumner episode in May, 1856. Until
these untoward events, it should be recalled, Simms had looked
forward to annual visits to the North, numbered many Northerners among his closest friends, and enjoyed popularity with
Northern critics and literary people in general. This is perhaps
the period in his career in which Simms showed impetuosity
and lack of judgment at its worst; the futility and tragedy of
hostile misunderstanding are nowhere better illustrated than
in Shillingsburg's article.

This first collection of studies on Simms closes with two
essays painted with broad strokes by master limners of the
Southern scene. In the first of these, "Biography and the Southern Mind: William Gilmore Simms," John M. McCardell states
in readable, polished prose the underlying reasons why a satisfactory biography has been so long in coming and so hard
to come by. Though potential biographers of Simms have no
unanimity of approach and purpose, McCardell focuses upon
problems that go beyond the writing of biography. His graceful
essay is sensitive to the issues confronting any Simms biographer, and perusing it will heighten any reader's perception of

the man and his times. In his forceful essay entitled "Simms, Charleston, and the Profession of Letters," Louis D. Rubin, Jr., convincingly uses *The Charleston Book*—a collection of writings by fellow Charlestonians put together by Simms in 1845— as the springboard for sprightly discussions of some of the reasons an accurate reassessment of Simms is so agonizingly difficult. Though he seems to lean heavily at times upon the Trent he grudgingly admires, Rubin is both provocative and hard-hitting, and his essay is intended to stimulate new ideas about an old writer—to put old wine in new bottles, so to speak. It is fitting that the final essay in a volume attempting to rekindle interest in a badly misunderstood writer of the Old South should challenge not only Trent, but those who would succeed Trent. Though some who read this book may conclude that Rubin perhaps underrates Simms the writer, no one would even hint that Rubin has failed to love or to understand his fellow Charlestonian of the previous century.

Collectively, these essays present various ideas about diverse aspects of a virile and versatile man-of-letters. William Gilmore Simms, more than a century after his death, remains relatively unknown, unread, and obscure. If this volume can arouse a new curiosity about Simms, his work and reputation, it will have accomplished its mission.

The Theme of Freedom in Simms's *Woodcraft*

JAMES B. MERIWETHER

William Gilmore Simms's novel *Woodcraft* has not lacked for critical praise. It has often been called his best novel, a judgment with which on the whole I concur. Donald Davidson, for example, in what is still the best general critical essay on Simms, his Introduction to the first volume of Simms's *Letters* (1952), says, "It is not too much to say that *Woodcraft* is Simms' highest achievement."[1] But despite the amount of praise it has been given, it has by no means yet received the full scholarly and critical treatment it deserves (a statement that could be made about most aspects of Simms's life and work). This essay examines just one theme of the book: the dual theme of freedom and its opposite, slavery. There are other themes in this long, rich, and varied novel that merit such examination, some of which are at least touched upon here. But freedom is in many ways the major theme of the work, and as Simms handles it, it is also a very complex one.

First, some background facts need be noted. *Woodcraft* is one of the series of eight loosely-linked novels about the Revolutionary War in South Carolina that Simms published between 1835 and 1867. It concludes the series, chronologically, although later he wrote three others that deal with earlier periods of the conflict. It was probably written entirely in 1851 and early 1852, and was published first as a serial and then in book form later in 1852.[2] It appeared, then, early in what was Simms's finest period as a writer, the decade of the 1850s, during which he produced what are probably his best four novels, beginning with *Woodcraft* and continuing with *The Forayers* (1855) and *Eutaw* (1856), the two Revolutionary novels which immediately precede *Woodcraft* chronologically in the series; and concluding in 1859 with *The Cassique of Kiawah*. The decade also saw the publication of that impressive, if hard to define, book *The Lily and the Totem* (1850), several fine works of shorter fiction, and two other novels of real if somewhat lesser accomplishment, *Katharine Walton* (1851; another of the Revolutionary series), and *As Good as a Comedy* (1852). In their variety as well as in their quality these works show Simms at his best. Most of them fall, too, within the period (1850–1855) which F. O. Matthiessen called the American Renaissance, and are a very substantial, if too often ignored, contribution to that period.[3]

Woodcraft begins with the withdrawal of the British forces from Charleston in December 1782, after the signing of the provisional articles of peace in Paris on November 30,[4] and ends a little over a year later. It is a period with which Simms's researches, as a biographer and historian, had made him thoroughly familiar, and it is worth quoting his description of it in his *History of South Carolina:*

> Covered with scars and glory, . . . the termination of the Revolutionary war found her [South Carolina] a wreck in fortune, and with a country most terribly demoralized by the progress of a long war, which had witnessed the total ruin of all her homesteads, and the disruption, everywhere, of the bonds of society. Wild passions had been let loose, and had fed on blood and rapine, for too long a season to be soon brought into subjection. The peace with Great Britain brought no absolute peace to her scattered communities, which sometimes glared on each other with the eager ferocity of the tiger. Lawless men traversed her forest-paths, for a time, with violence and impunity. Desperadoes, whom war and rapine had taught all their lessons, raged, torch in hand, around quiet and defenceless habitations. The old feuds of whig and tory were still unsatisfied. Old revenges were perpetually rising up to renew the bloody scenes of former sea-

sons; and, in some instances, the loyalist, notorious for crimes committed during the war, though discharged by court and jury, has been seized upon by a still infuriated people, and dragged, in the very presence of the judge, to the halter and the tree, allowed "short shrift," and shorter cord, and launched into eternity, in spite of the general amnesty proclaimed by the government. It required many years before the wild passions which had been stimulated by the bloody civil feuds of the Revolution, could be restrained by the arm of law, or subdued and soothed by the gentler offices of religion.[5]

Technically, then, *Woodcraft* is not a war novel at all, but a novel about the aftermath of war, or about war only in retrospect—the war seen through its results, its effects upon returning soldiers and upon the civilian population, like Faulkner's *Soldiers' Pay* and Hemingway's *The Sun Also Rises*.[6] But it differs significantly from those post-World War I (and post-*The Waste Land*) novels in that Simms's post-war world is seen ultimately in a positive light and the war itself, no matter how terrible, is seen as having been worth fighting, worth its cost.

Woodcraft is a long novel, over 500 pages, and its pace, like that of all Simms's longer fiction, is often leisurely—too leisurely, of course, for many modern readers, and for some critics, who have found fault with such interruptions in the action of the book as the lengthy expositions of a utilitarian philosophy of life by Sergeant Millhouse, and the equally lengthy rejoinders by Captain Porgy, who argues for a broader, more humanistic approach to life and making a living. Such criticism assumes that *Woodcraft* was intended to be, or should have been, a more straightforward novel of action, like *The Forayers* and *Eutaw*, with only brief philosophizing by the characters and commentary by the author. *Woodcraft* does in fact have episodes of stirring action. Many of the scenes involving the outlaw Bostwick, one of Simms's best-drawn and most complex villains, are among the finest of the whole Revolutionary War series for swift-moving, dramatic event, with dialogue and description nicely blended in a fast-paced narrative flow that still permits a considerable amount of change of pace and humor. These scenes show one side of Simms the novelist at his best.

But *Woodcraft* is only partly a novel of action, and it shows other aspects of Simms the novelist at his best too. By the time he wrote *Woodcraft,* Simms knew a great deal about writing novels, and about a great many other subjects too, including, most obviously, war and peace, and their connections; men and women, and their relationships; and that larger subject, which concerned him so deeply for so much of his career, and which might be called the single most important theme of his work as a whole: the process of the evolution, growth, and progress of a society and a culture from their crude beginnings—a theme which includes such matters as the relationship of the individual to a society, the relationship of parents to children, the relationships and responsibilities of the different classes in a society, and the means—including such arts as literature—by which barbarous and lawless nature can be tamed and made civilized. In *Woodcraft* authorial commentary and the soliloquies and debates of the principal characters allow Simms to treat such subjects with considerable philosophical weight and depth, as is appropriate for the work which concludes his long chronicle of the bloody struggles and terrible suffering of the rebellious colony of South Carolina during the Revolutionary War.

In Simms's view, this was the absolutely justifiable and proper struggle of the colony for its liberty, and throughout the Revolutionary War novels (and in his other writings as well) he accords little sympathy to the British or to their loyalist allies among the colonists. In a very real sense, then, one can say that liberty, or freedom, is the major theme of the whole eight-novel Revolutionary War series. But this theme is dealt with on an exceptionally broad scale in *Woodcraft,* where the subject changes from the struggle for liberty, to the problems that are consequent to that new-won independence.

This is made clear at the very beginning of the novel, where the description of the initial rejoicing at the departure of the British soon turns to a grim and sobering examination of the immediate postwar scene, when civil government has yet to be established, where lawlessness is to be found everywhere, and the most crucial problem of all may be that of the reabsorption of the returned veterans into a peacetime, civilian society. Freedom was a very simple goal to fight for, in wartime; or to fight for it was very easy and natural for a man like Captain Porgy. He had rendered his society significant service, as a soldier. But what are we to do in time of peace, Simms asks in *Woodcraft,* with veterans who seem able to consider only simple—*i.e.,* military—solutions to the complex problems of the post-war period?

Simms's original conception of this novel could not have envisaged anything like the thematic density and complexity which he finally accorded it. Writing his Philadelphia publisher, Abraham Hart, on September 27, 1851, Simms says, "I have more than half written, a novel entitled 'Fair, Fat & Forty; or the Sword and the Distaff.'" He had begun the work, he says, as a "nouvellette" for serial publication in the Philadelphia weekly, *Arthur's Home Gazette* (which had begun publication in September 1850 and which in 1852 published serially Simms's "Marie de Berniere"). However, he tells Hart, the book "has run out to a reasonable sized novel. It takes up the scene and action at the close of the revolutionary war in S.C., showing the fortunes, in love, of an old soldier, with broken fortunes, whose military occupation, like that of Othello, is gone." And he estimates that the book will "probably" be finished in January.[7]

Since Captain Porgy had appeared only as a minor character in three of the Revolutionary War novels written before Simms began the work which became *Woodcraft,* and since he was being placed at the center of a relatively short work of fiction—a "nouvellette"—it seems reasonable to guess that when it was projected this tale was only a by-product of the Revolutionary War series, rather than an integral part of it, and that putting the minor character Porgy at its center defined the work as originally a minor one.

Once into the writing of it, Simms clearly changed his ideas about the book, and about Captain Porgy. Presumably he finished it, as he had predicted to Hart, in January 1852, or close to that date, for in February it began appearing as a serial in the Charleston *Southern Literary Gazette,* which was published by the firm of Walker, Richards and Company. The title was "The Sword and the Distaff"; the subtitle was "Fair, Fat and Forty: A Tale of the South, at the Close of the Revolution."

With the title unchanged, it was brought out in book form by the same firm in September 1852, two months before the serial version was concluded.[8]

Despite the limited means for marketing such a book that were possessed by Walker, Richards and Company, *The Sword and the Distaff* must have sold reasonably well, for it was reprinted later in 1852.[9] The following year it was reissued, from the same plates, by the Philadelphia firm of Lippincott, Grambo; and a year later a new, revised edition appeared in the collected edition of Simms's work which was being brought out by the firm of Redfield in New York. This edition bore the title *Woodcraft; or Hawks about the Dovecote; a Story of the South at the Close of the Revolution.*[10]

Whether the original or the revised title is the better for this book is debatable. *The Sword and the Distaff* gives a clearer indication of the dual focus of the work—the sharply marked contrast between war and peace, with the major differences between these two worlds represented in the characters of Captain Porgy, the returned veteran, and the widow Eveleigh, who owns a plantation adjoining Porgy's on the Ashepoo River, near the coast and south of Charleston. The original subtitle, "Fair, Fat and Forty," is also appropriate, though Simms's devoted friend and frequent critic, James Hammond, may have been correct in protesting that it was in poor taste.[11] Perhaps it is, as a description of Mrs. Eveleigh, for throughout the book she is described as being of most pleasing and attractive appearance and figure, if inclining slightly toward plumpness. The description "Fair, Fat and Forty" (the phrase is taken from Scott[12]) is applied to her just once in the book, and this is on an occasion when Porgy, musing upon her attractions but trying, like the confirmed bachelor that he is, to resist them, thinks of that phrase in the context of his own gross corpulence, as a symbol of something he dislikes, knowing that it represents a weakness. Because the original subtitle, then, ultimately calls attention to Porgy's weakness and his tendency toward self-deception, I regret that Simms, presumably influenced by Hammond, abandoned it in the revised edition.

Whatever Simms's original plan for Porgy's place in this book may have been, he is far from being the hero of the work.

The central character, yes; but as Porgy's weaknesses and limitations are increasingly exposed, and as Mrs. Eveleigh's superiority is increasingly demonstrated, it becomes clear that this is a novel with a heroine but no hero.

Mrs. Eveleigh is the moral center of the book. As an individual, as a parent, and as a friend and neighbor she combines the qualities of head and heart that Simms finds most admirable, and most necessary for the soundness and growth of community and society. She has courage as well as intellect, imagination as well as the capacity for faith and loyalty. She is a wise and farsighted mother to her son Richard and foster-mother to Dory , the daughter of the villainous squatter Bostwick. She is the efficient manager of her plantation, and a generous neighbor to Porgy, whose lands are in ruins, and deeply mortgaged.[13] Some of Porgy's troubles can be blamed upon the war, but through laziness, carelessness, and self-indulgence, Porgy confesses, he was already well on the road to ruin before the outbreak of the Revolution (p. 206). Porgy is unmarried; and throughout most of the book, the advice of his friends and servants, and the twists and turns of the apparently conventional working out of the plot, lead the reader to expect the novel to end with Porgy's marriage to the widow.

Woodcraft is by no means a conventional novel, however. When Porgy finally manages to work himself up to proposing to her, Mrs. Eveleigh turns him down—very gently, but very firmly. "I have been too long my own mistress to submit to authority," she tells him. She admits to "a certain spice of independence" in her temper; while Porgy, she has noticed, has "a certain imperative mood" which would make him "despotic" as a husband (p. 513). Perhaps, too, as the original sub-title of the novel emphasized, Porgy's corpulence has something to do with the failure of his wooing of the widow. Imprisoned in excessive flesh that is the result of his inability to control his appetites within reasonable limits, he cannot be the man he knows he could be and should be. He cannot play the role that he knows is required of him if he is to be a proper match for Mrs. Eveleigh.

Porgy, escaping from the bonds of matrimony at the end of the novel, is free—free to eat and drink, to talk and carouse with his old army buddies.[14] And Mrs. Eveleigh is free to manage her own property, and manage it well; and to enjoy Porgy's occasional company and conversation without having to give him the power of managing her life. Independent and capable, she is free of the restrictions that marriage to Porgy would have entailed, just as South Carolina is free from domination by Great Britain.

What I have given here is an extremely condensed account of the relationship between Porgy and Mrs. Eveleigh, but it should be clear that Simms saw her as superior to Porgy, in this novel, in nearly every way—in every way, indeed, except for sheer physical strength and military skill. She has the cooler head, the quicker wit, the better judgment. She is farsighted and stable, a good administrator, and a good politician. She has in abundance the qualities that the former colony of South Carolina requires if it is to make a successful transition from war to peace, build up its shattered economy, and learn to get along with its neighboring states in the new federal relationship.

Porgy has some useful qualities too, it is true. But those that made him a good soldier are shown to hamper his becoming a good and law-abiding civilian. In time of peace perhaps his most admirable quality is his genuine devotion to literature, art, and beauty—so necessary as the counter to the American materialism which Simms deplored and attacked for so much of his career, and which characterizes the philosophy of the one-armed Sergeant Millhouse who becomes Porgy's overseer.[15] But in other respects Porgy is shown to require the civilizing influence of such fellow-citizens as Mrs. Eveleigh and the distinguished lawyer, Charles Cotesworth Pinckney, if he is to be of genuine service to his state in time of peace.

That freedom, real freedom, carries with it real responsibilities is strongly affirmed throughout *Woodcraft;* and Porgy's conception of individual liberty is shown to be far too close to license. In the earlier part of the novel, especially, Simms is at pains to show the dangers of an absence of restraint—the virtual domination of parts of the country by outlaws, in the immediate aftermath of war; and the opportunity to flourish that is afforded to such white-collar thieves as McKewn, who collaborated with the British during the war while amassing lands and mortgages that would make him wealthy afterwards. Too much restraint, too little liberty, we are shown, produce a revolution; but too little restraint, too much liberty, are responsible for the faults, and faulty actions, of the returning veteran, Captain Porgy. In one of the fine comic scenes of the book Porgy and his friends force the deputy sheriff, Crooks, to eat the legal documents he had brought to Porgy's plantation to enforce the foreclosure of the mortgage held by McKewn. Since McKewn's dishonesty has been shown from the opening of the novel, the reader's sympathy is likely to be entirely with Porgy. Yet the debt is a legal one, legally incurred; and Porgy's flouting of the law is behavior that cannot be tolerated in peacetime. Mrs. Eveleigh is aware of this and remonstrates with Porgy: "But, captain, is this not flying in the face of the law?" Porgy agrees that in the long run he will have to yield, but he intends to have his "fun in full" before succumbing (pp. 440–41). The proper perspective upon such boyish practical jokes at the expense of the law is provided by the brief but important appearance in the novel of Pinckney, who served his state and his nation with such distinction in both war and peace, and who here is the masculine epitome of what the devastated state of South Carolina needs, as Mrs. Eveleigh is the feminine.[16]

What is the opposite of freedom? To be a colony of a despotic central government; to be a plantation under absentee ownership; to be a woman trapped in a demeaning marriage; to be a man trapped within a mountain of flesh; to be a poor white trapped within that class by poverty, ignorance, and the habitude of lawlessness. Or to be a slave.

The subject of chattel slavery in *Woodcraft* is one aspect of the novel that has received a good deal of attention.[17] Here I shall discuss it only in the context of the broader theme of several different kinds of freedom and lacks of freedom. Simms brings the subject of slavery to the forefront of the novel from the very beginning, when the retreating British are shown attempting to steal as many slaves as possible, for subsequent re-sale in the West Indies. Through her quick wit and decisiveness, Mrs. Eveleigh frustrates the attempt to steal some of her slaves, and also Porgy's. Later, when Porgy's slaves are shown to be subject to a forced sale if the mortgage on his property is foreclosed, he sells his bodyservant, Tom, to Mrs. Eveleigh, and conceals the others in the swamp. The question of freeing them is debated at length. Often-quoted by critics is Simms's remark, in a letter to Hammond, that his novel "is probably as good an answer to Mrs. Stowe as has been published,"[18] and certainly in *Woodcraft* Simms is showing the institution of slavery at something close to its best—or is showing the relations between slaves and masters at their best. Nevertheless, he is also very much concerned to show the dangers inherent in the system: the helplessness of the slaves in a situation where by force (the British, the outlaws) they can be stolen and re-sold—or can suffer the same fate by quite legal means (foreclosure of a mortgage). They are entirely dependent upon responsible owners and a stable society. In the conversations about slavery that take place among the characters in the novel, great stress is laid, by both whites and blacks, upon the reciprocal obligations of slaves and owners in the system. If a pro-slavery argument is being advanced in *Woodcraft,* it is an argument carefully grounded in legality; that is, within a legal framework which spells out the obligations of the slaveowners and in which the slaves are well aware of what is due them.

I might note here, though, that I'm sorry that Simms made that remark to Hammond about *Woodcraft* being "an answer to Mrs. Stowe," for I think he meant it only in very small part as it has commonly been taken to mean. That is, I do not think that he set out, in *Woodcraft* (or in any other novel), to write a book which would in any sense be an "answer" to *Uncle Tom's Cabin*—a defense of the South and its peculiar institution. For one thing, the timing is wrong. *Uncle Tom's Cabin* was published March 20, 1852;[19] and as has been noted, we know now that Simms had written half of his novel by late September 1851 and presumably finished it by January 1852. It has been argued that he could have known the serial version of Mrs. Stowe's book, which ran in the Washington, D.C. *National Era* in 1851–1852,[20] but there is no evidence that he did and it seems more than a little unlikely. There is no mention of it in his letters or other writings until July 1852.[21] This is not to say

that he didn't know something about *Uncle Tom's Cabin* at the
time he was writing his own novel, about its subject and approach and popularity even during its serial publication. But I
doubt if more than an incidental remark or two in Simms's
novel is in direct response to Mrs. Stowe's.[22]

Another reason to doubt that *Woodcraft* was in any sense
written as a response to *Uncle Tom's Cabin* is that it is too big a
book, too important a part of Simms's most ambitious single
literary undertaking, his Revolutionary War series, to derive
in any major way from so narrow and inartistic and defensive
an original impulse. I think that what Simms meant by that
remark to Hammond was that if any reader of *Uncle Tom's
Cabin* wanted an antidote to it, *Woodcraft* would serve the
purpose very well—though several other of his novels, written
earlier, would do almost as well, in my opinion. I suspect that
what Simms had in mind was the overall picture he had presented of his society, and of the place of slavery in it, in his
novel—a book in which he dealt with that society as a complex whole, in process of rapid change and evolution, and in
which he dealt lengthily and realistically with man-woman
and parent-child relationships as well as those between master
and slave, between master and overseer, between overseer and
slave, and finally, with the relationships among various strata
of that society, both white and black. In short, his was a novel
solidly grounded upon complex historical and social reality;
and one which treated its major characters and themes with
far greater complexity than did Mrs. Stowe's passionate indict-
ments and oversimplifications.

Let me sum up by saying that the theme of freedom, in
Woodcraft, is a relatively simple one, considered as the goal for
which the rebellious colony of South Carolina and its citizen-
soldiers like Porgy had fought in time of war. Much less simple
is the problem of balancing the freedom of the individual citizen to protect his property against unjust seizure, in time of
peace, with the need to obey the law. Less simple yet is the
question of individual freedom, measured against legal and social responsibilities, considered in the light of what a marriage
between Porgy and Mrs. Eveleigh would have involved for
each of them. And freedom is very far indeed from being a
simple matter, when the subject of chattel slavery is dealt with

in this book. *Woodcraft* might have been just the same had *Uncle Tom's Cabin* never been written; but certainly Simms's thinking and writing about slavery and many other aspects of his native state and section had been shaped and influenced for almost two decades by the rising tide of abolitionism. If in *Woodcraft* Simms affirms the rectitude and propriety of the colonists' fight to gain their freedom, he had also to justify the denial of that right to the slaves of those colonists. His attempt to do so is based upon demonstrating the overriding need for a stable society, one in which all individuals and classes must obey laws that have been enacted for the common good. If Tom must obey the laws that govern the institution of slavery, with the loss of freedom that involves, the same is true, though to a lesser extent of course, of his master, for Porgy too must learn to obey the law, giving up some of his freedom to act in an irregular and individualistic manner.

It is very easy today to criticize Simms for his acceptance and defense of chattel slavery. In so defending it, Simms was simply being a man of his time, and place—just as Simms's critic of today is. But we should be very careful, in dismissing the validity of Simms's views of slavery, not to oversimplify them, or his fictional treatment of the subject. An examination of the two-fold theme of freedom and slavery, in *Woodcraft,* can reveal Simms in a rather different light than that in which he is generally shown in our standard textbooks and literary histories. It can also lead us a step or two further towards understanding a fine and complex novel, and towards understanding Simms himself—still, after all this time, after all the books and dissertations and articles that have been written about him in the nearly one hundred years that have passed since Trent's hastily written, uncomprehending, misleading, and condescending critical biography—still the most neglected and misunderstood of our important nineteenth-century American writers.

Notes

[1] Mary C. Simms Oliphant, Alfred Taylor Odell, and T. C. Duncan Eaves, eds., *The Letters of William Gilmore Simms* (Columbia: Uni-

versity of South Carolina Press, 5 vols., 1952–1956; vol. 6, 1982) (hereafter cited as *Letters*). The quotation is taken from vol. 1, p. xlv. A useful list of favorable modern criticism of the novel is provided by Charles S. Watson in the first footnote of his "Simms's Answer to *Uncle Tom's Cabin:* Criticism of the South in *Woodcraft,*" *Southern Literary Journal,* 9 (Fall 1976), pp. 78–90. Though it has received much less attention, *The Cassique of Kiawah* also represents Simms at the height of his powers as a novelist; a strong claim can be made for either as Simms's best, and an even stronger claim that they are his two best.

[2] *Letters,* VI, p. 118n.

[3] Matthiessen, *American Renaissance* (New York: Oxford University Press, 1941). The basis of his work is his study of Emerson, Thoreau, Hawthorne, Melville, and Whitman, but many other writers come in for at least brief examination. Of these, the only Southern writer is George Washington Harris, who receives a few appreciative pages. Simms is mentioned only once, in the prefatory chapter (p. x), as one of several writers active during this period.

[4] In *Woodcraft* Simms gives the date wrongly as November 13. *Woodcraft* (Spartanburg, S.C.: Published for the Southern Studies Program by The Reprint Company, 1976), p. 5. Further references to *Woodcraft* will be to this edition, cited by page number within the text of this essay. The text of this reissue of the novel is offset (but at an enlargement of 115%) from the New York, 1854 Redfield edition, which was revised and corrected by Simms from the first edition. This reissue is part of an eight-volume set which for the first time brought out all eight novels of the Revolutionary series together, with new, comprehensive annotations. The notes for *Woodcraft* were supplied by George F. Hayhoe and are valuable for an understanding of Simms's use of his sources as well as for identifying historical and literary allusions. See p. 521 for his note on Simms's error concerning this date; Hayhoe points out that Simms made the same mistake in the 1860 edition of his *History of South Carolina*. The error had in fact persisted from the first edition of this textbook (Charleston, 1840, p. 315; second edition, Charleston, 1842, p. 319). Presumably Simms was following David Ramsay's *History of South Carolina* (Charleston, 1809), a source he frequently used, where the same incorrect date is given (vol. 1, p. 475).

[5] *The History of South Carolina* (New York, Redfield 1860), pp. 394–95. This passage does not occur in the earlier editions (Charleston, 1840 and 1842), which give a milder description of the immediate postwar situation, particularly with regard to the treatment of the Tories. In the Preface to the work Simms discusses his intention in writing it

and his use of various published sources. See also his *Life of Francis Marion* (New York: H. G. Langley 1844); the prefatory Note listing his sources (p. [6]) includes Peter Horry's manuscript memoir of his life, and "five volumes of MS. Letters from distinguished officers of the Revolution in the South." In the Preface he also acknowledges oral sources: "Minor facts have been gathered from the lips of living witnesses," and states, perhaps surprisingly, that the laws of the biographer "are perhaps even more strict than those which govern the historian" (p. [7]).

[6] Davidson notes that the novel dramatizes "the now well-worn irony of 'soldier's pay," and that the novel shows qualities in its characters that are "so characteristically American that it would be very hard to find anywhere . . . a better representation of our supposed national temperament and principles." *Letters,* I, xlv.

[7] See note 2. This letter, so important for our understanding of the background and writing of *Woodcraft,* was not known until its publication in vol. VI of the *Letters* and has not been used in previous studies of the novel.

[8] *The Southern Literary Gazette* was a weekly journal; twice monthly there were supplements containing serials. "The Sword and the Distaff" appeared in eighteen installments in these supplements, beginning February 28 and ending November 6, 1852. (Its forthcoming publication had been announced in the *Gazette* for December 20, 1851. See *Letters,* III, 185*n.*) The serial text, obviously printed from standing type, appeared two columns per page of the supplement; subsequently the type was paged and plated for the book impressions. One page, or partial page, of the manuscript survives in a reproduction in *Homes of American Authors* (New York: Putnam, 1853), which also includes an engraving of Simms's plantation home, Woodlands. In a letter to Frederick Saunders at Putnam's dated from Charleston August 10, 1852, Simms says he is sending him "two scraps," one of verse, the other "prose from a novel now going through the press" (*Letters,* III, 190). The passage, from one of Porgy's remarks to Millhouse, is in chapter XLI (p. 283 of the Redfield edition, p. 319 of the Walker, Richards edition). It is presumably a fair copy made by Simms from the serial text; there are differences between the manuscript and the published text, with the manuscript readings superior. (There are revisions in this passage for the Redfield text, but none of them picks up the superior manuscript readings.)

[9] The title page of the first impresson of the book contains the statement *second edition;* obviously the serial text, printed from the same typesetting, was considered the first. A second book impression has *third edition* on the title page; both impressions have the date 1852.

[10] Redfield brought out a total of twenty-one volumes in this edition of Simms between 1853 and 1860. Along with sixteen other volumes of the fiction in this edition, *Woodcraft* was many times reprinted and reissued during the next half-century by a series of publishers, with ever cheaper paper and bindings and steadily worsening type batter. The textual reliability of these cheap reprints was further lessened by inept patching of the plates which occasionally offered corrupt readings in re-set lines.

[11] *Letters,* III, 243*n.* Hammond, writing on July 8, 1852, advised Simms to "strike out the "Fair, Fat & Forty.' It is *decidedly* vulgar and the *only* thing vulgar in the book. . . ." Hammond found several flaws in the novel, including "frequent violations of the unities of time, place & names. . . ." In an earlier letter (quoted in the same footnote), he had said the book was "full of petty blemishes" but still called it "fully equal to any" of Simms's novels. Presumably Simms's revisions for the 1854 Redfield edition corrected many, if not all, of the "petty blemishes," and it took care of the one inconsistency that Hammond noted, the fact that Millhouse is sometimes called corporal, sometimes sergeant, in the first edition. Paula Dean, in her 1972 Auburn University dissertation, "Revisions in the Revolutionary War Novels of William Gilmore Simms," states that there were "more than forty-one hundred changes" made in the 1854 Redfield edition, though some of them are undoubtedly to be ascribed to printers and proofreaders (p. 13).

[12] Hayhoe's notes on this subtitle and description (*Woodcraft,* pp. 524 & 543) give Scott as the original source for the phrase. Hayhoe shows that it was also used by Joseph Johnson in his *Traditions and Reminiscences Chiefly of the American Revolution in the South* (Charleston, 1851), in a passage which may have given Simms the idea for the creation of Mrs. Eveleigh.

[13] The best and fullest critical account of Mrs. Eveleigh's role in *Woodcraft* is the chapter devoted to that novel in Jacob F. Rivers, III, "Prominent Female Characters in the Revolutionary War Novels of William Gilmore Simms," M.A. Thesis, University of South Carolina, 1987, pp. 73–89.

[14] The fullest, and probably the most favorable, published examination of Porgy is in the introduction, "A Reappraisal of Captain Porgy," to Hugh W. Hetherington, ed., *Cavalier of Old South Carolina* (University of North Carolina Press, 1966), which collects the episodes of the other Revolutionary novels in which this character appears, as well excerpting and summarizing *Woodcraft.* I find his comments upon the Porgy of *Woodcraft* far less valid than what he has to say

about the Porgy of the other novels. Poorly chosen texts and many errors of fact further weaken this volume.

[15] In a short essay, "Labor—Its Value," published in Simms's collection *Egeria* (Philadelphia, 1853) but which Simms states was written in 1836 (see p. 155), he castigates the American love of gaining money and then irresponsibility in spending it. "With us the cry seems evermore for money. The want of money is the one want which we everywhere unite to deplore." But desire for greater wealth is "in proportion to our profligacy and vain pretension" (p. 152). In a passage that anticipates in part his characterization of Porgy, Simms recounts as typical the story of the father who acquires wealth which his "youthful heir" dissipates in "expensive frivolities" and a "meretricious life" (p. 154). The management of money "requires a previous training of head and heart, which cannot be too careful or too strict" (p. 152)—requires, then, those qualities which Mrs. Eveleigh possesses in abundance, but Porgy not at all. It is noteworthy that in *Woodcraft* Simms gives the explicit exposition of the materialistic or utilitarian philosophy to Millhouse, who is a Southerner. Had Simms written the novel as a narrowly conceived defense of the South, or of South Carolina, he could very easily have made Millhouse a Northerner, as so many overseers were.

[16] The role of the law in this novel is the subject of a fine article by E. Lynn Hogue, "The Presentation of Post-Revolutionary Law in *Woodcraft:* Another Perspective on the 'Truth' of Simms's Fiction," *Mississippi Quarterly,* 31 (Spring 1978), 201–210. As Hogue notes (p. 203 n.) his article was originally presented as a comment upon a paper by Herbert A. Johnson, "The Aftermath of the Revolution in *Woodcraft:* A Legal Historian's View," given at a conference on Simms and the Revolution in South Carolina at the College of Charleston, May 6–8, 1976. There is a copy of this paper in the William Gilmore Simms Collection, Thomas Cooper Library, University of South Carolina.

[17] Hetherington, pp. 38–50, usefully lists and summarizes previous critical examination of this subject, though his evaluations of them, and his own argument, are weakened by his unquestioning assumption that Simms undertook to write, and wrote *Woodcraft* as an answer to *Uncle Tom's Cabin.* See also Charles S. Watson, "Simms's Review of *Uncle Tom's Cabin,*" *American Literature,* 40 (November 1976), 365–368.

[18] *Letters,* III, 222–223.

[19] Joseph V. Ridgely, "*Woodcraft:* Simm's First Answer to *Uncle Tom's Cabin,*" *American Literature,* 31 (January 1960), p. 422 n.

[20] Ridgely. The serial version ran from June 5, 1851 to April 1, 1852.

[21] Ridgely.

[22] One example is the comment made by Porgy's bodyservant Tom, to another slave, Pomp, who is helping him in the kitchen, and who calls him "Uncle Tom." Tom's indignant reply is, "Don't you uncle me, you chucklehead!" (p. 179).

William Gilmore Simms's
The Cassique of Kiawah
and the Principles of His Art
ANNE M. BLYTHE

The Cassique of Kiawah, Simms's romance of seventeenth-century South Carolina, deserves far more attention than it has received in the years since its publication in 1859.[1] The novel was very well received, but its initial success was soon followed by neglect.

The immediate cause of this neglect was of course the coming of the Civil War. Soon afterward Simms's publisher, Redfield, failed, and *Cassique* was somehow omitted when later publishers reprinted the other novels that had been included in the Redfield collected edition of the 1850s. Though it was briefly reissued in the 1880s by the firm of Dodd, Mead and Company, the omission of *Cassique* from the collected edition doomed it to an unavailability and therefore a neglect that has continued until today.[2] Inexplicably, though other Simms novels have recently been brought out again—all eight Revolutionary romances were reissued in the 1970s, and *The Yemassee,* Simms's other colonial romance of South Carolina, has been brought out again no less than three times since 1950—*The Cassique of Kiawah* remains unavailable except in those few libraries and collections fortunate enough to possess the first edition of 1859 or its reissue by Dodd, Mead.

In 1892 W. P. Trent noted in his brief discussion of *Cassique* that it "had fallen upon bad times; for the country was too

much stirred up over the great questions of slavery and secession to pay much attention to literature." He pointed out that
sales of the novel, even in "stately Charleston," had been good
enough for the author to feel encouraged.[3] Then came the war;
and afterward *Cassique* shared in the general critical neglect
of Simms. As Jay B. Hubbell notes, in his own section of the
country Simms and his writings came to be considered "old-
fashioned" in comparison to the emerging writers of the New
South; and he was summarily dismissed by Northern critics as
a "rabid proslavery writer." Hubbell goes on to point out that
subsequently, most literary historians have not seemed to
know "quite what to make of him and . . . few of them have
read more than one or two of his books."[4] *Cassique,* then, though
it has often been called Simms's best novel,[5] has suffered from
the general neglect and misunderstanding of its author and his
writings,[6] as well as from the particular misfortune of its
unavailability.

But for a short time, when it first appeared, it was received
with acclaim by both critics and general readers alike. F. M.
Hubbard, reviewing *Cassique* in the *North American Review,*
praised Simms for "the range of characters he presents to us . . .
from the highest to the lowest, including almost every variety;
and he seems to be equally at home with them all. They are all
genuine flesh and blood." He particularly singled out the character of Zulieme (child-wife of the rover Harry Calvert), calling
her "a pure creation of the author . . . the author's masterpiece," and went on to say that since Cooper's death "there is no
one who can be reckoned his [Simms's] superior among American novelists."[7] The Columbia, South Carolina, *Courant* noted
that "Mr. Simms tells stories . . . he writes wild and stirring
tales of love and war, of ambition and action . . . ; [he narrates]
the joys and sorrows of love, the dangers and hair-breadth escapes of war, just as they might be expected to affect any man
or woman in our prosaic days."[8] *De Bow's Review* called *Cassique* "the best of his novels."[9] Yet Simms's headlong and often
full-scale depiction of passion and emotion sometimes left critics slightly shaken. A Charleston reviewer, for example, felt
that Simms went into a little more detail than was necessary
concerning "the social intercourse of the sexes,"[10] and Hub-

bard, in spite of his high praise of the novel, worried a little that "the genius of Mr. Simms leads him rather to sketch the darker and more agitating passions."[11] Yet *Russell's Magazine* commended in particular Simms's "ability to deal with subtile and violent passions."[12] It is interesting to note that the genteel tradition in American literary criticism, which has always been most uncomfortable with Simms, is to be found in both a Northern and a Charleston review of the novel; but that also the readiest acceptance of the novel's (and Simms's) earthiness comes from another Charleston review.

Simms's contemporaries, then, understood and for the most part praised his achievement—his ability to tell with historical accuracy a bold and vigorous story with characters of "flesh and blood," and with action scenes so intense that the real flesh and blood readers of the novel often found themselves agitated by Simms's revelation of the darker side of mankind. Presumably Simms himself understood and anticipated that part of the response to the novel which considered his treatment of violence and male-female sexuality as too powerful or explicit; consonant with his whole philosophy of art is Simms's belief that the reader should be moved by what he reads, and even those critics who thought he had gone too far in certain scenes had obviously been stirred by them.[13]

Simms himself said several times that he considered *Cassique* to be one of the best of his novels. Six years after its publication he described it in a letter to his friend Evert Duyckinck as "one of my most interesting romances."[14] Four years later, hopeful that a new collected edition of his books was "on foot," Simms wrote to his son Gilmore that "it is probable that we shall begin a new series with a fresh edition of the Cassique of Kiawah, one of my best romances."[15]

There are probably several reasons why Simms was particularly fond of this novel. One is that it is a story about South Carolina, and Simms in the decade of the 1850s devoted himself especially to historical fiction set in his native state. During a period of three decades, as a writer of fiction, Simms had placed many of his most memorable and daring heroes and heroines against a series of low-country backgrounds rich in history and in dramatic potential. But the best characters and scenes in *Cassique* are exceptional, perhaps unique. They are painted in colors so vivid and with such a confident and practiced hand that the result is a work in which the highly exciting and realistic narrative movement is enhanced by what may be Simms's finest achievement in description and imagery.

Especially in his descriptions of nature do Simms's knowledge of and love for the tideland's intricate waterways and the nearby deep, mysterious forests come through to the reader as a living and immediate presence. A particularly striking example of this appears at the beginning of the opening chapter, where Simms achieves majesty, awe, and a profound sense of the interdependence of land and people. It is one of the most effective openings of all his novels, with its emphasis upon untamed, primeval nature announcing a major theme of the book.

Perhaps another reason for Simms's special fondness for this, his last novel published in book form in his lifetime, was that he had planned and looked forward to writing such a story since he was a young man. In 1841, he wrote to his friend James Lawson that at about the age of eighteen he had written "10 or a dozen chapters of a novel called 'Oyster Point' founded on the early History of Charleston, which was built upon 'Oyster Point'." Four years later, in a letter to Evert Duyckinck he remarked, "I have in preparation a new romance in two vols. entitled 'The Cassique, a Tale of the Ashley River—' time somewhere about 1685." [16] Yet it was July of 1857 before Simms referred to the romance again, in a letter to Lawson in which he noted that he had "just laid the keel of a new romance." In December of the same year he lamented to Duyckinck that "my novel half finished & stereotyped, has not been touched for 2 months," [17] and, though he wrote Duyckinck that it was still unfinished in late April, 1859, [18] it was completed and published by late the following month. [19] The first reviews began to appear in early June of that year. Thus thirty-five years elapsed from the time when, as a boy of eighteen, Simms first began planning such a novel and the time when, as a man of fifty-three, he completed it. [20]

But even more than its long period of gestation, perhaps what sets *Cassique* apart from the rest of Simms's works is his achievement in accomplishing the work under enormously exhausting physical and emotional conditions. When one considers Simms's situation during the latter part of the creation of the novel, and the extreme effort he made under great difficulties to continue his work and to continue it at a high level, this novel emerges as a great personal as well as a literary triumph.

When Simms was writing this romance of early Carolina, although he was at the height of his creative powers as an artist—in "the meridian of life," as one reviewer of *The Cassique* put it [21]—he was also in the throes of deepest suffering. An outbreak of yellow fever had claimed the lives of two of his sons on the same day, September 22, 1858, a blow from which he apparently never fully recovered.[22] To complete his book and get the manuscript to the publisher was an almost unbearable strain. The dedicatory sonnet to Porcher Miles gives the best clue, apart from the *Letters,* of the conditions under which the novel was achieved.[23] In February of 1859 Simms wrote Mary Lawson, daughter of his longtime friend James Lawson, that his book was "nearly finished now . . . which has been lingering & languishing in my hands for almost a year. My griefs & miseries of the last year made me almost oblivious of what I have written, & in resuming my task I had to summon fancy against her will, & sometimes felt the necessity of writing sportively, with a head aching, a heart full almost to bursting, & eyes dropping great tears upon the paper even as I wrote." In March he wrote Duyckinck that "In a few days I hope to finish my novel . . . but now I feel that I am losing the wing for flight & the heart for song."[24] Yet the work of art that was created under such strain is rich with life, and with hope. Even in passages that are structured solidly along conventional lines there is a deeply moving emotional honesty that transforms the predictable scene, and gives it the power to strike the heart. It is this naked emotional honesty that, despite Simms's misgivings, does indeed give *The Cassique of Kiawah* "the wing for flight & the heart for song."[25]

The initial success of the novel is understandable. Besides the fact that it is a swashbuckling, colorful tale built on both of what another Southern writer, William Faulkner, would later call the only two plots for a novel, sex and money, it is also a reliable historical account of early South Carolina settlement and civilization. Indeed, the reviewer for the Columbia *Courant* praised Simms highly for his accuracy of detail, noting that young ladies and gentlemen who usually "dread Mr. Carroll's 'Collections,' or even Mr. Rivers' beautiful 'Sketches,' and the proceedings of the Historical Society, . . . may still be taught much of our history by Dr. Simms' romances, which, to say the least, are, as novels, highly interesting, while they are always correct and faithful in the facts, narrated as such."[26]

The storyline of the novel, when stripped down to outline form, resembles, if not epitomizes, a conventional plot of ill-fated lovers. A younger son strikes out to make his fortune, leaving behind the girl who has promised him her love. A vicious and conniving mother tells her daughter that her betrothed has died at sea, and pushes the stricken girl into marrying the first-born brother, a man of independent means. The younger son, shipwrecked off the Isthmus of Panama, deathly ill, and heartsick over his lover's marriage to his brother, is nursed back to health by a young and ravishingly beautiful girl of Spanish-Moorish descent, whom he marries in a moment of weakness. The brothers' discovery of the "betrayal," their eventual reconciliation, and their struggle for fairness and contentment form the heart of the story.

The main character and hero is Harry Berkeley, who, with his name changed to Harry Calvert, is captain of "The Happy-Go-Lucky," a sailing vessel with a "capacity for mischief" indicated by its "long brass cannon working upon a pivot amidships, and . . . six brass muzzles that grin significantly with open jaws on either side" (p. 22). Commissioned as a privateer by the English king, Charles II, to do as much damage as possible to Spanish commerce on the seas, Calvert is hailed as a hero until the British government declares privateering to be piracy, whereby Calvert becomes not a hero, but a criminal with a high price on his head. The governor of Carolina is instructed to capture Calvert the moment he enters the colony, but the captain's intimate knowledge of the waters and woods of the Carolina coastline keeps him confidently safe and always one—or two—steps ahead of the governor, who really does not want to capture Calvert anyway: his arrest would mean the loss of many beautiful silks and treasures and the potential of more money to be made. Here the reader is introduced to two of the worst aspects of the upper level of this early new-world society, one desperately striving for material gain but also for respectability at any cost.

When Calvert learns that his brother, Edward Berkeley, is the new Cassique of Kiawah, and that he has brought his wife, Calvert's once-betrothed, to the Barony to live, he determines to watch the residence until he can see Olive for himself. When he does see her, she is in a state of physical and mental decline, brought upon by the loveless marriage forced upon her by her mother. But she recognizes him and faints in his arms. They are discovered by Berkeley, who is as much overcome by remorse and anguish as is his wife when he discovers the manner in which they had been deceived. But Calvert, supposing deception in his elder brother, challenges him to a duel, which his brother refuses saying that he has done no intentional wrong. Eventually, in a tense and heated scene, Berkeley calms Calvert's passion and succeeds in proving his innocence, and the brothers are reconciled in one of the most moving scenes in the novel.

Meanwhile, Calvert has uncovered a sinister Indian plot to massacre all the inhabitants of the Barony and surrounding area.[27] Calvert arranges a preemptive attack, and the Indians are defeated in a reverse massacre that is chilling and blood-curdling in Simms's description. In the very moment of the Indians' defeat Olive Masterton Berkeley dies. In the end, Zulieme, Calvert's delightful child-bride (now with child herself), and Harry Calvert/Berkeley (having successfully put down an uprising among his sailors) set sail in "The Happy-Go-Lucky," heading South for "sunnier shores" (p. 600).

Moving in and out of this main love-triangle plot, however, are several episodes involving secondary characters that not only add color and spice to the story, but also broaden and deepen the treatment of the novel's major themes. For example, Molyneaux, the second officer of "The Happy-Go-Lucky," falls in love with Zulieme and unsuccessfully tries to woo her but is discovered in a treacherous conspiracy and dies in mortal combat with Calvert. And there is a melancholy tale involving a young Indian brave, Iswattee, whom we accompany in the solemn ritual of his coming into manhood and follow on to his untimely and tragic death; his story sounds an inexorable knell, first in the distance, yet becoming steadily closer and more foreboding as the novel progresses. Then there is the subplot involving Mrs. Perkins Anderson, doyenne of the new-world society of Charleston. Mrs. Anderson's social world shares the same values as the political world of the governor of Carolina who would prefer to continue illegally profiting from Calvert's sea missions than to see him legally hanged on the gallows. Mrs. Anderson's role in the novel is further complicated because she would like to seduce Harry Calvert whom she considers a conquest to be prized, though he rejects her.

Besides the flawed and partly corrupt upper-level Charleston political and social world of the Governor and Mrs. Anderson, we are introduced to two other microcosms at the beginning of the novel which are carefully woven into the design of the whole "fabrick" of the book, to use Simms's own word.[28] There is the high-seas world of "The Happy-Go-Lucky," a society with a population that is "to be relied upon when blows are heavy." The crew members are "English, Irish, Dutch, French—an amalgam of nations," but, Simms is careful to note, "these fellows are all picked men . . . rough sea-dogs . . . sturdy, cool, hardy, stubborn; capable of good knocks giving and receiving" (p. 23). This group of outcasts, though it gains from supplying the "respectable" world with finery and exotic spices, is independent within itself. Then, in almost direct contrast to the world of "The Happy-Go-Lucky," there is the dignified world of the Indian, who, though just beginning to learn the white man and his ways, as the story opens, already has been taught that first important lesson of distrust, and who, with characteristic patience in retaliation, is plotting one final, horrifying, and treacherous victory over the enemy.[29] Throughout the novel, each of these starkly different civilizations is seen moving steadily in its own independent direction, but the fates of each interlock and conflict with one another, and the resulting tensions rise inevitably toward the breaking point.

Simms, by this point in his life and career, had the vitality
and ripe wisdom of a good artist at the height of his powers, of a
man who is unafraid and unashamed of what he knows. As his
friends and colleagues knew so well, he held decided opinions
about the world, including "society" as he knew it—and voiced
these opinions freely and strongly at times.[30] A man of strong
and intense passion, he also possessed a genuine and hearty
sense of humor. In *The Cassique of Kiawah,* these individual
characteristics of the man radiate throughout the book, breath-
ing life into his characters and vitality into the scenes they
create. The mixture of passion and humor, one always balancing the other, is one of the finest achievements of *Cassique.*

Indeed, "balance" is a key word in understanding Simms's
method here. Throughout the novel, the characters are measured in terms of the balance they strike between the natural
and the civilized (or partly-civilized) world, by the harmony
with which their man-made laws are brought into accordance
with the laws of nature. The narrator tells us that Charleston
in 1684 was little more than "a scattered hamlet of probably
eight hundred inhabitants," and that most of the dwelling
places were generally "very rude," and "that a large proportion
of the people [were] quite as rude as street and dwelling"
(pp. 93–95). But he takes it all in stride, acknowledging that
"it takes a monstrous variety of all sorts to make up the com-
monest sort of world. . . . Blackguards, for example, are a necessary element. . . . There is a great deal of dirty work to be
done in new communities—" (p. 123). And it does not surprise
the reader to learn from the narrator that "there are lusts,
and vanities, and human passions; many vices, and . . . some
goodly virtues, scattered broadside among the goodly people of
the town" (p. 94).

We might assume that the worst vices are to be found among
the less genteel of this society; but we would be quite wrong.
On the whole, the "outlaws" of this society—the Indians, backwoodsmen, and the buccaneers of "The Happy-Go-Lucky" (who
do indeed have their lusts and vanities)—live in a world more

directly in harmony with nature than do the men and women of the township, and therefore tend to react honestly and straightforwardly toward one another rather than in the hypocritical social evasions so carefully practiced by their counterparts within the town walls. These ladies and gentlemen "show" well to one another, and they look after appearances in fastidious detail. But Simms is almost gentle here in his rebuke of these charlatans, for he leaves open the possibility that they are silly, childish, thoughtless, or perhaps stupid, rather than corrupt. He is gentle because, among themselves and to one another, playing the same games according to rules well understood by all, they are virtually harmless.

Simms's treatment of this full cast of characters is masterful and consistent throughout, usually graceful and humorous and gently mocking—until he encounters the more serious aberrations in mankind (or, in the case of Mrs. Masterton and Mrs. Anderson, womankind), at which point there is no mercy in his pen. When the narrator first introduces us to the women of Charleston going about their daily affairs, he dryly remarks that he doubts if "the world improves one jot from all the truths which are told it, especially of itself" (p. 109). We see the self-appointed "ladies" of Charleston adorning themselves in the splendor of smuggled silks and pearls, enjoying the "gallantries of the rover without asking to see too closely the color of his hands." We watch these ladies ("and no small number of a class besides, whom these good ladies universally voted no ladies at all" [p. 109]) playing at games of the heart, and games of power; and their games and desires are often described in words evocative of original sin. But Simms is equally rough with the men of this society too, for when we look to the courts of justice we find that "competence to office was no more the requisite in those days than in ours" (p. 111); and we learn even more when we hear the governor tell Harry Calvert that "we have to keep up appearances . . . this treaty is all a sham—a pretence . . ." (p. 117).

Several degrees more harmful than the Charleston society folk, however, are the degenerates, rogues, and reprobates who wander the outskirts of society, and who, if called upon, can mingle with the townspeople alarmingly well. Sam Fowler, pirate and traitor, who plots the takeover of "The Happy-Go-Lucky" when his captain is preoccupied with other matters, is a true blackguard and ruffian, an "old sea-dog, whose sentences . . . were so larded with oaths as to render them only in part intelligible" (p. 287). Though later on he gets his due in a graphically described murder scene, most of the time when he is plotting the conspiracy he is shown in a humorous light. The narrator wryly notes that "conspiracy . . . among pirates, is wonderfully helped by its potations," and when the plans are outlined, and the drunken, mutinous pirates are called upon to swear loyalty to the "Jolly Roger," they "grouped together in a circle, and joined hands . . . upon which they all swore horrible oaths of fidelity to one another, and to the more horrid purposes of crime . . ." (pp. 287–291). Yet Sam Fowler, by further revealing himself as a coward opposed to a fair fight with Calvert, at the same time reveals that he used to know what honor was, and though he now holds it "redick'lous," the reason he does so is fear: he knows Calvert would "slit your oozen as easy as he'd slice an orange" (p. 298). And Gideon Fairchild, that marvelous picture of Puritan hypocrisy ("rogue by instinct, but a saint by profession" [p. 414]), reveals himself as fool and coward when his bluff is called by the mulatto, Sylvia, whom he has promised to marry if she will help him escape. Nevertheless, in Fairchild as well as in Fowler, faint traces of instinctive honesty linger somewhere, redeeming them from total loss. Simms paints these creatures in harsh colors, but he paints them with humor, and usually with some sympathy.

But there is nothing gentle, humorous, or sympathetic in the portrayal of Mrs. Masterton, the mother who, because she was ashamed of their poverty, betrayed her daughter. Mrs. Masterton is described as having "no nature inconsistent with the rules of her circle," a woman "the natural man would never esteem a charming one" (p. 210). When Edward Berkeley, the deceived husband, reveals to the doctor his deep concern for his wife's life, he voices the suspicion that her mother is "at the bottom of all this mischief," and says coldly that Mrs. Masterton "is one of those fools of society with whom hearts are nothing" (p. 235). She is further damned when Berkeley confronts her with an appeal for honesty, but she only laughs in his face, exulting "that she had been able to lie successfully" (p. 244). She is a powerful and disturbing reminder that, silly and inconsequential as it can be, society can also be corrupt to the core. She is despicable and irredeemable.

However, with the exception of Zulieme, Simms is probably at his height as a character painter with the "macaronie" buccaneer, Molyneaux, the self-deceived, self-absorbed dandy who plots along with Sam Fowler to overthrow Calvert and to win not only "The Happy-Go-Lucky," but the grand prize—Zulieme herself, the captain's wife. Molyneaux, we are told, "prides himself on the having, and the making, of a leg" (p. 46), and, while Calvert is away scouting the coastline, Molyneaux plays with the captain's innocent wife, causing "his eyes to languish, looking deathly things into hers" (p. 47). And, later, trying to insinuate himself into Zulieme's arms with the help of Sylvia, her maid, Molyneaux becomes enraged by the news that Zulieme finds her husband, large man that he is, a lighter dancer than himself. He responds: "I can run as fast, bound as high, jump as far, hop as long, as any man of my size in Britain" (p. 173).[31] And then, to prove it, he says, "Look at that leg! . . . And he stuck his foot upon the gunwale, and stroked his calf complacently" (p. 174).

One of the merriest times Simms has with his secondary characters is with the two foppish courtiers, Craven and Cavendish, frequent callers on Mrs. Perkins Anderson in Charleston, with whom Zulieme is placed while Calvert is away. Having made a bet between themselves as to who will seduce Zulieme (and there is big money involved here too), Craven wins the chance to try. He calls upon her fully schooled in the conventions of "the simple world of Ashley river" and is thoroughly deflated when he finds those conventions of love-making "set in defiance" by the laughing and mocking Zulieme. There ensues a merry but exhausting chase around a cane settee (which Zulieme is winning), until Craven steps on and crushes some of her finest silks and brocades, whereupon she stops the chase, calls him a "great English elephant" and hurls at him furiously everything she can find at hand, including "one of the equivocal garments, of white linen"—at which point, our narrator observes dryly: "This was too much, even for a younger son"

(p. 354). Simms, in this outrageous passage, is at his very considerable best as a writer of comedy of manners.

Yet always before these colorful background characters are the four major characters whose lives, loves, and destinies are the heart of the novel. Three of these—Olive Berkeley, Harry Calvert, and Zulieme Calvert—form the love triangle of the story. Edward Berkeley, husband and brother respectively to Olive and Harry, is primarily a passive victim who, tormented by his wife's silent and mysterious deterioration, takes his frustration out on the land, physically trying to "make it a world to itself . . . [transplanting] civilization to the wilderness, and so train[ing] it as that refinement and art shall be triumphant without excess or sensualism" (p. 597). He is a good man who means well, but one who is incapable of understanding this wild new world as intimately as his brother.

Of the three lovers, it is Olive Berkeley who loses most, who is the tragic heroine of the story. Thomas L. McHaney correctly points out that Simms reverses the conventional tradition of the fair-haired heroine triumphing over her dark-haired counterpoint;[32] indeed, Olive Berkeley wastes away until she is almost a transparent apparition dressed in white, while Zulieme, with her abundance of wild dark hair, is physically strong and passionate throughout. Olive does not have the strength of will to withstand the relentless pressure exerted by her mother. She is ruined by the one who, above all human beings in the world, she should most have trusted. She becomes a sacrifice, the saint and martyr of the novel. The narrator, when he speaks of her, praises "the heart-instincts of Olive" (p. 369), but we see that while she is good, loving, faithful, and true, she is also weak. In her "unnatural condition of mind and heart" (p. 334) she rapidly deteriorates both physically and mentally from the time of her marriage. Resembling Ophelia on the verge of her death, she leaves the real world and wanders to the willows of her youth, singing woeful snatches of songs from her girlhood. She becomes a mere spectre in this world; one who, when denied her proper love, cannot survive. More alive in her subconscious dream world, at night she whispers her tragedy to her imagined lover: "It was for the cassique's gold, Harry! I was bought and sold, like an African from the Gold-coast, though

49

they did not call it selling—they only called it marriage!" (p. 245).

The nature of Harry Calvert when the reader meets him is a mixture of hot-blooded passion and stern discipline. Yet we meet him only after the heartbreak of his first love, after he has proved himself competent and deadly in battle, controlled in his conduct with his fiery new wife, and utterly capable of all that he undertakes to look after, protect, or accomplish. Calvert still loves Olive as he did before he left for adventure on the high seas; Olive still loves him the way she did before she became the wife of another man and bore him a child. Fate had altered their courses; and, subjected to radical change, both lovers pine for the past. Olive gives up and dies; while Harry, with his great physical and emotional strength, lives, though often wishing he could die.

Forced at an early age to seek his fortune elsewhere, Harry chose the freedom of the seas, as far removed from the "civilized" society of England as possible. Though he can return periodically to his former world and fit in comfortably, it is inevitable, now that he is in his own words "a freeman with Nature," that he can never endure "that Old World, with all its rotten conventions . . ." (p. 596). The battle raging within him while he is learning to accept the changes in his life makes him at times violent, murderous, and vindictive. But in the end, with the peace of Olive's death, and with all the promise of his new life with Zulieme, Calvert's tormented spirit comes to heaven.

But it is the character of Zulieme that lies at the heart of *The Cassique of Kiawah,* and she is perhaps the chief reason the book is so memorable. Simms's own description of her bears quoting in full:

> She is not a large creature as Cleopatra may have been—nay, *petite* rather—but full bosomed, with every look speaking passion—music's passion; the sun's passion; the passion of storm and fire upon occasion, ready to burst forth without warning and spoil the sky's face, and rage among the flowers.
>
> She is brown with a summer's sun; her beauty is of the dark; like a night without a cloud, far up in the sky, flecked with solitary stars. Her features are not regular, but, in their very caprice, they harmonize. Her large black eye dilates at every

glance, reveals every emotion, however slight, and passes, with the rapidity of lightning, from smiles to tears; from tenderness to a passion, which may easily be rage as well as love! It is keen, restless, jealously watchful, intense in every phase. The nose is small, but capable of sudden dilation; the lips voluptuous, pale, and soon shaken with a tremulous quiver, whenever the feelings are touched. The brow, whiter than the rest of the face, is marked by two blue veins above the eyes, that become swollen at a moment's warning. It is not high, nor massive, nor yet narrow; the eyebrows are thick and black, the lashes long; and when the orbs droop, in the languor of satisfied emotions, they form a beautiful and glossy fringe fit for hiding the fiery jewels that burn beneath. (Pp. 26–27)

The Charleston *Mercury* reviewer wrote in 1859: "We are inclined to consider Zulieme Calvert the most admirable female character ever drawn by the author, with its tropical languor and childishness, its unconscious voluptuousness, its self-will and difficulty of understanding the stern duties of life, and its true womanliness underlying all. We have seen more than one Zulieme Calvert, but few who could paint them."[33] These are high words of praise both for Simms and the woman he creates.

Zulieme is the character closest to nature in the story. She is also the one furthest removed from the civilized worlds of seventeenth-century Charleston; she is indeed the human counterpart of the primitive, voluptuous coastal lands and waterways that we were introduced to in the opening chapter. And, alone among the characters in this novel (with the exception of Calvert who changes at the end but remains static throughout most of the tale), Zulieme continues to grow, yet remains unspoiled and unhurt in any way. She is not of this civilized world, and in the true sense of the word, in the sense of lack of knowledge of evil, she is innocent. Though she may indeed flirt with powdered courtiers in society parlours, she does not yield to the temptations dangled before her. On the contrary, she mocks, taunts, and exasperates "society" when it takes itself too seriously. The narrator, wryly observing that "Zulieme is perhaps not half the fool which she appears—not half the fool, compared with some of her most self-assured neighbors," notes too that "an *honest* instinct is . . . a wiser guide for humanity"

(p. 319). With that we are reminded that Zulieme comes from a culture and society much older than the one newly taking shape in Carolina—and a traditional culture far more willing to accept a bouyant nature. Zulieme, a natural child, becomes an equally natural grown woman during the time that "The Happy-Go-Lucky" lies hidden in Charleston harbor. One of the things that separates her from the rest of the women in this town is the "warm current of healthy blood" flowing beneath her "exquisite skin" (p. 351). It is one of the features she shares with Harry.

Instinctively the reader knows that Harry Calvert, captain of "The Happy-Go-Lucky," is the rightful mate to Zulieme. He is a man of intense natural passions, "of manhood the most beautiful . . . full of blood as well as character" (p. 24); a man of "savage coolness" (p. 319), with a strong sense of duty, capable of doing almost anything in the name of that duty. But he is a man, too, who is capable of lighthearted as well as passionate love-making. Zulieme describes their courtship after his near-death recovery as a time of "playing in the orange-groves," although she does admit in her guileless way that she did most of the playing and "he suffered it" (p. 330). During the time they are in Charleston, when Harry is so inexplicably changed from the way he was on the Spanish Main, Zulieme remembers the times they shared and the sport they had. She exclaims to Charlotte Anderson, "Oh, . . . he can dance, I tell you!" (p. 330); and she recalls a little more slowly, "There's no person so quick to feel. He can change in a moment, like lightning; and he shows you, very soon, that he feels every change" (p. 328). Then she reveals, "When he made love to me, it was like a tiger" (p. 54). The very embodiment of sensuality, physical love, and beauty, Zulieme rejoices in her husband's manhood and physicality. Although her natural frivolity and playfulness frustrate Calvert to the point of distraction throughout this difficult time, it is important to remember that Zulieme, above all, remains steadfast and loyal to her husband—even in spite of his sometimes brutal temper and cruel neglect, and notwithstanding the calculated temptations presented to her by society.

Indeed, Simms finally equates the nature and passions of Zulieme, "child of Nature" who has no ties to conventional society, with Harry, "freeman with Nature," who rejects them.

Both have suffered danger and storm in this harbor, and both of them will suffer again in their lifetime together. But for now, as the novel draws to its close, the young man and woman, warm with the knowledge and promise of new life and hope, yield themselves "to those seductions with which Love subdues War" (p. 600), and "The Happy-Go-Lucky" turns southward.

———

The Cassique of Kiawah is consonant with all that Simms believed about the actual world, about its past, its present, and its implicit future—with its men and women busy creating their own present and their own past histories. It is also consonant with Simms's conception of the artist's all-important role in rendering such a world as truthfully as possible in fictional form.

Simms believed, in the spirit of Coleridge and Wordsworth, that the purpose of art is to elevate man's soul, to inspire him to transcend the coarseness and vulgarity of everyday life. It is the responsibility of the artist, possessing the inspiration of genius, to instruct his fellow man how to achieve proper morality and spirituality on this earth. He knew, too, that the first obligation of the artist is to capture the attention and interest of his audience. The writer's story, then, must be one that is both compelling and believable; fiction must be made from "the simple accumulation of interesting incidents, in relation to some hero in behalf of whom [our] sympathies are enlisted." [34] For the artist, the past—a mixture of known facts, probabilities, and imaginings—is of the highest importance. History, Simms consistently maintained, is the "raw material . . . to which the fire of genius imparts soul, and which the smile of taste . . . informs with beauty." [35] It is through art that the past, as history, lives "to the counseling and direction of the future."

Simms believed that "the true nature of man is art—that [man] is a builder and creator like his Sovereign Master," [36] and that the reason man builds is to strive towards some sort of immortality on this earth. Those who believe in such a philosophy of art, according to Simms, "care not so much for the intrinsic truth of history, as for the great moral truths." It is important for mankind to reason what *should have been*—that is, moral

53

truth—from the fragmentary records left to us by our forbears. Because history is left to us in fragments, in partial and conflicting accounts, the artist must take those shards of fact and supplement them by borrowing from "every department of human art"—from poet, painter, sculptor, dramatist, lawyer, and historian—to make his fiction "seem like truth."[37] For Simms fiction was "neither more nor less, than probable truth under intenser conditions than ordinary."[38]

An important point made by James E. Kibler is that the essential nature of Simms the man and Simms the artist centers upon "a philosophy which subordinates the material to the spiritual."[39] Simms had a strong belief in God and in the power of Nature. He abhorred the materialistic greed he felt was the all-consuming passion of his day, the "feverish, phrenzied passion for gain."[40] He stated emphatically in 1842 that "I do not believe that all the steam power in the world can bring happiness to one human heart,"[41] and Kibler notes that as his career progressed, Simms realized more clearly that "nature, as powerful as she is, might not be a match for man's greed."[42]

Simms deeply believed that "our business" on this earth and in this world was to work toward the attainment of "the highest good," and that "next to religion, the business of Literature is the noblest concern of human society. Nay, Literature is the religion of society; the handmaid of that spiritual nature, whose constant yearnings are for excellence."[43] This philosophy, so clearly expressed in his writings, so consistently held throughout his mature career, informs the world of *The Cassique of Kiawah* at every point. The novel is at once a major historical romance, a delightful novel of manners, and a realistic depiction of the early evolution of a society. It is also a final, full-scale revelation of Simms's profoundest thoughts on the principles of his art.

Notes

[1] William Gilmore Simms, *The Cassique of Kiawah* (New York: J. S. Redfield, 1859).

[2]When Redfield's house failed, it was taken over by William J. Widdleton, who then became Simms's publisher for books that Redfield had published; but for the ensuing five years, in Simms's words, "the whole business of his publication arrangements seems one inextricable snarl." Mary C. Simms Oliphant, Alfred Taylor Odell, and T. C. Duncan Eaves, eds., *The Letters of William Gilmore Simms* (Columbia: University of South Carolina Press, 1952), IV, p. 281. Hereafter cited as *Letters*. See also *Letters*, IV, p. 250n. for further discussion of the Redfield situation, as well as letters to James Lawson between October 1860 and 1865 for attempts to unravel the problems. (For most of the bibliographical data here I am indebted to James B. Meriwether, who kindly made available to me his unpublished bibliography, "The Books of William Gilmore Simms.")

[3]William P. Trent, *William Gilmore Simms* (New York: Houghton, Mifflin and Company, 1892), p. 242.

[4]Jay B. Hubbell, *The South in American Literature 1607–1900* (Durham: Duke University Press, 1954), p. 596.

[5]James Henry Hammond writes Simms that *Cassique* "is perhaps superior in genius & ability to any thing you have done in prose." The novel is also highly acclaimed by such periodicals as the Charleston *Mercury,* the New York *Leader, Godey's, Russell's Magazine,* and *De Bow's Review.* See *Letters,* IV, p. 152n. for the quotation from Hammond's letter and a useful discussion of the contemporary reviews this novel received. Mary Ann Wimsatt, in her essay "Realism and Romance in Simms's Midcentury Fiction," *Southern Literary Journal,* 12 (1980), 29–48, lists the modern criticism the novel has received (p. 41n).

[6]Wimsatt's essay "Realism and Romance in Simms's Midcentury Fiction" is the fullest treatment of *Cassique* in recent years. It is a useful explanation of Simms's use of both romance and realism in several of his novels, but I disagree with her conclusion that "although he was intrigued by the newest trends in the realistic tradition, he was basically a romancer who tried to accommodate these trends to the conventions of his major genre." Simms's artistic aim was to make his fiction "Seem like truth" and to do so it was essential that he cloak his romantic "moral" in abundant realistic detail. See Simms's essay "Modern Prose Fiction," *Southern Quarterly Review,* 15 (April 1849), 41–83, for his philosophy as a writer of romances. Robert Bush has pointed out with reference to Simms's comedy that "to Simms, the comic writer begins as the observer of truth, not as the creator of humor"; I think his comment is equally applicable to Simms the creator of romances. Simms begins with his observation of the truth (i.e., real-

istic detail), rather than adding it on later as an accommodation to current literary trends. (Robert Bush, Introduction to *As Good as a Comedy,* in *The Writings of William Gilmore Simms,* ed. James B. Meriwether [Columbia: University of South Carolina Press, 1972], III, xiii).

[7] *North American Review,* 89 (October 1859), 559–561.

[8] Columbia *Courant,* 1 (June 9, 1859), 45–46.

[9] *De Bow's Review,* 27 (July 1859), 123.

[10] The Charleston *Mercury* (June 7, 1859). This reviewer continues to praise the novel highly and in great detail, calling it "one of great vigor and attraction" and reporting "the avidity with which it has been sought and read, both here and elsewhere." However, being a careful Charleston gentleman, he notes with a furrow in his brow that "there is some disparagement, however undesigned, of the tone and condition existing in the colony even at that early day."

[11] *North American Review,* 89 (October 1859), 559.

[12] *Russell's,* 6 (December 1859), 276–277.

[13] The reviewer for Charleston *Mercury* (June 7, 1859) for instance, praises Simms for doing what "general history cannot do," that is, to "picture American life and scenes—the manners, the habits, thoughts and pastimes of the people." This, he acknowledges, "cannot easily be done. The scenes must all be elaborated and mingled with the great ruling passions that move the human breast." At the same time, however, he frets that "there are some strong expressions and ideas in regard to the social intercourse of the sexes that are disagreeable, and in our judgment, had better been omitted."

[14] *Letters,* IV, 519.

[15] Letter to William Gilmore Simms, Jr., August 3, 1869, *Letters,* V, 240.

[16] *Letters,* I, 285; II, 81.

[17] *Letters,* III, 504; 520.

[18] Letter to Duyckinck, April 22, 1859, *Letters,* IV, 146. The dedicatory sonnet to W. Porcher Miles carries the date April, 1859.

[19] The novel was listed among new works in *American Publishers' Circular and Literary Gazette* (May 21, 1859). For a listing and brief discussion of the reviews of *The Cassique of Kiawah,* see *Letters,* IV, 152n.

[20] In September of 1865, after Sherman's army had destroyed Woodlands, including Simms's library "which numbered some 10,700 vols." (*Letters,* IV, 501), Simms wrote Duyckinck asking if he could "procure me a History of the Pyrates . . . [which], with all my books, has been destroyed. . . . It gives me great material, which I have long desired to

work up into a standard romance of Pirate life & practice" (*Letters,* IV, 519). Because he requested the volume specifically for work on a new romance entitled "The Brothers of the Coast," it is reasonable to assume that he drew from the "History of the Pyrates" for his colorful and lively depiction of the pirates in *Cassique.* See *Letters,* IV, 519n. The volume he requested was probably Capt. Charles Johnson, *A General History of the Pyrates* (London: T. Warner; T. Woodward, 1724–1725).

[21] *De Bow's Review,* 27 (July 1859), 123.

[22] Simms writes to Lawson of his children in February, 1859, "I have had *thirteen* of these but six remain. I have buried *seven*" (*Letters,* IV, 123). Trent records that both boys died on September 22, 1858 (p. 240).

[23] On the occasion of the unveiling of the bronze bust of Simms at Charleston, on June 11, 1879, Porcher Miles remembered his friend as "a Carolinian of Carolinians" and recalls: "It was my sad privilege to watch with him and his estimable wife by the deathbeds of their two darling boys. I have known him, therefore, in the bitterness of grief and the desolation of bereavement, as well as in joy and prosperity and successful achievement, and can bear witness to the real nobility of his nature; his brave, *manful,* tender heart; his truthful, earnest, ever-aspiring soul." *Ceremonies at the Unveiling of the Bronze Bust of William Gilmore Simms at White Point Garden, Charleston, S.C. June 11th, 1879* (The News and Courier Book Presses, Charleston, 1879, reprinted by the Southern Studies Program, University of South Carolina, 1979), p. 57.

[24] *Letters,* IV, 128; 138.

[25] William Peterfield Trent, on the other hand, reports with facile oversimplification the circumstances of the completion of the novel, suggesting that after such bitter and tragic losses, "in such a state of mind it was natural for him to turn for relief to his proper and congenial occupation of writing romances." He continues glibly: "He took up the unfinished 'Cassique of Kiawah,' and by the spring of 1859 had it ready for the printers" (p. 240).

[26] Columbia *Courant* (June 9, 1859). The reviewer in this instance is most probably Simms's friend, William James Rivers, who was professor of history at South Carolina College at the time of this review. There is a letter from Simms to Mr. Rivers, dated June 13, 1859, which thanks Rivers for "your kind estimate of my volume. . . . " and notes that Rivers is "one of the few, whom I know, capable of following me along the route which I pursued." Trent, too, remarks that "Professor W. J. Rivers, perhaps the best informed man in Carolina on matters of local history, wrote to bear his testimony to the accuracy with which

Simms had delineated the historical period in which he had set his romance" (p. 240). If the review were written by Rivers, one has to appreciate the high esteem with which he regards his own work. The "beautiful 'Sketches'" refers to Rivers' *A Sketch of the History of South Carolina to the Close of the Proprietary Government by the Revolution of 1719* (Charleston: McCarter & Co., 1856). *Letters,* VI, 199.

[27] Albert Keiser, in his chapter on Simms in *The Indian in American Literature,* provides a sound and knowledgeable discussion of Simms's treatment of the Indians in *Cassique.* He commends Simms for his foresight concerning the eventual plight of the Native Americans and for his sympathetic and realistic depiction of the Carolina Indians of this period. See "Simms' Romantic Naturalism," *The Indian in American Literature* (New York: Oxford University Press, 1933), pp. 154–174. In direct contrast to Keiser's judicious and thorough study is Richard Drinnon's treatment of Simms in *Facing West: The Metaphysics of Indian-Hating and Empire Building* (Minneapolis: University of Minnesota Press, 1980). In Chapter XII, "An American Romance in Color: William Gilmore Simms," he shows little knowledge and no understanding of Simms's various writings on the subject, misrepresenting Simms's attitude towards the Indians and their culture in an attempt to fit Simms into a thesis which, no matter how applicable to the other writers he treats, ignores the balanced picture Simms is always careful to give of the complex and ultimately tragic relationship between Indian and white man.

[28] Simms's philosophy of art and the artist falls into the classical Aristotelian (and later Romantic) tradition which suggests that genius provides the inspiration for creativity, and fancy (the imagination) embellishes the creation. Simms writes about the artist: "Thus, the *tout ensemble* of his fabric will awe with its magnificence, yet with such exquisiteness of detail, that its cunning joinery will scarcely be perceptible to the nicest examination. The first great evidence of his superior art, will be the manifestation of design. It is in this particular that we are made to see the genius. It must be seen that he is working out a purpose." "Modern Prose Fiction," *Southern Quarterly Review,* 15 (April 1849), 47.

[29] Keiser, in his rich and detailed discussion of the Indians in *Cassique* writes of this plot: "The description of the assault and defense ranks with the best found in American literature." *The Indian in American Literature,* p. 160.

[30] Wm. Porcher Miles, in his tribute to Simms on the occasion of the unveiling of the bust in 1879 notes that Simms "was criticised as lacking tack and *savoir faire* in social intercourse, and not without justice. His truthfulness, his frankness and boldness in uttering his opinions,

always and everywhere—giving his manner an aggressive air—were not always to the taste of the frequenters of *salons,* where 'that repose / Which stamps the caste of Vere de Vere' is strictly required and considered to be *de rigeur.* Simms certainly was a man who had 'the courage of his convictions.' And in avowing them he cared little about conciliating men, or women either. In his scorn and contempt for the little, the false, the mean—for *simulacrums,* and 'shams' of all sorts, he reminded me often of Carlyle . . ." *Ceremonies at the Unveiling of the Bronze Bust of William Gilmore Simms,* p. 57.

[31]Though anachronistic, this quotation is reminiscent of the later Southern "brag" literature that Simms and his readers knew and appreciated for its realistic humor.

[32]Thomas L. McHaney, "William Gilmore Simms," *The Chief Glory of Every People,* ed. Matthew J. Bruccoli (Carbondale: Southern Illinois University Press, 1973), p. 185.

[33]The Charleston *Mercury* (June 14, 1859).

[34]Simms, "Modern Prose Fiction," p. 43.

[35]William Gilmore Simms, "The Epochs and Events of American History, as Suited to the Purposes of Art in Fiction," in *Views and Reviews in American Literary History and Fiction,* First Series, ed. C. Hugh Holman (Cambridge: Belknap Press of Harvard University Press, 1962), p. 34. Hereafter cited as "History for the Purposes of Art." For a thorough and illuminating discussion of Simms's use of history in the creation of his art, see Nicholas G. Meriwether's essay in this volume.

[36]Simms, "Modern Prose Fiction," p. 65.

[37]Simms, "Modern Prose Fiction," pp. 44–45. Also, Simms would remind us that as "truthfulness is never without its moral, and as the great end of the artist is the approximation of all his fiction to a seeming truth, so unavoidably, he inculcates a moral whenever he tells a story."

[38]Simms, "Modern Prose Fiction," p. 52.

[39]James Everett Kibler, Jr., *The Poetry of William Gilmore Simms: An Introduction and Bibliography* (Columbia, S.C.: University of South Carolina Southern Studies Program, 1979), p. 24.

[40]William Gilmore Simms, *The Social Principle: The True Source of National Permanence. An Oration, Delivered Before the Erosophic Society of The University of Alabama, December 13, 1842* (Columbia: University of South Carolina Southern Studies Program, 1980), p. 43.

[41]Simms, *The Social Principle,* p. 53.

[42]Kibler, *Poetry of William Gilmore Simms,* p. 22.

[43]Simms, *The Social Principle,* p. 25.

American Gods and Devils in Simms's *Paddy McGann*

LINDA E. MCDANIEL

In a series of essays published in 1846 on "The Epochs and Events of American History," William Gilmore Simms observes, "It is in the god and devil of a race that you can behold the truest picture of themselves."[1] In his 1863 novel, *Paddy McGann; or, The Demon of the Stump,*[2] Simms develops the narrative by portraying the hero's encounters with gods and devils in different stages of the American experience. Under the influence and advice of various "authorities" and guides, Paddy moves from the age of the hunter step by step to the Civil War. He battles in the swamp and then on the river and sea with a demon avenging the destruction of the wilderness—first by hunters, then by commerce. After he arrives in New York, Paddy discovers new versions of priests, prophets, and devils who exert their powers through newspapers, books, and "swarrays." In the final episodes of his career, Paddy sees his old familiar spirits at home gradually superseded by those of nineteenth-century religion and rationalism. Though Paddy's adventures perhaps appear uneven and disjointed,[3] they follow Simms's earlier analyses of the development of the American nation as it moved from the imaginative superstition of the woods through later phases of religion, commerce, art, and science.

Paddy's swamp adventures correspond with Simms's previous discussions of the early stages of the American nation. In his essay, "The Four Periods of American History," Simms examines first the age of colonization, "when there were witches in the land—sorcerers needing to be baffled—devils to be cast forth—all angrily striving for continued possession of their ancient strong-holds in the troubled heart of man."[4] Sam Hartley serves as Paddy McGann's instructor through these early periods of superstition and religion. After the hero fails repeatedly to shoot birds and animals with his usual skill, Sam advises that the gun may be jinxed and directs Paddy to a backwoods wizard to break the spell. Despite the good money paid for the services, the bad luck continues. As the bullying Isaac Clymes observes, first Paddy tries the "witch doctor" and then he tries God (p. 274). Drinking whiskey and reading Scripture, Hartley instructs his friend concerning the witches in the Bible (such as Saul's Witch of Endor) and the various forms devils take. Sam also functions to present Simms's theme about the gods and demons of each period. In Sam's words, "'instead of one devil, there's a thousand,'" according to the time and location: "'Jest as they live, according to the place, or element, so they have a perticklar nather, for that same place or element'" (p. 259). In *Paddy McGann,* Simms illustrates Sam Hartley's generalization.

As Robert Bush and Simone Vauthier observe, the first demon Paddy encounters differs curiously from the usual literary diabolical spirit.[5] Though he appears in the various forms of big red eyes or phantom beasts, Paddy's fiend most often manifests himself as a "Hoo! Hoo! Hoo!" or as a stump or a log. His peculiar form represents the destruction of the forests as Americans cleared the land to establish homesteads and to supply materials for commerce and industry. In an analysis of Thomas Bangs Thorpe's "Big Bear of Arkansas," Leo Lemay notes similar relevant symbolism: "The cutting down of the trees of the American wilderness had been viewed as the primary symbol of the destruction of the wilderness and as the end of the American paradise since at least the early eighteenth century."[6]

In *Paddy McGann,* this symbolism fuses with myths and traditions of supernatural forces inhabiting forests and trees. Simms alludes in his poetry to forest spirits, ranging from the cultures of the ancient Greeks to those of the American Indians. In "Haunted Woods.—A Fragment," for example, Simms muses on the effects of these universal superstitions on the European hunter in the New World. Bringing their own dryads, gnomes, and fairies into the wilderness with them, the white hunters found the Indians' spirits already haunting the woods—"Mischievous elves" to trick the hunter, and demons to cast "spells that haunt" and "inspire terror." [7] The colonists' beliefs in supernatural "races" added to their sense of danger from very real hostile Indians and predatory beasts in the pathless primeval forests. In one of Simms's early stories, for instance, a magic pine can imprison a human being. When an Indian finds himself entrapped by the great tree, the author explains that the hunter "was in the power" of "the Grey Demon of Enoree": "In these traps for the unwary the wicked demon caught his victim, and exulted in his miseries." [8]

Paddy's demon is a literary descendant of tradition and myth; and he specifically recalls certain Germanic wood spirits whose duties included, according to one folklorist, "looking after the forest in general and shielding the trees from injury" and chastising "those who stole wood or did injury to the forest trees." [9] The demon of the stump also chastises Paddy for "murdering" the wildlife in the woods and protects the "children" and "pets" raised by the forest spirit's own hand (pp. 315–316). Thus, in the demon of the stump, Simms embodies a symbol of the destruction of the wilderness and universal superstitions about tree spirits; and the unusual devil provides a means of depicting the end of the age of the hunter.

From the early phase of hunting and superstition, Sam Hartley directs Paddy toward a more civilized and religious way of life. When Paddy's hunting no longer provides enough food for him and his mother, Mrs. McGarvin, Sam advises Paddy to leave off hunting independently and to compete instead in a socialized, ordered competition for a prize beef, where contestants pay for chances to shoot at an ace of hearts nailed to a tree. Even with the best quality gun and powder, however, Paddy completely misses the tree. When the hero later rides in hot pursuit of a "devil buck," Simms symbolizes the effects of the industrial forces overtaking the hunter: a long train on the railroad track interferes with the chase (pp. 291–292). Paddy can no longer depend on his rifle for survival.

The ex-hunter adjusts to these changes during a transition period by turning to religion.[10] As he gives up his primitive way of life, Paddy also begins to turn from his old superstitions and to study the Bible on his own "like a young student." He becomes a Soldier of the Lord before he returns for another wrestling match with the burnt stump (pp. 332–333). But in the last scene in the swamp at this stage of Paddy's career, no devil appears in any form. Finally, before he leaves the scene of his encounters with the demon stump, Paddy kneels to pray.

Immediately upon Paddy's arrival home, Simms changes the scene to the period of commerce, urbanization, and industrialization by moving his protagonist from the farm to the river. Sam Hartley awaits his friend with a message from a lumberman who wants Paddy to command a fleet of rafts down the Edisto River to Charleston. Though Paddy extols the "sweet" pure beauty of the Edisto, his description indicates the changes that have occurred in the forty years since a hunter on the river first shot at an eagle and startled the bird into dropping its fish; man has been robbing the eagle of its food ever since, observes Paddy (p. 335). Now the waterway has also become a means of robbing the forest of more trees, a highway for moving timber to populated areas like Charleston, which, as Paddy remarks, "gits all the trade of the Edisto, and it's the great lumber river for the city" (p. 338).[11] Moreover, civilization has brought a new kind of moral pollution to the river: the bawdy-houses of Nelly Miller and Mother Jordan.

Even on the river, fallen trees have the ability to avenge the losses of their species. Paddy describes the dangerous trees "throwed down by Harricanes and lying secret in the river, with jest a snout and a horn riding up and hooking your timbers" (p. 336). The "snout" and "horn" suggest another form of the devil. Once past these and other dangers, if "nothing goes wrong with the machinery," the rafts reach a civilized, Christianized urban center: the city of Charleston, "lying like a great tarrapin in the water, with a world of steeples and churches and houses on her back" (p. 337).

Paddy, however, does not reach Charleston at the end of his

most unusual voyage. Because he has turned from the "murder" of partridges and other wildlife nurtured by the forest only to participate in a trade based on wholesale destruction of trees, the hero does not escape the demon of the stump by leaving the swamp. At first, the journey down the Edisto proceeds smoothly. At one stop, Nelly Miller and "her gals" provide an evening of "frolic." Eventually, the raftsmen reach White Points safely, though thunder and lightning rage around them. After joining the party at Mother Jordan's, however, Paddy remembers his responsibilities for the timber and the men. He realizes that the rising wind makes White Points, where the Edisto joins another river and runs out to the ocean nearby, an even more "dangerous" place "for a raft to be in." He leaves off the "drinking and dancing, cussing, and swearing, whooping and fighting" to check on the rafts. In the dark, foggy night, however, Paddy feels "mighty lonesome" and takes a few consoling drinks before he falls asleep on the job (pp. 340–342).

In Paddy's subsequent dream of riding on "the biggest owl in the world" going "full speed down the river, fast as he could fly," the author effectively employs different versions of owl symbolism (p. 342). In the novel, Simms associates the devil's "Hoo! Hoo! Hoo!" with owls; and as Paddy dreams of flying with an owl, the demonic stump pilots the raft full speed toward the gulf. According to various traditions, just dreaming of an owl meant bad luck and foretold the traveler's shipwreck; and owls could represent either death or wisdom [12]—Paddy's options after he awakes to find himself lost at sea. The owl's speeding flight also suggests that the dangerous and irresponsible rush toward "progress" and "civilization" could sweep the American into a gulf before he could gain control.

At sea, instead of drowning himself, Paddy undergoes initiation into a higher wisdom in the one episode in which he depends on no human guide or adviser: "I was out at say, me one,—one alone,—on my poor pilot raft; going out fast as I could drive," headed for the "gulf," a name "to terrify of itself!" (p. 343). All alone, Paddy finds comfort in the eye of the sun, the angels and the staff of God seen in the stars, and in the four moons. His tribulations and visions lead to personal revelations of his own individual God who will keep him from drowning and help him withstand further trials.[13] Buoyed by a new independence, Paddy experiences a change in his relationship with the demon of the stump; and he finally embraces and dances with the protecting spirit of the wilderness before a ship rescues the hero and carries him into another stage of American history with its own brands of gods and devils.

The period of commerce and trade, according to Simms, was "followed by the gradual steps of art and science."[14] Through imagery and puns, Simms presents, in Paddy's New York adventures, the gods and devils of the important era of artistic and literary development during the two decades before the Civil War. Though his guides point out to Paddy the local philosophers, "choice sperrits," and "glories" of New York, Simms implies that at this stage of the American experience, the gods and devils become difficult to distinguish from the "fools."

Simms continues the devil motif in the discourse of the captain of the ship that rescues Paddy. Aboard the brigantine, the hero awakes to find himself under the care of Mr. Thompson and Captain Wilson, both Scotsmen, who will advise and interpret for Paddy during his New York sojourn. Hearing the Captain's description of the city, Paddy remarks, "'Why, Cappin, it's a sort of hell on airth, 'cording to this charackter'" (p. 383). After the Captain agrees, saying, "'You'll lose yourself,'" Paddy links his forthcoming trials to his old demon in the swamp: "'Lord,' says I, 'lose myself in the streets of a town, when the Divil himself, trying to mislead me, would niver lose me in the woods of the swamp'" (p. 383). In New York, new kinds of devils attempt to mislead Paddy.

Simms begins this episode with Paddy's harassment by representatives of the diabolical New York press. Three editors have already featured Paddy's adventures in their newspapers and board the ship to "pump" the hero of the "shipwreck." In his explanatory notes to *Paddy McGann,* Robert Bush names likely candidates for Simms's satire. Editors who had attacked the South over the years include Horace Greeley of the *New York Tribune,* whom an Arkansas Congressman "severely caned" in 1856. The journalist who "calls himself a *philosopher*" is based on James Gordon Bennett, editor of the *New York Herald,* who ranked himself with "Zoroaster, Moses, Socrates, Seneca and Luther." Simms also "despised" the *Enquirer* editor, James Watson Webb, and the *New York Daily Times* editor, Henry J. Raymond (p. 529). Though these editors envision themselves as great prophets and philosophers, Mr. Thompson expresses another opinion: "'Them three newspapers are pretty much the rulers of these people. They lead 'em back and for'a'd as they please. . . . They are jest hurrying them on to the Devil!'" (p. 382). After Paddy receives unfair treatment in the press, he wants to go after the man who wrote the article; but his advisors tell him "to grin and bear it" because that journalist is "not a human at all." Still Paddy longs for "a chaince for a clip at the infarnal editor, who was ividently inspired by the devil" (p. 410).

Though Paddy finds the New York newspapers generally fiendish, no editor riles him more than a "smooth, smiling gintleman" who jumps up from the wharf when Paddy first goes ashore (p. 384). In his biting satirical portrait of Lewis Gaylord Clark of the *Knickerbocker Magazine,* Simms renews attacks on the editor with whom he first became embroiled nearly two decades earlier.[15] The editor who greets Paddy promises to show him the "glories of New York," which include Wall Street (where "they settle all the affairs of the world") and Barnum's Museum (p. 385). Clark also takes Paddy to a restaurant, where the two eat a fine meal before the editor sneaks off, leaving Paddy stuck with the bill. When the waiters tell Paddy that he has been "*sold,*" and explain the con game of the "sponge," Paddy can only exclaim, "'The devil he does,'" and pay the bill (pp. 387–388).

Following further episodes with "philosophers" and a "generous" con man, Paddy encounters a votary of a new religion. The hero meets the fat and feathery Fourierite, Anne Statia, at a tea in Brooklyn where she monopolizes him with her talk of "fair sperrits," ecstasies, souls, prayers, and flames. Her conversation combines Fourierism with Byronic romanticism and lascivious innuendoes. Supposedly fascinated by the ecstasy Paddy must have felt alone at sea, she rhapsodizes: "'But had you no longings of the soul, Paddy—no grand hopes and inspirations—no great imaginations—no prayers for wings to fly to that beautiful sphere—to soar away from this lowly orb, and bask in the etarnal light of moon and stars!'" (p. 414). She gushes over Paddy's romantic South Carolina log cabin and over his native foods: "'How I do relish those delicious Carolina potatoes, as far as I kin hev a taste for any more mortal food!'" (p. 418).

If Anne Statia implies that she is a goddess, Paddy sees signs of another kind of spirit. According to him, she speaks "with the eyes of a hungry sarpent" (p. 414), and later her eyes have "a softness and a fire mixed together that would have melted the bowels of an alligator" (p. 419). More than once, he feels her "hot breath" on him. When they move to the dining table Simms makes a pun on the word "sand-witches": "I only knowed about one sort of witches," says Paddy, implying that Anne falls into that category (p. 416). On his departure, Paddy questions the Captain about the woman. Wilson explains that she is a "Furey-ite," who "'preaches the doctrines of a Frenchman named Furey, who denounces marriage.'" Paddy's response links Miss Statia to other figures in the novel: "'The divil!'" he says. And his adviser agrees: "'Paint and powder, Paddy. She's a made-up thing, and as impudent as the divil'" (p. 421).

Anne Statia invites Paddy to attend a "swarray" where she says he will meet all the "choice sperrits of New York" (p. 420). In the earliest extended commentary of the novel, Robert Bush interprets Simms's treatment of the soirée as a satire of New York literary life and goes on to criticize Simms's effort as "ineffective" because "he chooses to lampoon not the culture of the 'sixties, but that of the 'forties when Poe and Margaret Fuller were alive."[16] Simms, however, selects a distinct phase of American intellectual and literary history to develop his theme of American gods and devils. And as early as 1845 he had expressed his concern about the kind of "gods" worshipped in America when he wrote of American writers who were "feeble" in "imaginative endowment," but who had become "thy Gods, Oh! Israel!"[17]

As if supplementing remarks made almost twenty years earlier about America's literary gods, Simms uses religious imagery to draw the soirée guests. Anne Statia first points out Fanny Osgood: "'She's a beauty; and angel; the wittiest, gayest, best-hearted creature in the world—all soul—all heart—spiritual quite, and writes like a fairy!'" In the company of this "angel" is Edgar Allan Poe, a "divine" being whom women "worship": "'Eddy is a dangerous fellow among us women. We all worship him. He is so divine a poet; and so handsome!'" (p. 427). Eventually, Fanny ushers "Eddy" over to meet the Edisto Raftsman, suggesting to Poe that Paddy's shipwreck "would make a glorious subject" for a "mystic and supernateral" poem. Poe, however, dismisses the notion of a poem based on a real shipwreck. Like a god, he will create his own men and worlds: "'I kin make grand poems without the man and without the wrack. I kin make wracks enough, and men enough for myself. I don't need the actial, to make the idee.'" According to Paddy, "This was going it a huckleberry or two above Miss Anne Statia. But she looked delighted" (pp. 429–430).

Other spiritual creatures also appear at the "swarray."[18] The author of *Greenwood Leaves,* like a "grace" or a goddess, can create golden light. Anne Statia introduces her as "'our grace— Grace Greenwood'" and informs Paddy that she is "'the writer of all those beautiful poems of sentiment that make goulden light for the magazines'" (p. 430). The "huge and fat" Mrs. Caroline Kirkland, author of *Forest Life,* has the power to change forms. Though she is "going on sixty," she has had an engraving made picturing her "like a slender young girl of seventeen, reclining in a bower!'" (pp. 427–428). Instead of a goddess, Margaret Fuller, "famous female metaphysician," acts like a prophet: "'When she speaks to you she does it in a way that seems to say, "young person, listen! you now hev an opportunity of listening to words of wisdom for the first time in your life"'" (p. 428).

Additional portraits include further ironic religious allusions. Simms lampoons Rufus Griswold, whom Anne Statia describes as "'our Bishop—Bishop Grizzy, as we calls him. But he's no Bishop—only a Parson. . . . He is our famous Editor of authors'" (p. 428). The Bishop makes a hasty exit when another Reverend appears—"the Rev. Mr. Headley," author of *Napoleon and His Marshals* and *Washington and His Generals.* Joel Tyler Headley has the power of raising a real-life hero like Paddy "'to the attitude and altitude of a God controlling the tempest!'" (p. 429). Later George Pope Morris (author of "Woodman, Spare That Tree") and his "boy," N. P. Willis, arrive. They edit the *Home Journal,* which, according to "General" Morris, is an oracle: "'The orakil of the fashionable; the maker of the fashions; the ruler of taste'" (p. 431). Captain Wilson's comments on the "swarray" sum up the author's views and provide a foreshadowing and transition to Paddy's final episodes. After he calls Anne Statia "a fat fool," the Captain says that he needs "'some consolation, after this long three hours in a house of fools—'" (p. 432).

When Paddy returns to South Carolina, Simms introduces yet other phases of the American experience. The demon of the woods resumes taunting Paddy when he hunts, fishes, or chops down trees, but leaves him alone when he works at a *"rigilar* job." Since Paddy's efforts at hunting still prove luckless, he contracts with the railroad to furnish timber, and with the money earned buys stock for the farm (pp. 444–445). In the closing scenes of his narrative, Paddy follows the counsel of his mother and the pseudo-religious Salley Hartley—and marries a "fool." Incidents and imagery suggest that a variety of new gods and devils have manifested themselves—in Paddy's marriage, in Salley's religion, and in new scientific attitudes— before Paddy leaves for the Civil War.

On his return from New York Paddy finds his old friend Sam Hartley changed—by his new wife Salley and her dogmatic religion. Mrs. Sam Hartley's creed replaces superstitions about witches and spirits of the night with a worship of appearances and respectability, the kind of religion Huckleberry Finn associates with "civilization." The Hartleys and his mother begin to harass Paddy as relentlessly as the demon of the stump had—this time to "git a wife." While Mrs. McGarvin expresses the traditional views of an aging mother, the Hartleys base their counseling on "religious" arguments of decency and respectability: "'It ain't decent and respectable,'" or, "'It is sinful and onnatural.'" When Salley continues talking about the "sin of it" since he naturally wants a wife, Paddy connects her god of respectability with his old swamp devil: "'There's the stump in your road, Salley Hartley. It's bekaise I don't feel the want of the thing'" (pp. 454–455).

Though Paddy's mother sees Susan Heffernan Pogson as an

"angel," Paddy's descriptions link her with other devils. Initially, he speaks of his future bride in unimaginative, apathetic terms: he is "jubous" of her "breed"; he admits to regarding her as if she were a farm animal on sale. As a man of a new realistic age, Paddy no longer fosters the kind of romantic dreams he once had of Kitty Moore. Though Susan takes more interest in her own appearance than in housecleaning, he reluctantly goes through the courtship ritual and learns too late that she is "a sort of divil-snake" (p. 457).

The accounts of Paddy's courtship and marriage into the Pogson family at first suggest an anti-Union or anti-Northern allegory. But the referent for the episode lies closer to Simms's home. The author provides no Northern relatives, connections, or political views for the poor white Southern clan; and Paddy's own mother and friends push the "middle-aged" man into wedlock. Despite his own feelings and despite voices urging him to turn back because he is "going too fast," Paddy continues his courtship. A message supposedly from a man long dead warns Paddy that this "bad business" will "bankrupt" him (pp. 476–477). But Paddy nevertheless proposes to Susan Pogson, explaining later that he had made his "detarmination, and . . . was ashamed to back out" (p. 483). During preparations for the wedding, he discovers that the Pogsons have no meat and poultry for the wedding supper—"a *bad sign*" (p. 484). Paddy furnishes food for the supper and, ultimately, will have to feed and clothe the entire Pogson family.

In his descriptions of the improvident Pogsons, Simms may be expressing criticism of devils and false gods of the Confederacy. A letter written by Simms about the Southern government's impressment of crops suggests parallels with the Pogsons' confiscation and theft of Paddy's victuals and whiskey. On March 26, 1863, the Confederate States Congress passed a law ordering landowners to supply crops and labor for military needs. The authorization "aroused considerable protest in South Carolina." [19] In 1864 Simms's close friend, James Henry Hammond, had apparently expressed his determination "to resist the Impressing officer by force of arms." The author wrote him, advising "a patient submission to the extortion & injustice which we may expect, and which we cannot easily escape."[20] In this context, the courtship and wedding represent a former Unionist's interpretation of the Confederacy's ill-prepared management of a war "bankrupting" its supporters.

At the wedding, yet another kind of devil arrives to cause havoc. Paddy's friend, Jim Meredith, the "Napoleon of the rail-road," brings with him to the ceremony a pet monkey—which represents another development in the American experience. The controversy over evolution began long before the American edition of *Origin of the Species* appeared in 1860, and in the periodicals he edited, Simms included reviews of the works of Darwin's forerunners. For instance, Simms praised a review of Robert Chambers' *Vestiges of the Natural History of Creation,* which he included in an 1845 issue of *The Southern and Western.* In the essay, J. L. H. McCracken observes, "It is shameful to be descended from actual ancestral monkeys"; yet he concludes with a moralistic, optimistic view of man's natural progress.[21] In an 1850 review entitled "Lyell's Second Visit to the U.S." in *The Southern Quarterly Review,* another essayist discusses the religious controversies occurring in "the present eventful era of scientific attainment" and censures sectarian "dogmatism" as "worthy only of a Puritanical age." The writer supports his argument by quoting Charles Lyell's views on society's use of religion "'as a mere piece of machinery—like a police, for preserving order, or enabling one class of men to govern another.'"[22]

Colonel Meredith's monkey functions to unmask the kind of hypocritical religion Salley Hartley represents and to introduce a new scientific era. When the monkey escapes from his owner's pocket, he lands on top of Salley. As she yells to Meredith to get "the dreadful beast" off her, the monkey escapes with Salley's red wig. No observer feels a greater shock than her husband on discovering that the pious Salley Hartley is "as bald as a pumpkin" (pp. 487–488). The final paragraph of Paddy's narrative ends with a report of Salley's views of this latest devil of the times: "To this day Mrs. Sam Hartley abuses Jim Meredith, for an infidel and monster. . . . She goes so fur as to say that she believes the monkey is a sort of pet divil; and she shakes her head as ef to say the divil's got a tighter hold on Jim's soul than iver he hed in her wool" (p. 490).

When Paddy's auditors complain about the abrupt ending of his narrative, the hero explains, "I've only got to say, as I said before, that I warn't going to tell you a *story,* but a *history!*" (p. 491). After his departure, Wharncliffe relates the unhappy husband's disillusionment in marriage, and the parties discuss Paddy's experiences. As if to emphasize Simms's method of development, the recently arrived Father Abbot ends the novel with his discourse on the stages of man. Reviving his self-satirical title character in his 1849 *Father Abbot* for a last-hour appearance in *Paddy McGann,* Simms gives the new arrival the final thematic words. The burden of his discourse is that each person must go through a step-by-step process from childhood through old age to attain an independent vision: "To shake off mere external authority, and assert his own mind and moral independently." Father Abbot further expounds on the "middle life" of man, the period in which "the gifted man invents, originates, broaches new philosophies, embarks in daring speculations" (p. 508). Despite superstitions, "external authorities," and other gods and devils of the past and present, an individual or a nation gradually moves through the "several steps in a regular progress, each of which steps argues an advance, and each advance develops new characteristics and powers" (p. 507). As Simms develops the novel, he presents Paddy's "step-by-step" process of freeing himself from devils and false gods in the swamp, on the river, in New York, or in his own home. Americans, however, Simms implies, will continue their submission to spurious powers—when they fall for Fourierism, Barnum's mermaid, or religious and political cant, or when they permit Wall Street, newspapers, home journals, literary divinities, or outside "authorities" to control their thoughts, their literature, their lives.

In *Paddy McGann* Simms contributes to the continuing dialogue on the American hunter, farmer, and industrialist, and examines concomitant developments in the national experience. In his treatment of the wilderness theme, unlike James Fenimore Cooper, Thomas Bangs Thorpe, or William Faulkner, Simms exhibits little nostalgia or regret for the changes in the American landscape. Rather, like Henry Clay Lewis in "The Indefatigable Bear Hunter,"[23] Simms implies that the ravished wilderness and wildlife may ultimately avenge its destroyers. Like John Gardner in *October Light,* Simms suggests that Americans too often wax elegaic and nostalgic over a naïve, primitive past instead of recognizing and adapting to the potentials of "new characteristics and power." Simms also in 1863 foresaw likely "places and elements" from which would spring later varieties of American gods and devils. Twentieth-century commentators indicate the continued relevance of Simms's concerns in their ongoing discussions about the machine in the garden, ecological necessities, the power of the press and other media, the protracted conflict between Darwinism and religion, and the rise and fall of multitudes of American gods and devils.

Notes

[1] William Gilmore Simms in *Views and Reviews in American Literature, History and Fiction: First Series,* ed. Hugh C. Holman (Cambridge, Mass.: Belknap Press, 1962), pp. 80–81.

[2] Simms, *Paddy McGann; or, The Demon of the Stump,* in *The Writings of William Gilmore Simms,* ed. James B. Meriwether. Introduction and Explanatory Notes by Robert Bush (Columbia: University of South Carolina Press, 1972), III, pp. 213–509. Subsequent references are to this edition and appear in the text.

[3] The only extended critical discussions of the novel appear in Robert Bush, "*Paddy McGann,* William Gilmore Simms's Devil Story," *Bulletin of the New York Library,* 69 (1965), 197–204, much of which Bush incorporated in his Introduction to the Centennial Edition; and Simone Vauthier, "Une Aventure du Recit Fantastique: *Paddy McGann; or, the Demon of the Stump* de William Gilmore Simms," *RANAM,* 6 (1973), 78–104. Both Bush (*Bulletin,* p. 203) and Vauthier (p. 84) find in the New York episodes a flaw in the unity of the work.

[4] *Views and Reviews,* p. 79.

[5] Bush, Introduction, pp. xxii–xxiv; Vauthier, *RANAM,* pp. 84–86.

[6] J. A. Leo Lemay, "The Text, Tradition, and Themes of 'The Big Bear of Arkansas,'" *American Literature,* 47 (1975), 332.

[7] Simms, *Poems: Descriptive, Dramatic, Legendary and Contemplative* (1853; rpt. New York: Arno Press, 1972), II, 75–77.

[8] Simms, "The Arm-Chair of Tustenuggee," in *The Wigwam and the*

Cabin (1845; rpt. Ridgewood, New Jersey: The Gregg Press, 1968), p. 149.

[9] Alexander Porteous, *Forest Folklore, Mythology, and Romance* (London: George Allen & Unwin Ltd., 1928), p. 90.

[10] As Leo Lemay, p. 332, parenthetically remarks, "The institution of religion" is "a chief mark of civilization and a natural concomitant of the destruction of the wilderness."

[11] Again, Lemay's remarks, p. 336, apply: "The river, which becomes in *Huckleberry Finn* a symbol of nature, is accurately viewed in 'The Big Bear of Arkansas' as the highway, the carrier of civilization. Suitably, the river symbolically destroys the wilderness."

[12] Beryl Rowland, *Birds with Human Souls: A Guide to Bird Symbolism* (Knoxville: University of Tennessee Press, 1978), pp. 115–117.

[13] Vauthier examines the events at sea as an initiation journey, p. 89.

[14] "Americanism in Literature," in *Views and Reviews*, pp. 26–27.

[15] Simms's letters indicate that he and Lewis Gaylord Clark had begun on reasonably civil terms after Simms became friends with Clark's twin brother and made contributions to their *Knickerbocker*. According to Simms in 1836, he had sent the magazine articles after Lewis Clark had written requesting submissions and "*hinting* at pay." Simms had received no acknowledgment or pay from Clark (Mary C. Simms Oliphant, Alfred Taylor Odell, and T. C. Duncan Eaves, eds., *The Letters of William Gilmore Simms,* [Columbia: University of South Carolina Press, 1952–1956, 1982]), I, 80. Hereinafter cited as *Letters*. In 1840 Simms was still disposed to offer articles to Clark (*Letters*, I, 187), though the *Knickerbocker* editor "has shown very little regard for my labors" (*Letters*, I, 231). After Simms published his *Southern Literature* series in 1841 in the *Magnolia,* his own journal, the *Knickerbocker* criticized Simms's views on sectional literature and his "'lots' of labored romances." Simms's alliance with the Young America group advocating a national literature involved Simms in further battles with the conservative Clark, who made vitriolic attacks on Simms in print (See *Letters*, I, 320–321, n.73; and Hugh Holman, Introduction to *Views and Reviews*, pp. xxii–xxxi). By 1845 Simms was referring privately to the *Knickerbocker* editor as that "dirty crawling creeping creature, Clarke" (*Letters*, II, 107).

[16] *Bulletin*, p. 203.

[17] *Letters*, II, 90.

[18] Bush's Explanatory Notes provide additional details about the lives and work of the literary figures satirized in the New York episode.

[19] *Letters*, IV, 457n.65.

[20] *Letters,* IV, 457–458.

[21] *Southern and Western Magazine and Review,* 1 (June 1845), 377–378. Simms praises the essay twice in *Letters,* II, 70–71, 83.

[22] C. A. W[oodruff], *Southern Quarterly Review,* n.s., 1 (July 1850), 406, 424–425.

[23] In *Odd Leaves from the Life of a Louisiana "Swamp Doctor,"* (1843; rpt. Upper Saddle River, N.J.: Literature House/ Gregg Press, 1969), pp. 165–171.

Simms's *The Lily and the Totem:* "History for the Purposes of Art"

NICHOLAS G. MERIWETHER

In November of 1850, a brief notice appeared in *Sartain's Magazine* announcing the publication of a new work by William Gilmore Simms. The book was called *The Lily and the Totem,*[1] and its publication represented something of a triumph for its author, in part because of the difficulties he had encountered in trying to find a publisher. The work was well received initially, and some of Simms's best critics have praised it. But, unfortunately, after a brief period of being in print, it dropped from sight. Never included in the collected edition of Simms's writing, which began in the 1850s with Redfield and was often reissued in the next half-century, *The Lily and the Totem* has received only brief critical attention for over one hundred thirty years.[2]

Its status as a forgotten work, however, is perhaps the least important reason for renewing critical interest in the work. Intrinsically, *The Lily and the Totem* has much to recommend it, not only in the writing—for it contains some of Simms's best prose—but more importantly in nature, for Simms did not write *The Lily and the Totem* as an ordinary romance. Indeed, part of Simms's high estimation of *The Lily and the Totem* probably stemmed from the effort he had made in writing it— and it had placed unusual demands on his talents. Simms envisioned his book on the sixteenth-century Huguenot settle-

ments in the American Southeast not as a traditional historical romance, but as a new way of combining history and fiction,
one shaped by the critical theories he had developed during the
preceding decade. Thus *The Lily and the Totem* is particularly
interesting to Simms scholars, for it not only illustrates several of his most important critical theories, but it also shows
how those theories fit together. Indeed, John C. Guilds has said
that in this work "Simms makes his clearest statement concerning his technique of enhancing history with art."[3]

Before examining *The Lily and the Totem,* one must take
brief note of Simms's critical theories. The three principal ones
most useful in analyzing *The Lily and the Totem* are his theories of art, history, and fiction. None can be given the extended
attention they merit in this essay; however, it is possible and
informative to indicate how these theories affected *The Lily
and the Totem,* and how that work shows the degree to which
those theories are interconnected. In brief, Simms's theory of
art requires that the artist's goal be the elevation of man,
through the presentation of an ideal, moral, or truth.[4] This is
a responsibility for both the historian and the imaginative
writer,[5] for Simms viewed historical writing as art, too. In addition, the imaginative writer must be realistic; this is logical,
for Simms defined the ideal as "nothing more than the *possible
real.*"[6] Therefore, in order for the artist to elevate, he must be
realistic. For the historian, this translates into the obligation
to be accurate with his facts.[7] Lastly, the historian has one further obligation: he must show progress in his analysis of history. Like many of his day, Simms believed that man's history
was one of progress, and he therefore felt it important that the
historian frame his examination of history in that light.[8]

Tracing Simms's progress with *The Lily and the Totem* from
earliest thoughts to publication not only reveals the extent of
Simms's interest in his subject but also explains much concerning the book's purpose. Simms first mentioned the concept of
such a book in an April 1845 letter to his friend Edward Duyckinck, enthusiastically describing an ambitious project: a book
about the Huguenot settlements in the Southeast in the late
sixteenth century. The subject itself was not so unusual (although Simms considered it one of the finest subjects for Ameri-

77

can art),[9] but Simms's proposed method of dealing with it was. Rather than write a strictly factual history, like his textbook history of South Carolina, or even a historical romance like those of his Revolutionary series, Simms wished to make *The Lily and the Totem* an unusual amalgamation of the two. As he explained to Carey and Hart, who had published several of his books, the work would contain "the history of a most exciting and interesting endeavor of the French to colonize Florida, with Huguenots, all enveloped in an atmosphere of fiction."[10] Essentially, this was one step short of actual historical writing: more factual than historical fiction, but less so than history.

Simms had not arrived at this formula at first. His initial conception of the project was as an epic-length poem, an attempt he abandoned for lack of interest in such a venture from both the publishing world and the general public.[11] Despite his attraction for a work on this subject, he did not begin the prose version until later. In that April 1845 letter, Simms told Duyckinck that he had "the scheme of it" in his head, but it was not until September that he committed an outline to paper.[12] He had originally planned to write it for Wiley and Putnam's Library of American Books, but a dispute with the publisher involving another of his works put an end to the possibility.[13] But by this time, Simms was committed to the project. In the literary wars of the 1840s he had taken a strong stance, arguing for the establishment and support of a uniquely American literature, one which drew upon her history as a rich source. Set forth in several essays, Simms's opinions on the issues of the literary wars first appeared in various Southern literary journals in the early to mid-1840s, and were subsequently collected in *Views and Reviews in American Literature, History and Fiction: First Series,* published by Wiley and Putnam in 1845. In one of these essays, Simms described several examples of epochs in American history as particularly compelling subjects for her authors, with the Huguenot colonies of Admiral Coligny as one of the best.[14] Not surprisingly, among these essays was his famous defense of historical fiction in general, published in the *Southern & Western* magazine that fall.[15] By November, he had completed at least one chapter of what would become *The Lily and the Totem,* which also appeared in the *Southern & West-*

ern.[16] Problems, both professional and personal, delayed Simms's final completion of the project. Professionally, publishers were exceedingly reluctant to publish the book; Wiley and Putnam had balked and dragged their feet, despite Simms's persistence, as did Carey and Hart, when Simms turned to them.[17] Baker and Scribner finally agreed to publish *The Lily and the Totem* and were the only publishers ever to set it in type.[18] Other distractions, such as family troubles and other work, kept Simms from the book. His *Life of the Chevalier Bayard,* published in 1847, was a major competitor for his time,[19] as were his legislative duties in Columbia.[20]

Critical reception of the book was generally positive.[21] *Sartain's* called it a history "in the form of a very charming fiction"; *Holden's* brief notice went so far as to say that it was "a narrative of rare interest"; and Simms's friend James Hammond, to whom it was dedicated, wrote him and quoted the *Richmond Examiner* as saying it was among Simms's finest works.[22] *De Bow's Review* gave it more attention, calling it one of Simms's "very best productions," lauding its author as "a man who has, at an early age, attained very high laurels in our literary world, and whose industry has exceeded that of almost any of his contemporaries."[23] Simms himself noted with pleasure that it was "considerably praised," and he seems to have thought highly of it himself—a fact that his efforts to publish the book after the war further underscores.[24]

Baker and Scribner gave Simms's unusual book two printings, both apparently in 1850, and their successor firm, Scribner, another in 1854.[25] After the war, Simms went to considerable trouble to procure the plates from Scribner, and had them shipped to the Charleston printing firm of Walker, Evans, & Cogswell, who agreed to print a limited run.[26] Under this imprint it appeared in 1871, a year after Simms's death. Apparently they made only one impression. Thus *The Lily and the Totem* had only four printings. Unfortunately, we do not know exactly how many copies of *The Lily and the Totem* were printed, or how well they sold; we can assume that Baker and Scribner printed about 3,000 copies, based on 1,500 copies per printing, and that they had sold out by the time Scribner reprinted the book—presumably in another 1,500 copies.[27] We know that the second printing did not sell out, for Simms asked that Scribner send him all unsold copies.[28] For the 1871 Walker, Evans, & Cogswell edition, information is even more sparse.[29] Probably the only point that can be made with any certainty is that their press run was approximately 1,500 copies. This re-issue had no changes from the original edition, and although Simms feared that the plates had been damaged during transit, extant copies reveal only slight if any deterioration in print quality.[30]

It seems strange that a book by an author who was both popular and critically acclaimed would not sell well, or at least would be passed over in selecting that author's works for a collected edition. The unusual structure of the book would explain at least part of its mixed reception. Arranged into twenty-five chapters, the book's ostensible chronological scope covers only the French Admiral Ribault's two voyages to the southeast coast of America, each of which comprise one section. The first section is eight chapters and gives a general overview of the first colony, describes the Huguenots' interaction with the Indians, and discusses a few of the colonists in detail. The most prominent of these are the gentle violinist Guernache, whose story comprises half of the section, the heroic Lachane, a friend of Guernache's, and the evil and sadistic governor of the colony, Albert. In general, Simms describes the failure of this first settlement as the result of Albert's mismanagement of the colony, exemplified by his mistreatment of Guernache and Lachane. The latter's revenge upon him leaves the colonists without their tyrannical governor, and they decide to abandon the colony and return to France. In their ill-equipped, ill-prepared bark, they are becalmed, and Lachane proves his heroism by sacrificing himself so that his comrades might live.

Despite the misfortune which met the first attempt to colonize the Southeast, the great Huguenot leader and Admiral Gaspard de Coligny pleads to the court of King Charles IX to send another expedition, again under Admiral Ribault's supervision. This second colony's story comprises the remaining seventeen chapters, the bulk of the book. Simms has a greater number of characters and describes his major ones in more detail: the weak commander Laudonnierre; his able lieutenant and the hero of the section, Alphonse D'Erlach; and the ambitious but twisted Le Genre, who conspires to overthrow Laudonnierre. There are other elements in this second section as well, including a deeper analysis of the differences between European and Indian, especially in the interlude-like chapter "Iracana," which describes the colonists' discovery of a New World Eden. Simms also makes a powerful statement about religion, comparing Spaniard to Huguenot and contrasting both to Indian, not only in the final chapters, which describe how the Spanish slaughtered most of the French settlers, but also with "The Narrative of Le Barbu," an almost wholly independent vignette of a Spaniard who has lived for several years with the Indians, and whom Laudonnierre arranges to be brought to La Caroline. The final chapter is the epilogue-like story of Dominique de Gourgues, a valiant Gascon who takes it upon himself to raise a crew and sail to the New World and avenge the deaths of his countrymen.

Interspersed throughout these vignettes are chapters that Simms entitled "Historical Summary," which give the factual skeleton that he fleshed out with his creative powers. This choppy, strange blend of fact and fiction that characterizes *The Lily and the Totem* foils efforts to classify the book according to existing literary categories, for although it can hardly be classified as merely fiction or simply history, neither can it be accurately summarized as *historical fiction*. Although Simms says that this appellation "will justly apply" to *The Lily and the Totem,* it is plain that he thinks it does not suffice; nor is the book representative, in his view, of such works. As he notes of most practitioners of the genre of historical fiction:

> Where the author, in this species of writing, has employed history, usually, as a mere loop, upon which to hang his lively fancies and audacious inventions . . . I have been content to reverse the process, making the fiction merely tributary, and always subordinate to the fact. (P. iv)

The difference between what Simms termed "historical fiction" and *The Lily and the Totem* is that whereas both used historical settings and facts to paint a convincing backdrop for the action and characters, *The Lily and the Totem* also relied on history to provide the plot and characters. Simply put, *The Lily and the Totem* is too much history to be fiction, too much fiction to be history, and uses history in a different and more demanding fashion than does historical fiction.

The lack of an existing specific category or genre in which to place it, however, does not mean *The Lily and the Totem* is impervious to analysis. In fact, its definition of an extreme in Simms's blending of history and fiction suggests that Simms was creating a new genre, which we may term *fictional history*. This genre could be defined, in simplest terms, as occupying the gulf that Simms notes exists between contemporary historical fiction and *The Lily and the Totem*. As with any genre, fictional history should have its own criterion for evaluation, which Simms provides: the reader should judge *The Lily and the Totem* by how well Simms links what he terms "the certain" and "the conjectural" together; or, how well Simms integrates his fiction into the history. "Upon the successful prosecution of this object, apart from the native interest which the subject itself possesses, depends all the merit of the performance," he states (p. v). While this is the only standard upon which to judge the book's merits, it need not proscribe more general analysis. Indeed, since fictional history is an amalgam of history and fiction, it is appropriate that both of these two elements receive critical attention in *The Lily and the Totem*. As fiction, it has several prominent strong points, among them Simms's portrayal of character, his realism, his literary themes, and his narrative technique.

An important part of Simms's theory of fiction is the need for elevaton and the need for realism. Consequently, Simms employs heroes to fulfill the former, while nonetheless attempting to maintain the latter. Alphonse D'Erlach, Guernache, and Lachane are three representative heroes. Unquestionably the best developed of them, D'Erlach appears in more vignettes than any other character and occupies the most central position of any character in the narrative framework of the book. D'Erlach's heroism is constantly displayed, in his support of the *status quo* (even though that means supporting an incompetent commander), in his prowess as both leader and soldier, and in his strong sense of ethics. He is also the level-headed leader who safeguards his followers not only from disaster at the hands of savage Indians but also from even more deadly Spaniards. Perhaps most importantly, however, he serves as the pivotal character who ties the last vignette into the narrative framework of the book, as the mysterious white Indian chief who leads the avenging party of Dominique de Gourgues in exacting vengeance upon the Spanish for slaughtering the Huguenot colonists.

Although he portrays D'Erlach in an uncompromisingly heroic light, Simms also has lesser heroes. Guernache is the epitome of a good but weak spirit. Without D'Erlach's strength, Guernache is a pitiful but not tragic figure. His tortures by the tyrant Albert invoke an interesting comparison: Guernache is as guileless and at least as much victimized by the white man— in the form of Albert—as his Indian compatriots. This comparison is further heightened by the Indians' acceptance of Guernache, as evidenced by his marriage to Monaletta, one of the local chief's daughters. Lachane is another minor but significant hero, who exhibits more of the heroic ideal than does his friend Guernache. Albert's brutal treatment of both Guernache and Monaletta extends to Lachane, who escapes death by hanging or flogging but is exiled to a tiny island, no more than a sand-bar with scant vegetation. Rescued by his comrades, Lachane plots the execution of Albert with the assistance of his friends, and personally throttles him. When the remnants of the colony, on the return voyage to France, are blown off-course and becalmed, Lachane sacrifices himself to save his companions. As a hero, Lachane exhibits both the noble compassion for his fellows and the unhesitating ability to avenge wrong that Simms's conception of heroism requires. Of these three characters, Guernache is the most appealing, partly because of the close adherence to the heroic ideal exhibited by Lachane and especially D'Erlach. In comparison, Guernache, the gentle, wrongly persecuted musician, has more depth than his fellow heroes.

Overall, Simms's portrayal of his heroes is stylized, but realistic, for it shows the many levels of good in man: Guernache is weak, D'Erlach is tough, but both are good. Likewise, Simms's depiction of the evil characters in the book is stylized but realistic. Albert, the garrison commander of the first settlement, is purely one-dimensional: his petty tyrannies and cruelties are those of a child elevated to power, and equally conscienceless. His persecution and final execution of Guernache are unjustifiable, as is his scourging of Monaletta and attempted abandonment of Lachane to starve on an island. He is the alter-ego of Laudonierre, the commander of the second settlement, who is equally simple and one-sided, but essentially good. Le Genre, by contrast, is an excellent villain. As a convincingly evil plotter against Laudonierre, he conspires to take over the fort, foiled only by D'Erlach. Fleeing the fort after his coup fails, he becomes wracked by sorrow and contrition, causing his unrepentant former comrades-in-arms to abandon him. They then stage a successful mutiny without him. Ultimately Le Genre takes refuge in the wilds, and there, he makes his presence known to D'Erlach, who is leading an expedition north from the fort. Le Genre then aids D'Erlach in defeating the Indians and returns to the fort, an expiated sinner. Far from being a flat character, Le Genre is a tragic hero with a twist: he is a good man with a flaw—his greed for power—who undergoes a downfall and realization, but unlike his classical counterparts, he has the chance to redeem himself and does.

That Simms's villains range from flat to three-dimensional illustrates an essential feature of his critical theories of fiction and history: the romancer's and the historian's responsibility to be accurate and realistic. Just as people range from good to bad, so too do they range from simple to complex. By showing several variations in each category, Simms's characters in *The Lily and the Totem* are excellent examples of this theory put into practice. Consequently, the critic who concentrates on D'Erlach and Albert as examples of Simms's inability to draw realistic characters should be wary. In the first place, Simms placed a severe limit on his use of imagination to color his portrayals by never violating his sources. Thus, for example, for Simms to have created an unpleasant childhood for Albert might have made him a more interesting and credible villain, but it was beyond the bounds Simms set for himself. Furthermore, it is doubtful that the flatness of some characters was unintentional or unnoticed on Simms's part. To judge from the amount of space Simms devotes to them, Guernache is the central figure and hero of the first section of the book, and Le Genre is the best villain overall; the fact that these are two well-drawn characters undermines the theory that Simms could not draw living characters. However, this standard of prominence unquestionably makes D'Erlach the hero and protagonist in the second section, which is a problem, for he is an undeniably flat character. However, the resolution to this problem may be found in Simms's theories of art, history, and fiction, for as the central figure in the book, D'Erlach must embody the elevating ideal of art—he must epitomize the heroic ideal. He does, and is consequently afforded none of the weaknesses that make Guernache, by contrast, so human. While Simms fails to draw convincing characters in individual instances, when taken as a whole, the cast of *The Lily and the Totem* is certainly true to human nature and consequently fulfills the responsibility of the artist to be realistic, yet elevate.

While playing an essential part in Simms's theory of drawing character, realism as a distinct responsibility of the artist can be seen clearly in Simms's description of the Indians, his discussions of sex and violence, and his language in the book. The Indians in *The Lily and the Totem* are especially noteworthy for their realism, for Simms avoids stereotypes, portraying them as being neither exclusively Pocahontas-like nor completely blood-thirsty.[31] Simms's sources provided him with ample material for both stereotypes, and the result was his unflinching descriptions of not only the Indians' kindness to the settlers but also their savagery when provoked. When Laudonnierre arrives with his small band of settler-soldiers, the Indians meet the Europeans with a mixture of fear and awe, which is rapidly transformed into friendliness when the Huguenots make peaceful overtures. Instances of Indian kindness and courtesy appear throughout the book, culminating in their assistance of the Gascon, Dominique de Gourgues, in his attack upon and defeat of the Spanish at the end. However, Simms also presents the other side of the coin and meticulously records those instances of Indian hostility and cruelty to the Europeans.

Simms portrays the Indians as three-dimensional characters

on a level deeper than simple behavior, too. Although he notes their crude manners and customs, he is also quick to point out the virtues of naive simplicity. The obvious, blunt comparison Simms draws in the latter half of the book between the corrupt and decadent Spaniard and the honest, simple Indian underscores this pointedly. Simms even draws comparisons between Indian and Huguenot, unfavorable to the latter, pointing out their fondness for gold as a uniquely European fault, and emphasizing the settlers' indolence and arrogance in expecting their Indian friends to provide for them. A reasonable conjecture drawn from *The Lily and the Totem* is that Simms saw the Indians as completely human, sharing all of the emotions, motives, and skills of the European, but on a more primitive level. Likewise, while the European may appear more advanced, elevated, and "civilized" in comparison to his "savage" counterpart, Simms is quick to point out how this posture can conceal as base, savage, and cruel a nature as could ever be found among the Indians. In short, Simms treats the Indian evenly and realistically. Even to Oolenoe, the chief who deceitfully misled and attacked D'Erlach on his journey, Simms ascribes some probable cause for hating the white man: the latter's encroachments on Indian hunting grounds. In *The Lily and the Totem,* Simms presents human nature as basically the same, regardless of the trappings of civilization.

With regard to sexuality, Simms's realism is even more noteworthy, given the publishing codes of the time. Indeed, Simms's graphic realism concerning sex contributed to his neglect and dismissal by "genteel" critics, such as William Peterfield Trent.[32] In *The Lily and the Totem,* the most impressive example of this realism is Guernache's marriage to Monaletta. Not only does Simms make this marriage plausible by describing the hardships and exigencies of the settler's life (which explains why such a union is natural), but he moreover states that it was a pagan ceremony that united the two lovers. That this was an interracial marriage as well as a pagan one makes Simms's boldness in mentioning it particularly significant; that he does so in highly favorable terms is even more noteworthy. Nor does Simms neglect the earthy aspect of sexuality. Guernache and Monaletta share the joys of marital bliss, in

Simms's words, in "nightly meetings" between "the lovers," concluding of Guernache that "his, indeed, were nights of happiness" (p. 65). In another sensual scene, Simms describes the earthly pleasures of the New World's paradise, Iracana. In their peregrinations, a detachment of the Huguenots discover this land, where "soft breezes played ever in the capacious forests, always kindling to emotions of pleasure, the soft beatings of the delighted heart" (p. 297). In a memorable passage, he describes the celebration given for the Huguenot soldiers by the natives of Iracana:

> Half the night was consumed with dancing; then gay parties could be seen gliding into canoes, and darting across the stream to other villages and places of abode. Anon, might be perceived a silent couple gliding away to sacred thickets. . . . (P. 301)

The implication in the passage of natural, human sexuality is undeniable, as is the favorable terminology Simms employs in his depiction. Nor is Simms condescending in his portrayal of Iracana Indians' way of life; indeed, he makes his preference for their values plain when he describes how delighted the Huguenots are with Iracana. The soldiers found Iracana Indian maids with whom they "waltzed and wandered," and each "had his share of the delights and endearments which made the business of life in Iracana" (p. 301). Simms makes the comparison of the two groups' values more pointed by stating that the relationships that blossomed between Indian maid and soldier "opened a new idea of existence to the poor Huguenots who, hitherto, had only known the land of Florida by its privations and its gold" (p. 301). That the Huguenots responded so readily, and favorably, to the Iracana Indians and their way of life indicates how natural, healthy, and good that life was— and how flawed, by contrast, was the colonists' approach to life in the New World. Pagan, artless, and innocent the Indians may be, but that seems superior to the Europeans' worship of an organized religion which slaughters innocent people, and to their sophistication, which thinly masks an all-consuming, destructive lust for gold.

Simms's graphic descriptions of violence in *The Lily and the Totem* are striking and quite justifiable (for all except the more genteel or squeamish readers) on the grounds that such descriptions are essential if Simms is to fulfill his obligation to be realistic: violence was, after all, an integral part of the early settlers' lives. Thus in one scene Simms describes D'Erlach not as simply killing an Indian but as taking a hatchet and driving it "into his brain" (p. 210). Examples such as this abound in Simms's descriptions of the Spaniards; their horrible betrayals of the Huguenots' trust, not to mention their even more ghastly executions and mutilations of the French Protestants, represent the worst of human nature in the book. When Ribault's shipwrecked soldiers seek Melendez's aid, the *adelantado* shows them "the exposed, the bleached and decaying bodies" of the other colonists, saying, "I have punished all these with death" (p. 373). Rather than bludgeon the fort's defenders to death, Melendez opts for a mass hanging, leaving the bodies "hanging in the sun and wind, destined equally as trophies to the victor, and warnings to the heretic" (p. 362). A more extreme example of graphic language occurs in the final chapter in the first part of the book, when Simms describes the privation and ultimate degradation of the starving colonists, becalmed in their bark en route to France:

> With each of these last words, the brave fellow—thence called "Lachane, the Deliverer"—struck two fatal blows, one upon his heart, and one upon his throat. He leaned back between the two famished persons whom he had especially addressed, and, while the consciousness was yet in the eyes of the dying man, they sprang like thirsting tigers, and fastened their mouths upon each streaming orifice. The victim, smarting and conscious to the last, sank in a few seconds, into the sacred slumber of death. (P. 108)

Their final cannibalistic feast on the still-warm body of their compatriot is perhaps the most graphic scene in the entire book and is a superb example of Simms's realism.

Simms's comparison of the Indians to the Europeans highlights one of the central themes in the book, religion. This should come as no surprise, for religion was an important underpinning for many of Simms's critical theories. Evidence of religion's centrality in the book can be seen in the fact that *The*

Lily and the Totem both begins and ends with it: the Huguenots leave France because of the religious persecution, and it is in the name of religion that Spanish *Adelantado* Melendez slaughters their second colony in the New World. One possible interpretation is that Simms is denouncing organized religion in general throughout the book. Several points can corroborate this view. The most obvious example is the behavior of the Spanish at the book's end. In a grotesque parody of religion, after the Spanish have taken the fort at La Caroline, the *adelantado,* Pedro de Melendez, screams to his men, "Slay! Slay! Smite and spare not! . . . The groans of the heretic make music in the ears of heaven" (p. 356). Even the Huguenots' behavior could be interpreted as a denunciation of organized religion, for they make no effort to convert the Indians, allowing them only to observe some of their ceremonies. In fairness to the Huguenots' religiosity, however, when given the choice between death and conversion by Melendez, all but four of the colonists opt for death, saying, "We are of the church of Messer Luther, and no other; if death's the word, we're ready. We're not the men, at the end of the reckoning, to belie the whole voyage" (p. 362).

The Huguenots' stake in their religion is obviously strong; it is ironic, as Simms is pointing out in this scene, that an equally strong commitment to religion guides Melendez. Independent of their religious faith, however, it must have been clear to these colonists that Melendez was their enemy and not to be trusted, even though he said those who converted to Catholicism would be spared. When Melendez pursues the remnants of the settlement, he informs them of the fall of the fort and, promising nothing, asks them to submit to his mercy. Some follow Admiral Ribault, who chooses to submit; others follow Alphonse D'Erlach, and leave at night. Those who submit, Melendez butchers, systematically and without compunction.

This is yet another denunciation of organized religion, whose influence upon these men's minds has been to stop them from thinking. Those colonists who follow Ribault place their faith in Melendez's mercy, in his religion. They blind themselves to the evidence of his brutality, which he makes no effort to conceal from them: rather than view his massacres of their fellow colonists as evidence of his untrustworthiness, they instead believe that he is showing them the bodies of their slain comrades as proof that his lust for blood is sated. The group of settlers that follows D'Erlach, by contrast, is thinking in terms of human nature, and not religion; they place their faith in Melendez's actions, which have been murderous, not his professions of Christian belief. "I will sooner trust the incarnate devil himself, than this Melendez," D'Erlach summarizes (p. 376).

Simms, then, seems to offer compelling evidence that organized religion can be a pernicious institution. It is responsible for the intolerance which drove the Huguenots out of France; it is responsible for the arrogance and complacency which allows Melendez to justify any act, no matter how barbarous, with the maxim that he is responsible to God alone for his actions, and not man; in sum, organized religion seems to be responsible for turning off men's minds, eradicating the impulse to think rationally and compassionately. Intolerance and complacency, encouraged by religion, are much easier attitudes to assume than rational open-mindedness, which carefully considers opposing views.

However, the significance of these examples notwithstanding, to portray Simms as anti-religious is an oversimplification. Nor is such a conclusion consonant with the clearly religious attitude Simms expresses in his critical theories and letters. One way of determining Simms's attitude toward religion in the book is to compare his descriptions of the religion of the Indians to the religion of the Europeans. Certainly, some pagan Indians behave with more intelligent thought and compassion than do the Europeans—Monaletta, for example. It would be shortsighted, however, to conclude from this one incident that Simms is voicing a preference for the pagan religion of the Indians over all organized religion, or even over Catholicism in particular. After all, Simms describes only one pagan ceremony in *The Lily and the Totem,* and when the Europeans violate the secrecy with which their primitive counterparts guard their rituals, the Indians react with a fury reminiscent of the blood-lust of the Spanish. The crux of Simms's point on religion is that behavior, not belief, should be the criterion for humanity. There are some good Indians, and some bad, just as is the case with the Europeans in the book. Therefore, Simms is not delivering a broadside against organized religion, or even Catholicism, only a blunt warning concerning its dangers; specifically, its tendency to eliminate the concept of responsibility to one's fellow man.

To support this thesis, one need only examine the heroes in the book. D'Erlach's religious beliefs, for example, are not what makes him a hero. Stripped of them, he would still be a leader. The last part of the book offers final substance to this thesis: the reason the Huguenots are not avenged, Simms concludes, is that the kings of France and Spain are at peace. Moreover, as Melendez notes to some of his victims, the mother religion in both of their countries is Catholicism, which would make Philip even less interested in avenging the Huguenots' murders. Melendez informs an incredulous Frenchman that he can slaughter the French without fear of reprisal because the alliance between King Charles IX of France and King Philip II of Spain "is an alliance between members of the true Church, both sworn against heretics" (p. 369). The most startling example of an organized religion's ability to pardon temporal wrongs can be seen by the manner in which Melendez eliminates the Huguenots. After storming the fort and slaughtering the males over fifteen there, Melendez arrives in his camp to be greeted with the chant of *Te Deum,* honoring him as the savior of the "True Faith," a ritual repeated when he dispatches Ribault's men: "All perished, to the number of two hundred; and Pedro Melendez returned to his camp at St. Augustine, again to be welcomed with *Te Deum,* and the acclamation for good Christian service, from a Christian people" (p. 371). De Gourgues' statement that his avenging of his countrymen's murders is justified, however, speaks volumes, for he is not simply saying that the bonds of humanity must transcend the differences imposed by religious belief (it should be remembered that de Gourgues was a devout Catholic); he is also asserting that man must ultimately be responsible to his fellows for his behavior. For de Gourgues, the Huguenot colonists were Frenchmen first and foremost, a bond which called for their murderer to be punished. But de Gourgues' deed is not merely a blow for national honor, it is also one of simple decency: a righteous act of punishment for a brutal, deceitful crime. As Simms notes of de Gourgues, "His crimes, if his warfare against the Spaniards shall be so considered, were committed in the cause of humanity" (p. 462). Dominique de Gourgues is a hero for avenging the deaths of his countrymen, an action independent of religion.

With regard to religion, then, *The Lily and the Totem* is an excellent example of Simms's putting his critical theories into practice. This does not mean that he wrote *The Lily and the Totem* according to a formula, for he could not warp his facts or distort them in any way. He could, however, frame his analysis of the facts according to the standards and principles outlined in his critical theories. Two primary points corroborate this view. First, religion is an ever-present theme in the book, although it is only explicit in a few instances, such as the descriptions of Melendez. The same may be said of religion's role in Simms's critical theories. Religion's status as a foundation of several of those theories makes it implicit in many, if not most, of them, but explicit only in some, such as in his theories of art, fiction, and history. Secondly, *The Lily and the Totem* expresses Simms's own view of religion, which is embodied in his critical theories. In a letter to Hammond, Simms wrote: "I will not trouble you with my theology, which, if not orthodox, is without a shade of irreverence." [33] The uniqueness of his religious views can be clearly seen in his positive portrayal of a pagan marriage; only with a non-doctrinal, or as Simms prefers, an unorthodox, view of religion could such an act be not only condoned but approved. Simms's realism would accept the marriage, for it is unrealistic to expect the standards of civilization to apply in a wilderness; his religious views, however, would approve of such a marriage as being not only natural but good.

An examination of Simms's narrative technique in *The Lily and the Totem* illustrates the problems he encountered in creating this new genre, for the demands of narrative technique for history and for fiction are different. A historian has the obligation of telling all the significant, pertinent facts as he knows them, essentially in a chronological framework. In fiction, however, the author has considerably more flexibility. With no obligations to following the facts of a known history, he has complete freedom to create material and alter chronology.

In *The Lily and the Totem,* Simms made his primary obligation the telling of the history of the Huguenot settlements.
This obligation resulted in a dilemma for Simms. He could either tell the stories of all of his subjects, whether groups or individuals, in one strict chronological account—an almost day-
by-day account—or he could follow his subjects separately,
telling each of their stories separately from start to finish, and
then backtracking in time to begin with the next subject. Both
approaches presented Simms with some problems in narrative
structure and continuity. The first method, simultaneously
telling all subjects' stories in a strict chronological progression,
all but completely sacrifices the narrative continuity of the
overall story when working with several subjects. This method
preserves the chronological integrity of the colonists' history
but reduces the story to a diary-like journal of various subjects'
daily exploits. With many subjects, this is almost certain to be
confusing. The second approach, telling a subject's story from
start to finish and then backtracking to begin the next subject's
story, results in a series of loosely-linked vignettes, or a tale
that hop-scotches around chronologically, and thereby risks
confusing the reader.

Simms was keenly aware of the dilemma posed by these
choices in narrative technique—it was a dilemma he embraced,
with his dedication to telling the history of the Huguenot colonists and his equally strong commitment to being a good story-
teller. In the first part of the book, Simms did not have much of
a problem with this dilemma, for the people and events that he
had to deal with were few. This allowed him to follow the second type of narrative technique, telling the stories of Guernache, Lachane, and the other colonists from start to finish,
without resorting to chronological backtracking and with no
loss of narrative continuity. This is why, perhaps, the characters of Guernache, Lachane, and Albert are so memorable, for
Simms weaves their stories together well, forming one contin-
uous tale. With the second part of the book, however, the problem of narrative continuity was probably Simms's most pressing concern—it certainly is to modern readers. With a more
complete—and more complex—picture of the second voyage of
Ribault, as provided by his sources, Simms had a concomi-

tantly greater problem with maintaining the narrative continuity of his tale. Maintaining the same narrative technique used in the first part of the book, Simms told the stories of his subjects in part two from start to finish, vignette-fashion. Chapter twelve, "The Conspiracy of Le Genre," is an excellent example of this narrative technique, for it is a major break-point in the book, setting several different stories into motion. Their first attempt at mutiny having been thwarted by D'Erlach, the mutineers escape to the wilds and in chapters fourteen and fifteen stage another mutiny, this time successful, and extort a pirate's commission from Laudonnierre. Their exploits as privateers and final retribution complete this strand of the story. Their former leader, Le Genre, plays no part in this second mutiny, however. Le Genre appears in the next story strand, chapter sixteen, which follows D'Erlach's adventures on an expedition. Simms repeats this pattern of fragmentation, explication, and reunification of his subjects' stories several times throughout the story of the second colony, in varying degrees of scale.

Chapters twelve through sixteen show Simms's use of this pattern on a small scale, but he exploits it on a larger scale as well. The first example of this large-scale application is his use of the "condition of partial obscurity" on the final disappearance of D'Erlach to tie the final chapter, "Dominique de Gourgues," to the preceding section. Having detailed D'Erlach's final disappearance, after Melendez has butchered all but those few Huguenots who placed their trust in D'Erlach, Simms unites the final chapter with its predecessors by speculating that D'Erlach survived to witness, and assist in, the French revenge on the Spanish. This chapter is particularly susceptible to the accusation of breaking the book's narrative continuity, for it concentrates on a Gascon, who was not a colonist, and his tale moreover occurs after the destruction of the second colony. Simms's historical tie between this subject and the history of the colony is only that this Gascon, Dominique de Gourgues, took it upon himself to avenge the murder of his countrymen. Simms strengthens this tie by speculating that D'Erlach reappears to aid in the defeat of Melendez. Rather than letting his subject matter—the history of the two colonies—or simple chronology be the sole points of unity in his story, Simms instead made every effort to strive for narrative continuity as well, both within the individual stories of his characters, as evidenced by his decision to tell their stories from beginning to end, and also by weaving their stories together—a luxury afforded him, in this last instance, by the "partial obscurity" surrounding D'Erlach's demise.

In *The Lily and the Totem,* then, Simms's narrative technique is part and parcel an expression of his goals in writing the book: to be true to the history of his subject but to "enliven" it with fiction. The pattern of fragmentation, explication, and reunification represented the best compromise Simms felt he could make with the problem of narrative continuity, and his exploitation of the "partial obscurity" in the history provided by his sources enabled him to use fiction as the cement to bond together the places where the inviolability of his facts inevitably resulted in a break in narrative continuity. As good a solution as this narrative technique is, it is the fiction, especially in this last instance, that maintains the narrative continuity of the story as a whole.

Simms uses one further—and essential—device to maintain the continuity of his tale: the chapters of "Historical Summary." By adopting the narrative technique of telling the stories of individual subjects to their completion and then backtracking to begin with another, Simms knew he risked confusing his reader. However, by including the chapters of "Historical Summary," Simms could provide not only an outline of the facts but also a brief synopsis of what was to come. In brief, they are a roadmap of the book. More importantly, they are also a logical device for Simms to use in this fashion, because of their historicity: after all, history is Simms's paramount concern in *The Lily and the Totem.*

One additional result of Simms's narrative technique in *The Lily and the Totem* is that several episodes are excellent short stories in their own right. Defining what constitutes a short story within an episodic work like *The Lily and the Totem* is a difficult task; Simms's technique could allow classifying most of the book's vignettes as short stories. If the standard employed is a story's independence from the rest of the work, however, only two of them qualify: chapter seventeen, "The Narrative of Le Barbu," and chapter twenty-five, "Dominique de Gourgues." Each of these has little to connect it with the rest of the work. The only tie between "Le Barbu" and the rest of the book is that Laudonnierre sent for, and ransomed, the ship-wrecked and enslaved Spaniard Barbu from the hands of an in-land Indian tribe. The story of his shipwreck, and subsequent enslavement and adventures among the Indians, has nothing to do with the story of the colonists. Only in the end of Barbu's tale, with his emancipation, do the Huguenots come into play— a comparatively small role indeed. Similarly, the ties between chapter twenty-five, "Dominique de Gourgues," and the rest of the work are weak. Only in furnishing a motive for de Gour-gues' voyage of retribution do the colonists play a part in the story, a link so weak that Simms created the fictitious charac-ter of the White Indian chief, supposedly Alphonse D'Erlach, to strengthen the story's link with the rest of the work. Given the obvious independence of both stories to the rest of the book, it seems strange that Simms would leave them in. Again, how-ever, Simms did not feel justified in swerving from his in-tention to tell the story of the two colonies from beginning to end, and as his sources indicated, both of these stories were an indisputable part of that history. It is interesting to see how this situation allowed Simms to create two good short stories, a genre in which he excelled, as scholars are increasingly noting.[34]

Simms's narrative technique in *The Lily and the Totem* also shows the degree to which his theories of art, fiction, and his-tory fit together. One obvious point of comparison is his use of the heroic ideal, a concept which is an admirable bridge be-tween his theories of art and history; D'Erlach would seem to be the best example of this, for he is, after all, the epitome of the hero. However, another hero also springs to mind: Domi-nique de Gourgues, whose vengeance upon the Spanish Simms goes out of his way to applaud, not only in his authorial com-mentary but in dramatic revelation as well. If Simms had so chosen, de Gourgues' adventure could occupy considerably less space, resulting in much less of a break in the book's continu-ity. His decision to make de Gourgues' story so prominent in the book illuminates the second, and most important, way that

The Lily and the Totem bridges Simms's theories of art, literature, and history. As Simms states, de Gourgues' revenge is
justified even if it seems to violate the laws of man. He is an-
swering a higher call, in Simms's opinion: the law of "humanity" (p. 462). With de Gourgues, then, Simms ends his story on
a positive note: justice has been served, and thus Simms has
fulfilled his responsibility as a historian and as an artist, for he
has embodied an elevating moral in his tale.

On a small scale, Simms has certainly fulfilled his obligation
to history, literature, and art with de Gourgues. However,
there is still one problem: the obliteration of the two Huguenot
colonies. While de Gourgues' story places the end of the book in
the proper historical, artistic framework, it does nothing to resolve the problem created for Simms by the fact that the Huguenot colonies, his basic subject, were extinguished, one of
them by an evil force. In the resolution to this problem, the sophistication of Simms's practice of his critical theories becomes
clear. Simms has to justify the Huguenots' deaths in the book,
for if he does not, then the law of history as progress has been
violated, and he as a historian has failed in his responsibility
to portray his story in those terms. One possible reason for the
Huguenots' massacre at the hands of the Spanish is their blind
faith in religion. Desperately trusting Melendez's pious declamations, the Frenchmen (except for D'Erlach and his followers)
forsake their reason, and die as a result.

This is an unsatisfactory answer, for no matter how histori-
cally accurate a lesson this may be, the extermination of an entire colony for temporarily abandoning reason seems overly
harsh. Moreover, it still leaves the problem of the first colony's
demise with no solution. The answer lies in the values of the
Huguenots themselves. Although they fled from religious persecution in France, their activities in the New World are almost wholly concerned with searching for gold. Their fatal
error lies not in their forsaking reason and trusting Melendez,
although that certainly represents their graver error in a most
blatant fashion. Rather, their fatal mistake is not recognizing
the falseness of their values. In their search for gold, they neglect to plant crops; even the resulting famine does not teach
them the error of their ways. Even when an American Eden,

Iracana, dangles alluringly under their noses, they turn back to their search for gold, despite the happiness they experience there. Ultimately, the Huguenots are unteachable. They perish as a result. In the form of de Gourgues, we see the right values; thus he triumphs. He is not motivated by gold but by honor. The same is true for D'Erlach, who, as the sole survivor of the second colony, witnesses the final justice paid to Melendez. With Simms's exercise of his imagination to fill the gap in his records concerning D'Erlach's demise, D'Erlach emerges as an example of heroism being rewarded as well.

Thus historical writing can embody an elevating moral, just as purely imaginative writing can, and in fact the two can be synonymous, as *The Lily and the Totem* proves. Ultimately, the distinctions between the two types of writing dissolve into common purposes and devices, as the example of D'Erlach and de Gourgues shows: D'Erlach is rewarded for his heroism through Simms's use of art to fill in a gap in his history; de Gourgues illustrates the same lesson, drawn straight from history. A more graphic example of Simms's belief that history and fiction are not very far apart would be difficult to find.

Analyzing the history in *The Lily and the Totem* further highlights the complexities of this genre of fictional history. In the first place, the history in *The Lily and the Totem* is inextricably intertwined with the fiction, and on a level deeper than simply the narrative flow. True, Simms had to work particularly hard to join fact and fiction smoothly together in his story, but the marriage between the two was logical, for Simms's critical theories supported it. For example, Simms considered a chief responsibility of historians to be the instruction of present generations in the achievements of the past;[35] his use of the heroic ideal, a literary device, also fulfills this obligation. Thus divorcing history from fiction in *The Lily and the Totem* is difficult due to the interdependence of the critical theories that shaped the work. Moreover, there is a danger in isolating the history in the book from the fiction, since such an approach could portray Simms as a historian. Because Simms wrote the factual, historical account of the Huguenot settlements in the Southeast in other works, such as his *History of South Carolina,* his primary purpose with *The Lily and the Totem* was not to demonstrate his proficiency as a professional historian. Rather, it was to demonstrate how art could "enliven" history, bridging the gaps between facts with plausible fiction, providing characters with conversation and life; in short, his purpose was to make his subject "come alive." The settlements of Coligny, Simms felt, were particularly suitable for this purpose; as he notes in *Views and Reviews,* "in the employment of historical events, for the purposes of art in fiction, a condition of partial obscurity and doubt in history being that which leaves the genius most free to its proper inventions, is the one most suitable for its exercise."[36] The vagueness of Simms's sources, then, was essential for the success of his fictionalized approach, and fortunately, his sources for *The Lily and the Totem* left him with that necessary vagueness.

Thus, while the historical aspect is crucial to the book's analysis as a whole, it should not be evaluated by the same standards as a conventional history. The difficulty of finding a suitable standard to evaluate the history in *The Lily and the Totem* Simms thoughtfully obviated, for he himself establishes it: accuracy. As long as his fiction does not contravene his known facts, and his conjecture in the absence of facts—be it conversation between characters or speculation concerning the disappearance of them—remains plausible, he has lived up to his standard (p. v).

As he notes in the introduction to the book, Simms never took liberties with the facts as he knew them. The historical evidence in *The Lily and the Totem* is confined to the "Historical Summaries" and to Simms's documentation. The former tend to be brief outlines of the facts, which not only give the reader an indication of what is to come but moreover indicate the boundaries between fact and fiction that Simms blurred (p. v). As can be expected, they are not the best display of Simms's talents as a historian, nor are they particularly interesting, especially in comparison with the rest of the book. Simms even remarked to Hammond that the first chapter was "unavoidably dull" because of the necessity of providing so much history in it.[37] Much more interesting and revealing are Simms's techniques of documentation in *The Lily and the Totem.* Since this was not to be a conventional history, yet not completely removed from that realm either, the problem that documentation posed Simms must have been great. His use of sources and his footnotes are the obvious method of analyzing his answer. Unfortunately, Simms never states what his sources were in his preface; however, in his *History of South Carolina* he lists three primary sources for this period in history, and, following the common practice of midnineteenth-century historians, refers to them only by surname: Adair, Hakluyt, and Charlevoix. From his footnotes in *The Lily and the Totem* we learn the titles of two works by Charlevoix, "Feste Chronologiques" and *New France*. Of these, *New France* is by far the most important, as it incorporates the accounts of Hakluyt, Loudonnierre, and others. Although a comparison of Simms's sources versus *The Lily and the Totem* is beyond the scope of this essay, it is important to note that Simms did, in fact, live up to his promise of not straying from the facts as he knew them. Charlevoix alone provides the basic plot and stories of the various characters in the two voyages, from Guernache to Gourgues. The best method of determining when Simms was indulging in "conjecture," as he put it, is to read the "Historical Summaries." As he notes in the dedication, they indicate to the reader "upon how much, or how little, he may properly rely as history" (p. v).

Given Simms's intention not to write a scholarly account, his footnotes are relatively extensive. They can be grouped into four categories, the first and most common of which is the simple documentation of facts, much as in any modern historical account. Although this kind of footnote is the most conspicuous type of notation, Simms nonetheless does not use it often—after all, this was a work of fiction. More interesting is the second type of footnote, which provides supporting quotations from his sources. For example, when Simms feels that his fictionalized descriptions of people could be questioned, he quotes the passage from his sources that provided the basis for his exposition. Thus, after thoroughly derogating the character and morals of Captain Albert, Simms cites a lengthy passage from Charlevoix to corroborate his characterization (p. 79). A third type of footnote is the simple explanation of terms, occurring fairly frequently because of the problems in translating

Indian names and terms, particularly since Simms used both French and English sources. Last, Simms footnoted controversial facts, as indicated by contradictory evidence from his sources, providing his own interpretation and the rationale behind it. These are the most interesting of all the footnotes in the work because they demonstrate the author's skill as a historian. In several instances, Simms cites the contradictions between sources and offers a practical explanation for their resolution. Thus, while *The Lily and the Totem* is not the best indication of Simms's abilities as a historian, by analyzing his historical scholarship and techniques therein, the reader gains a sense of the difficulties Simms encountered in attempting to create such a hybrid of fiction and history.

Any estimate of a book's merits normally assumes that the work in question belongs to some established literary genre which provides guidelines for critical evaluation. With *The Lily and the Totem,* this is obviously a problem, since no one existing genre properly defines it. As short fiction, a couple of the vignettes can be considered excellent short stories in their own right. As history, although it cannot be compared to the type of rigorously documented historical writing that modern scholarship requires, it is nonetheless impressive. As fictional history, of course, it stands as the epitome of the genre—a genre established by Simms in this work. And as historical fiction, aside from its significance in the literary history and theory of the historical novel, *The Lily and the Totem* can be considered successful, despite its problems with narrative continuity. However, if viewed as a romance, these problems with continuity relegate *The Lily and the Totem* to second-rate status. While this opinion cannot be found in any of the contemporary reviews of the book, perhaps this is one reason for its relative neglect subsequently.

For an understanding of Simms, *The Lily and the Totem* is indisputably important for its illumination of several of his critical theories. That these theories accurately describe the imaginative and historical elements in the book is apparent; among other points, Simms's portrayal of character, his realism, his use of sources, the major literary themes of the work, and the complex narrative framework all have their basis in his theories of art, fiction, and history. Perhaps even more importantly, the book also provides an excellent illustration of how well these apparently distinct critical theories actually mesh in Simms's thought. And while it is important to recognize that *The Lily and the Totem* demonstrates Simms's considerable powers as a critical theorist, it needs to be remembered too that much of it also shows Simms at his best as an imaginative writer.

This makes its dismissal as a second-rate romance unacceptable. True, perhaps part of the lack of continuity in the book may be attributed to Simms's own fashion of writing—the lament that he wrote too quickly springs to mind, for at one point he was writing a staggering forty manuscript pages a day.[38] But most, if not all, of the reason for the lack of narrative continuity must be traced to Simms's choice of narrative technique. *The Lily and the Totem* was a literary experiment on Simms's part, an attempt to combine history and fiction in a more rigid framework than traditional historical fiction. If the rigidity of that framework exacted a certain toll on the literary merits, as conventionally defined, of the work as a whole, that toll should be viewed as inherent in the genre, for a new genre is in fact what Simms was attempting to create.[39] And when evaluated within the bounds established by this new genre, *The Lily and the Totem* shows a mature author using all of his powers of creativity and scholarship in a first-rate work of fictional history.[40]

Notes

[1] *The Lily and the Totem, or, the Huguenots in Florida. A Series of sketches, picturesque and historical, of the colonies of Coligni, in North America, 1563–1570* (New York: Baker & Scribner, 1850).

[2] The only extended treatment of the book is in an unpublished dissertation. Mary Crow Anderson, "The Huguenot in the South Carolina Novel," Ph.D. dissertation, Univ. of South Carolina, 1966.

[3] John C. Guilds, "Simms's Use of History: Theory and Practice," *Mississippi Quarterly*, 30 (Fall 1977), 510.

[4]William Gilmore Simms, "Bulwer's Genius and Writings," *The Magnolia,* n.s. 1 (December 1842).

[5]"Modern Prose Fiction," *Southern Quarterly Review* (April 1849), 43. (Hereafter abbreviated *SQR.*)

[6]Magnolia, n.s. 1 (December 1842), 331. Italics in original. Cf. *SQR,* 15 (April 1849), 52.

[7]William Gilmore Simms, *Views and Reviews in American Literature, History, and Fiction. First Series,* ed. C. Hugh Holmann (Cambridge, Mass.: The Belknap Press of the Harvard University Press, 1961), 42.

[8]*Views and Reviews. First Series,* 33–35. Cf. *SQR,* 15 (April 1849), 52. Cf. *SQR,* 7 (April 1845), 316.

[9]"The Epochs and Events of American History, as Suited to the Purposes of Art in Fiction," *Southern & Western,* 2 (September 1845), 145–154.

[10]Mary C. Simms Oliphant, Alfred Taylor Odell, and T. C. Duncan Eaves, eds., *The Letters of William Gilmore Simms,* 5 vols. & supp. (Columbia, S.C.: University of South Carolina Press, 1952–56, 1982), VI, 93. All further references to this source will be abbreviated *Letters.*

[11]*The Lily and the Totem,* p. vi. All further references to this work will be by page number within the text.

[12]*Letters,* II, 55, 105n.

[13]*Letters,* II, 170.

[14]Simms, "The Epochs and Events of American History, as Suited to the Purposes of Art in Fiction," pp. 145–154.

[15]Simms, "The Epochs and Events of American History, as Suited to the Purposes of Art in Fiction," published in four parts in *Southern & Western,* 2 (February 1845), 109–127; 2 (March 1845), 182–191; 2 (April 1845), 257–261; 2 (June 1845), 385–392; 2 (September 1845), 145–154.

[16]*Southern & Western,* 2 (November 1845), 324–332. *Letters,* II, 106n. This later became chapter fourteen of *The Lily and the Totem.*

[17]*Letters,* II, 55, 147, 170–171, VI, 93.

[18]*Letters,* III, 36.

[19]*Letters,* II, 140, 118, 178, 234, 273, 286.

[20]Jon Wakelyn cites this as contributing to a marked decrease in the quality and quantity of the fiction Simms produced during the 1840s. Jon Wakelyn, *The Politics of a Literary Man: William Gilmore Simms* (Westport, Conn: Greenwood Press, 1973), 80. Most Simms scholars, however, would take exception with Wakelyn's remark.

[21]*Literary World,* 7 (September 7, 1850), 189–190; *Democratic Review,* 27 (October 1850), 379; *Harper's New Monthly Magazine,* 1 (Oc-

tober 1850), 718; *Sartain's,* 7 (November 1850), 318; *Holden's Dollar Magazine,* 6 (December 1850), 758–759.

[22] *Holden's Dollar Magazine,* 6 (December 1850), 758. *Sartain's,* 7 (November 1850), 318. *Letters,* III, 61n.

[23] *De Bow's Review,* 9 (November 1850), 574.

[24] *Letters,* III, 79, 60–61.

[25] Baker and Scribner distinguished the second printing from the first by adding the words "Second Edition" to the title page plate. Four years later the firm of Charles Scribner reissued the book, with the title and subtitle reversed, as *The Huguenots in Florida; or the Lily and the Totem;* it is called the "Third Edition" on the title page.

[26] *Letters,* V, 229, 231, 259.

[27] For the size of the press runs of Simms's romances, see *Letters,* II, 385. No printing later than the third by Scribner has been noted.

[28] *Letters,* V, 259.

[29] Most records of the Walker, Evans & Cogswell firm were destroyed by fire in 1879. There is only one extant volume of customer orders prior to that date.

[30] *Letters,* V, 271, 271n.

[31] Albert Keiser has said that Simms's portrayals of the Indians throughout his works, from *The Yemassee* to *The Cassique of Kiawah,* are generally accurate, and he compliments Simms on not depicting them as either the 'noble savage' or the 'blood-thirsty savage' stereotypes. See "Simms' Romantic Naturalism," in Keiser's *The Indian in American Literature* (New York: Octagon, 1970), 154–174.

[32] See William Peterfield Trent, *William Gilmore Simms* (Boston and New York: Houghton, Mifflin, 1892), 88.

[33] *Letters,* II, 385.

[34] John Caldwell Guilds, "Introduction," *Stories and Tales,* in *The Writings of William Gilmore Simms* (Columbia: University of South Carolina Press), V, xii, xxiv. Cf. John C. Guilds, "The Literary Criticism of William Gilmore Simms," *South Carolina Review,* 2 (November 1969), 49.

[35] *Views and Reviews. First Series,* p. 38.

[36] *Views and Reviews. First Series,* p. 76.

[37] *Letters,* III, 82.

[38] *Letters,* II, 438.

[39] This is corroborated by Simms's comments in the "Epistle Dedicatory" to Hammond, where he states that *The Lily and the Totem* will be viewed as "Romance of History," whereas it actually has much higher aspirations (p. v).

[40] If postscript were to be added to this, it would be that the next big

project Simms embarked upon after *The Lily and the Totem* was the Revolutionary romance *Katherine Walton*. Published serially in 1850, it appeared in book form in 1851. In 1852 followed another outstanding contribution to the Revolutionary series, *Woodcraft*. It almost seems that Simms, with the completion of *The Lily and the Totem,* felt that he had proven his point, and demonstrated not only that America could indeed provide suitable subjects for historical romance but also, and most importantly, that his conception of the use of history by art was valid. After uniting history, biography, and exploring the relationship between fiction and history so thoroughly in the 1840s, Simms now returned with new energy and conviction to the novel form and to the Revolutionary Romances that he had begun with the publication in 1835 of *The Partisan*. It is significant that his best historical fiction, if not his best fiction ever, was forthcoming.

Perceiver and Perceived: External Landscape as Mirror and Metaphor in Simms's Poetry

JAMES E. KIBLER, JR.

William Gilmore Simms probably wrote more poems descriptive of nature than any American poet before or after him. His natural scenes are most often very carefully described pictures which reveal that their painter was both a good observer and a sensitive reporter. His knowledge of nature was extensive, owing to early horseback and flatboat journeys through the southern states to the southwestern frontier, forays into the lowcountry swamps of his home, and habitual camping trips to the mountains of South Carolina, North Carolina, and Georgia. He knew well the tidal marshes and the sea beyond them. Simms's love of hunting and fishing also brought him into the woods. He thus knew nature from experience, but also from the explorations of naturalists before him. Through their works, he had more than a passing book-knowledge of the flora and fauna of his native land. William Bartram was one of his favorite naturalists and the one he mentions most frequently.[1] Of contemporary treatments of nature, he knew, for example, Thoreau's *Walden*[2] and contributed information on the practical properties of plants to Francis Peyre Porcher's *Resources of the Southern Fields and Forests* (1863).[3] Among those local naturalists whom he knew and encouraged were John Bachman (1790–1874), friend and collaborator of Audubon; Joel Roberts Poinsett (1779–1851); William Summer (1815–1878), horticulturist and nurseryman; and Henry William Ravenel (1814–1887), botanist and authority on fungi.

Considering this deep and abiding interest in the natural scene, it is small wonder that this romantic poet devoted so many of his energies to describing it. On the basis of his descriptions alone, he is sufficiently interesting. He does, however, much more. The goals of his descriptions are not to provide pictures, no matter how charming or picturesque he might be able to make them. Investing nature with charm is simply not enough. His descriptions are not ends in themselves, but instead go to the heart of his concept of man, nature, and God.

In 1846, in a letter to a fledgling Southern poet seeking advice from the established author, Simms addresses the subject of nature poetry. He demands that the poet should "only not forget in merely describing its actual features to say how these impressed him," in other words, show what this natural scene reveals by "associations, analogies, &c." Doing so would be thus "associating the moral with the physical, as is done by Wordsworth, Bryant &c."[4] It is clear from these comments and similar ones elsewhere that it is not enough for him to catalogue the "external" subject. He is quick to point out that the external is in want of the "moral" (spiritual or psychic) life residing within, which the true poet reads through physical nature's "innate suggestions."[5] By "moral," he does not mean didactic or moralistic poetry, which he spurns. If the aim of the writer is truth, he states, truths greater than the single maxim will be inherent in an imaginative work.[6] Instead, he defines the "moral" part of a work as the ability to "awaken thoughts, interests and inquiries in the mind, which hurry the spectator far beyond the scene." To "awaken into stir the spiritual mind," he says, is the chief role of the artist.[7] The true poet of nature must "try" the moral, or internal-spiritual life, in connection with the external, that is, to merge the two, "as Bryant does, as is done by Wordsworth, Thomson, &c."[8]

Simms thus shows that he understands a primary aim of the nature poet in the romantic period. His constant praise of Wordsworth hinges partly on the English writer's ability to "invest the sun, stars, the air and vernal woods . . . with something of a spiritual instinct."[9] Simms likewise does so in his verse. This study will explore three of the techniques by which he accomplishes his goal. It will not treat the verse in which he flatly states the idea, for many poems like "Carolina Woods"[10] exist in the canon to declare, "These woods have all been haunted, and the power / Of spirits still abides in tree and flower." Nor will this essay deal with Simms's frequent and effective personification of nature, or how he uses objects in nature as simple similes and metaphors. In "Elegiac,"[11] for example, the speaker's young wife hangs upon his bosom like a flower. In "The Western Emigrants,"[12] an old man leaving home is compared to a tree that can "take no root again," having "snapp'd off / His ancient tendrils, and in foreign clay / His branches will all wither." It is significant that almost exclusively, his similes and metaphors will have a thing of nature as one of their two terms. The poet is constantly tying man to nature; with these comparisons; and this fact is interesting in its own right. This study, however, will address itself to how external nature is made relative to the world of spirit by its perceiver.

There are three techniques by which Simms yokes the outer world[13] to the inner world, or (put a different way) the world of external physical nature with the mind of the individual or the spiritual world to which it is allied: (1) the perceiver draws an analogy between his natural world and the world of the spirit; (2) the perceiver shapes the perceived by infusing his own life into the object perceived; and (3) the perceived is the metaphor for the feelings of the perceiver. All three thus result in the inextricable binding of man to nature; and the last, in fact, accomplishes a merging of the two, a blurring which successfully images the divine unity, or oneness of all things, a concept so central to the Romantic.

1. The perceiver draws an analogy between his natural world and the world of the spirit.

In this technique, the viewer recognizes that nature is emblematic, or symbolic. Physical nature mirrors truths of the spirit. In "Harmonies of Nature,"[14] Simms summarizes this concept by saying that nature is the "type of the Eternal" and teaches spiritual truths. The poem's final stanza states that nature is the robe that dresses the spirit. In his "Forest Worship,"[15] the poet specifically names nature's "rude scatter'd emblems," showing once again an indisputable awareness of the emblematic nature of the world. One should also recall in this context Simms's advice to poets of nature that they must draw analogies and make associations, not merely describe "literal" nature. For to be "literal" in poetry, he says elsewhere, "is always apt to be untrue."[16]

This drawing of analogies is an old method in American verse, going back to Anne Bradstreet and Edward Taylor. It was current in Simms's own day in the works of Freneau, Bryant, and Emerson. In the prose of Thoreau, Hawthorne, and Melville, it had a flowering during Simms's maturity. The method is not original with any of these writers; it simply shows that they are similar in their use of it and therefore working in a tradition that provides one of the continuities in American literature from its outset through Simms's day and beyond. In this respect, Simms is in the broad American mainstream. That he has not often enough been taken in his American context is one of the great oversights in American criticism.

With these authors, the analogy is *of* a common enough physical event, process, or object in nature *to* a higher law or spiritual truth. There is frequently, then, as in Freneau and Bryant, a lesson to be gleaned from the analogy. A few examples should suffice to show Simms's particular manner in handling the technique.

In his "Flowers and Trees,"[17] the "grandsire oak," which he further personifies as a gray-haired, moss-draped "Druidpatriarch" with arms "out-stretched" in benediction, is an emblem of endurance:

> March is profuse in violets—at our feet
>> They cluster,—not in pride, but modesty;
>> The damsel pauses as she passes by,
> Plucks them with smiles, and calls them very sweet.
> But such beguile me not! The trees are mine,
>> These hoary-headed masters;—and I glide,
>> Humbled, beneath their unpresuming pride,
> And wist not much what blossoms bud or shine.

I better love to see yon grandsire oak,
  Old Druid-patriarch, lone among his race,—
  With blessing, out-stretched arms, as giving grace
When solemn rites are said, or bread is broke:
Decay is at his roots,—the storm has been
Among his limbs,—but the old top is green.

Undoubtedly the Southern liveoak—one of the common moss-swathed trees from Simms's low country environment—speaks the universal lesson of endurance. It is a common object in nature which becomes symbol of this particular virtue, one that the speaker, through the poem's tone, shows that he extols. Although the poem is not didactic, as Freneau's or Bryant's might have been if they had treated the subject, it has moral truths implicit. Literature, Simms states, "should never be written with reference to a specific moral." If composed "with due heed to *general truth*," works of art "carry with them a thousand wholesome morals, which are superior to maxims."[18] Simms's anti-didactic mode is thus more in keeping with modern taste.

"First Day of Spring"[19] begins with a description of the resurgence of life in nature. In its fifth stanza, the speaker goes from a description of the external landscape to a portrayal of the poet's inner life. His feelings "bound," "break chains," and "leap," thus utilizing the same diction which describes spring's "bursting buds," "leaping birds," and "tender shoots" that "spring to birth." The external landscape is thus made analogous to the inner, and provides a mirror for it. The statement is implicit; the analogy is drawn only from a close reading of the diction. More often than not, the theme of a Simms poem is not on its surface.

In "The Streamlet,"[20] the brook becomes the emblem of continuity and timelessness amid the flux of an unstable world. As a symbol of immortality, it is well-chosen, for though the stream is flowing like life (in the manner of the cliché of "the river of life"), it remains inexhaustible in its deep banks from age to age. In "Stanzas,"[21] dashed hopes are analogous to "deep planted oaks," which storms have uprooted and destroyed. In "The Memorial Tree,"[22] a green, fruiting tree is "linked with," that is, made analogous to childhood and "the first dear throbs of feeling in thy heart"; its summer leaves are analogous to first love and the promise of love; its autumn foliage is linked with grief over loss and the death of loved ones. The lesson of nature is mutability, but she has "memorials" which "are taught" to "bring our sweetest histories back to thought." There is one ancient tree in the forest which has become a record tree, carved upon first by Indians and now by white men. The speaker, too, leaves his record of love on the tree and knows that when he and his loved one will decay in the grave of that same hillside, other young lovers will read that record:

> We shall leave ours,
> Dear heart! and when our sleep beneath its boughs
> Shall suffer spring to spread o'er us her flowers,
> Eyes that vow love like ours shall trace our vows.

The memorial tree is a complex emblem. It symbolizes the transience of life, but, at the same time, the preservation of human values in and through nature. Nature bears the message of continuity or immortality transcending the short-term shifting and vanishing forms. It is an excellent poem.

Another work that makes use of the analogy, but in a slightly different way, is "Heedlessness":[23]

> We see the flow'r decaying as we pass,
> Pale with the coming cold, and, on the grass,
>   Write ruin, with our footsteps, every hour,
>   Yet pause not in our progress, though a pow'r,
> As much superior to ourselves, as we
>   To these dumb suff'rers of the predestined earth,
>   Beholds us rapidly passing from our birth,
> To a like ruin with the things we see;
> And, from our side, as little heeded, goes,
>   Drawn by invisible cords, the treasured thing
>   That has our heart, in keeping;—yet we sing
> As idly as if life were free from foes,
> And love were sure 'gainst danger;—there is one,
> Who, speaking near me now, of death, is heard by none!

Man's own mortality is analogous to the transience of the things of nature; but here the analogy is only observed by the superior "power." Man himself is heedless of the truth even while the lesson of mutability is clearly spoken in his ear. In this poem, the speaker has gained distance from his subject, and the work's tone is more objective and matter-of-fact than in the usual Simms poem in which the "I" observes the analogy and brings it home to himself. One of the themes of "Heedlessness" is that men resist the truths placed before them in nature. Man's refusal to see beyond the literal surface in this poem mirrors Simms's general belief that literalness has become the cardinal sin of the era.

In "Harbor by Moonlight,"[24] the poet is again voicing the same theme:

> The open sea before me, bathed in light,
>   As if it knew no tempest; the near shore
> Crown'd with its fortresses, all green and bright,
>   As if 'twere safe from carnage ever more;
> And woman on the ramparts; while below
>   Girlhood, and thoughtless children bound and play
>   As if their hearts, in one long holiday,
> Had sweet assurance 'gainst to-morrow's wo:—
> Afar, the queenly city, with her spires,
>   Articulate, in the moonlight,—that above,
> Seems to look downward with intenser fires,
>   As wrapt in fancies near akin to love;
> One star attends her which she cannot chide,
> Meek as the virgin by the matron's side.

The natural scene is likely an actual, specific one. It is the Moultrie House Spa, on the beach north of the city of Charleston and site of Fort Moultrie, famous for the Revolutionary War battle of the same name. The "ramparts" are thus of the fort; and one can look across the harbor to see the city's spires. The "thoughtless" spa-goers see the beauty of the calm moonlit scene; but the sea is known for its tempests; and the very boardwalk of ramparts is the symbol for "carnage."[25] Heedless man never looks behind the placid mask to see reality. The sonnet then shifts to the city in its sestet. The poet means for the reader to perceive that the scene in the octave parallels that in the sestet. Thus, the city, too, suffers under a delusion, thinking the very sky looks down on it "with intenser fires . . . near akin to love." The city's delusion of safety and divinely-favored status closely parallels the "thoughtlessness" of the vacationers on the beach, who never stop to consider one important fact of life: violence and destruction, described here as "tempest" and "carnage." In less than two decades, the guns of Sumter in this same harbor would prove the poem to be prophetic. Thus, both this poem and "Heedlessness" reveal that the poet feels most men are unable to see beneath the literal surface and thus are unaware of the abundant lessons residing in the physical forms. Only the heedful poet can be an interpreter.

With the poet's inspired ability to see analogies, nature becomes an inexhaustible "soul-garden."[26] In exploring nature, the poet feels he is a "dreamer / In the world's notion," but realizes that his "mute converse" with woods and waters frees him from literalness, gives him insight, broadens his spirit, and makes it "fruitful." His soul "grows lifted into stature" through nature's teachings. The lessons are ever-present in her visible forms; imaginative man has only to open eyes and hearts. Nature thus "wings us to a spirit world," and this "lowly world" is thereby linked with heaven. The analogy is one way in which the inspired poet-perceiver aids nature in the linking process.

2. The perceiver shapes the perceived.

In this concept, the active observer casts or infuses his life into the object he views. Nature *is* as the viewer perceives it. Nature and the viewer, therefore, are bound through the viewer's mind and invigorate each other in a symbiotic relationship. Without man's active contribution, nature would fall lifeless as a hollow, dead shell without a kernel of spirit. This belief, perhaps best expressed by Coleridge, is centrally Romantic. Unlike the analogy, which, although Simms adapted it to his Romantic purposes, was found in American writers over a span of three centuries, this concept of perceiver creating the perceived shows the poet to have been abreast of current English Romantic thought. In America, this trait was certainly not as widespread as the first. Although Emerson, also taking the lead from Coleridge in his essay, "Nature" (1836), is another American practitioner of this view, I cannot suggest a third who so clearly states it.

For Simms leaves no doubt as to his adherence. In his 1829 essay, "Poetry and Painting," he writes that the poet, "like the all-animating principle of nature," infuses "his own essence into his creations" and transfuses "his very being into the elements around him until he becomes a portion" of all nature. In his novel, *Katharine Walton,* he claims that "the heart gives its character to the scene always."[27] In "Moral Change,"[28] he directly states the theory in verse. The poem's speaker, who has lost his early hopes and is now an "incomplete" person, has brought "a worse change in nature." For nature, he says, will "bloom" only "to bless a kindred spirit," flying the home "that yields no worship":

> She is seen
> Through the sweet medium of our sympathies,
> And has no life beside. 'Tis in our eye
> Alone that she is lovely—'tis our thought
> That makes her dear.

Nature thus takes its life from man, whom it reflects. For the process to be benign, or actually, in Simms, for it to work at all, the perceiver must be a "complete" man, an integrated, whole personality, not the "incomplete" utilitarian—materialist—rationalist—literalist—scientist—atheist. As a whole man, he can in turn see the wholeness of nature (matter and spirit integrated); but it is absolutely essential that he be whole in order to do so. If he is a fragmented man, he loses the ability to view nature properly, that is, to see both its physical and spiritual sides. The consequences of the fragmented personality are separation from nature, and a general alienation and isolation that is a torture. The end result of the actions of the fragmented perceiver of nature is a fragmented nature, or one robbed of anything but literalness in a denial of its spiritual side, which is for Simms the besetting sin of the age. This tragic consequence is that outlined in the poem.

"Moral Change" bears close resemblance to Coleridge's "Dejection: An Ode" ("Oh Lady we receive but what we give, / And in our life alone does nature live"). Both poets are saying essentially the same things. Although borrowed, it is obviously a more daring concept for Simms to put forward than that of the analogy, and provides a far better key to his general theory of poetry. That theory, along these lines, has been outlined elsewhere.[29] Briefly stated, the poet feels that the cardinal sin of the era is literalness, or the failure to see beyond the physical or material. Science has been a culprit in causing the problem; and now spirit, since not "susceptible of proof," is denied.[30] That "cold-blooded demon called Science" has destroyed belief in all but empirical reality. It is left to the imaginative, whole man to project life back into a dying nature. By no later than 1829, Simms shows that he is well aware of the essential role the poet has in shaping the world. A case in point is "Moral Change," which exhibits the central importance of man's inspired consciousness as a creative, harmonizing power. The "Moral" of the title means simply, as Simms defined the term on many occasions, the "spiritual" side, the ability to "awaken into stir in the mind" a process that would "hurry the spectator far beyond the scene."[31] Thus, the poet becomes minister to man, performing a religious role, saving him from the idolatry of objects, awakening his spiritual sense, and invigorating nature with that sense. The street is two-way. Imaginative man is inspired by the lessons of nature, which in turn put his active mind into play, projecting that life back into nature.

As a result, nature lives through the imaginative power of man's mind. Man's mind mirrors itself in nature and *vice versa,* for if the mind projects itself into nature, nature must of necessity reflect it. Again, as in the concept of analogy, the physical and the spiritual unite, and man and nature are bound. So many examples can be cited in Simms's poetry that one might say the process becomes a habit of mind for the poet. A few such examples should suffice. In "The Cassique of Accabee,"[32] the landscape takes on the traits of those who have lived in it. The physical world is thus enlivened and humanized through human associations. In "La Bolsa de las Sierras,"[33] the setting is an Edenic landscape of perfect oneness owing to a "commerce of kindred things." Man and nature commune; each "requites" the other and blessings are "ever circling" from one back to the other. It is Simms's picture of a prelapsarian ideal. In "Harmonies of Nature,"[34] Simms shows that nature fades as man's soul fails to appreciate it. In "Ashley River,"[35] the speaker relates that since "dark clouds have come about me," the river has also "felt the change." In "Dear Harp of the Forest,"[36] the gloominess of the forest "had birth" "in thy master's own sorrows." In "The Inutile Pursuit,"[37] the speaker, who praises the visionary and damns the materialist, notes that the true artist "would impart to things around," "his own bright hues . . . the glories that are growing in his heart." The examples could continue over pages, to a degree unknown in the verse of Coleridge himself.

Basil Willey has written of Coleridge that in freeing nature from the literalness of the atheist, the utilitarian, the materialist, and the empirical scientist, and in reinvigorating nature through the poetic imagination, thus disimprisoning "the soul of fact," he has focused on "the deepest meanings of romanticism."[38] Simms likewise has the inspired seer-minister-poet do the same. He is thus also aiming at "the deepest meanings of romanticism." Through the workings of his mind, the perceiver creates life in the perceived. He invigorates dead matter with spirit, which in turn provides inspiration and higher truths, resulting in more powerful focusing of life on the object in turn. The symbiotic process is thus unending; it only intensifies if the perceiver, as a whole man of imagination, can look at nature aright. Nature then becomes the perfect reflection of man's inner being, as it is also a reflection of God, who, after all, has made man in his own image. Man, nature, and God, therefore, merge through man's inspired perceptions of nature.

3. The perceived is the metaphor for the feelings of the perceiver.

Stated slightly differently, the landscape becomes a metaphor for the speaker's state of mind. The result is that the external and internal become fused. The process again ends in unity, with a blurring of the outer and inner. There is now no distinction between the two. The latter is spoken of directly in terms of the former.

Examples in the canon abound. "The Peace of the Woods"[39] ends with a description of a seascape:

> Thou hast enamor'd me of woodland life,
>> Good shepherd, for thou showest me, in thy faith,
>> More than thy argument, how free of scaith
> Thy cottage—how secure against the strife
> That beats on prouder dwellings. So I glean
>> Thy secret from thee, of true happiness,
>> Inbred content, and quiet humbleness,
> That striving only at the golden mean,
> Can never be o'erthrown by soaring high,
> And vexeth not the glare of envious eye.
> Thy blessings are of that serener kind,
>> Which, as they rouse no passions up, must be
>> Liked to that breeze benign that strokes the sea
> From rages into murmurs. No rude wind
> Disturbs thy placid waters, and deforms
> The glory of thy peace, with its unreckoning storms.

The subject's mind is like a placid sea that a benign breeze (the blessings of contentedness) calms. The subject has no high ambitions for wealth, power, or fame, which are equated in an implicit metaphor to raging winds that would "disturb" and "deform" his peacefulness. An external landscape thus becomes a metaphor for the state of mind of the subject—and, by *contrast*, of the state of mind of the speaker himself, who admires and longs for such calmness, but does not quite have it in his life. The poem's theme is that the simple man in nature, who is never ambitious for wealth and fame, is rewarded by peace of mind. This idea is dramatized through metaphor.

In "The Wilderness,"[40] similarly, the poet differentiates two casts of mind by use of natural landscapes. The speaker states that "there is a chilliness in lofty thoughts" and cold, "proud intellect" that is like the "mountain's brow" which "forever wears / A wreath of frostwork," and forbids approach. This man of impersonal, icy reason will not go to nature with "feeling or of joy"; and the speaker distrusts him. In contrast to the

117

landscape of the remote, frozen mountain peak, the speaker
chooses the scenery of the mountain's familiar base to image
his mind:

> I would mark its base, where falls the stream
> And buds make merry with the gliding drops,
> That steal into their open bells, at morn. . . .
> There is a melody in waterfalls,
> A sweetness of repose in solitude,
> In the far windings of untrodden wilds—
> Where nature is the same, as at her birth
> . . . and I become
> A member of the scene, I but survey!

The two landscapes thus mirror two contrasting mind-sets: the
impersonal man of reason's remote, clinically objective, and
unfeeling attitude (hence, Neoclassic view) versus the personal, gentle, warm, heart-felt, and familiar approach (hence,
Romantic view). The speaker, of course, opts for the latter. And
the rest of the poem then goes on to demonstrate a true, imaginative response to nature and the results thereof. "The Wilderness," written some time before September 1826,[41] is particularly significant as the earliest instance I have found of
Simms's use of this metaphorical technique.

In "Stanzas by the Sea-Shore,"[42] a poem written a few years
later, a seascape of dreary and "restless" waters is the metaphor for the speaker's own restless, hopeless state of mind. The
last line slightly varies the first in having "sleepless" waters
replace "restless" waters. The sea thus becomes a metaphor for
"sleeplessness" and "desolation." That the landscape is one of
desolation ("Roll / Dread ocean to thy drear extreme") under-
lines the figure; and the external landscape thus again becomes the metaphor for a state of mind. It is interesting to note
that although Simms borrowed his line, "Roll on, ye restless
waters!—Roll," from Byron's *Childe Harold* (IV, stanza 179),
Byron provided no such metaphor.

In "Stanzas to a Lady Who Asked Why My Verses Were Always Sad,"[43] the speaker explains through external landscape
why his verse is frequently melancholy:

i

The mournful God of Florid's cape
      Has taught his woes to me,
And all the strains my fancies shape,
      Must share his destiny.

ii

He looks o'er weary wastes by day,
      And with its mournful flight,
To mocking winds and storms the prey,
      He breathes the drearier night.

iii

What other song should then be mine,
      Thus taught by kindred grief,
O'er memory's waste by day to pine,
      Nor find in night relief.

iv

My lyre like his, upon the rock,
      What should its music be,
Thus smitten by each tempest's shock
      That sweeps along the sea.

In "memory's waste," the lonely seascape of waste and tempest is equated to his state of mind. The landscape is personified as "the mournful God" of the cape, who is like the poet. Both are destined to watch over desolation, one a desolate landscape, the other "o'er memory's waste." Their music must therefore be plaintive, thus taught by "kindred grief." A barren external landscape of tempest and "shock" therefore describes both the speaker's inner life and his poetry's tone. This is achieved through implicit metaphor in stanzas iii and iv.[44]

"Memory"[45] provides perhaps a clearer and more effective example of this metaphorical technique:

There is a moonlight in the heart,
      A lonely, sad expanse of light;
Cold as the meteors that impart,
      Strange lustre to the wintry night:
A vacant being, which though lit,
      By gleams that haunt it from the sky,

119

Still feels cold phantoms o'er it flit,
　　The shapes of those who should not die.

These are the memories of the past,
　　Gray watchers on the waste of years,
Shadows of hopes that could not last,
　　And loves, forever born in tears.
The mellowed music that they bring,
　　Falls sweet but sad upon the heart,—
Around whose brink they sit and sing,
　　Of death,—and will not thence depart.

Here, the speaker's state of mind is vacancy of feeling, lone-
liness, emptiness. It is described through the metaphor of a
barren winter landscape, whose vacancy is broken only by cold
meteor flashes of sad memory (relative to death). The poem's
first stanza is, on its surface, largely a description of external
landscape; but it is the internal one that matters. The external
landscape is merely the metaphor for it. The poem thus depicts
the landscape of a desolate heart in terms of a physical one
from nature. In method, one is reminded of the poetry of Robert
Frost in our century. The technique seems quite modern.

In "Sympathy with Nature,"[46] the theme is of the oneness of
man and the physical world, of how man loses self and partakes of the life around him. Appropriately, the poem ends
with a metaphor from nature to show man's oneness with it:
"Thus we range, / Capricious, still obedient to the tides / That
chide or soothe our streams, as winds impel the sea." To para-
phrase, our feelings are affected by nature as the sea is affected
by tides or winds. External landscape is the metaphor for the
process; and, thus, "we share / The life that is about us."

The list might again continue for pages. In "Promise,"[47] the
entire poem is built on the metaphor of a bright landscape to
image inner hope. In "Harbor by Moonlight,"[48] moonlight becomes a metaphor for a state of mind: delusion, a false assur-
ance that all is peace, beauty, and happiness. Moonlight's unre-
ality images the romantic views of the "thoughtless" strollers
along the beach who do not go behind the beautiful mask which
hides scenes of "carnage" owing to battle and tempest. In "The

Close of the Year 1861,"[49] the outer landscape shapes and mirrors the inner. The poem's theme is that man's will can triumph over external influences. Only the "animal" part of man is totally subject to environment. The soul or will can shape its own destiny. This poem is particularly interesting because it shows Simms still using the same basic techniques treated in this paper, but moving from his early romanticism. Man is to be *over* nature now, more than *with* it in oneness. The poem reflects an important shift in view.

"Harmonies in Nature"[50] perhaps best states the idea behind this use of metaphor. Here, Simms writes that nature is the robe that dresses the spirit, and the mirror to man's inner self. If the perceiver would only look, he would see that she reflects "with perfect sympathy" and gives meaning to "each yearning passion lonely in our hearts." Physical landscape expresses man's innermost feelings in its visible forms. Hence, it is only a small, natural step for Simms to use external landscape in the metaphorical way described here. His technique grows from his theory and is perfectly and harmoniously suited to it, illustrating by poetic craft what he communicates in theme. Craft and theme could be no more closely allied. In general, this might also be said of all three of the techniques discussed in this essay, for they all link man to nature. As man and nature become one thereby, so do craft and theme.

Simms's poetic canon demonstrates the basic romantic assumptions, both American and English. The poet should be considered as directly at the center of the tradition, perhaps in a way unsurpassed by any of his American contemporaries, for his verse extols imagination, spontaneity, organicism, freedom. He praises simplicity, and free-thinking. He dislikes artificiality and orthodoxy. But his way of looking at nature as being one with the individual in a symbiotic relationship, with perceiver creating the perceived, and finally fused with the perceived through metaphor, is more directly at the center of his thinking and places him most clearly in his romantic context. One might regret that he did no more with the last of these three techniques described here; but that he came upon this method at all is rather astonishing. At the least, Simms's effective use of the external world as mirror and metaphor for the inner, distinguishes him as a romantic poet deserving of serious consideration.

Notes

[1] For references to Bartram's and Simms's close knowledge of the natural scene, see James Kibler, "Simms as Naturalist: Lowcountry Landscape in His Revolutionary Novels," *Mississippi Quarterly,* 31 (Fall 1978), 499–518. Thanks are due Mary Ann Wimsatt, Rosemary Franklin, Anne Williams, and Rayburn Moore for their kind suggestions.

[2] Review in Charleston *Mercury* (February 5, 1855).

[3] Mary C. Simms Oliphant, Alfred Taylor Odell, and T. C. Duncan Eaves, eds., *The Letters of William Gilmore Simms* (Columbia: University of South Carolina Press, 1952–1956), IV, pp. 376–77. Hereinafter cited as *Letters.*

[4] *Letters* II, p. 137.

[5] *Letters* II, p. 156.

[6] Charleston *Mercury* (February 6, 1856). Simms writes that works "should never be written with reference to a specific moral." Written "with due heed to *general truth,* as they were designed to be, they carry with them a thousand wholesome morals, which are superior to maxims."

[7] William Gilmore Simms, "The Writings of Washington Allston," *Southern Quarterly Review,* 4 (October 1843), 378.

[8] *Letters* II, p. 156.

[9] William Gilmore Simms, "Poetical Works of Wordsworth," *Southern Quarterly Review,* 2 n.s. (September 1850), 20.

[10] The poem first appeared in, Henry W. Herbert, ed., *The Magnolia* (New York: Bancroft, 1836), p. 36.

[11] Charleston *City Gazette* (April 14, 1832). It is more accessible in *The Magnolia,* 4 (March 1842), 154, and Charleston *Mercury* (September 28, 1858).

[12] First appeared in *Southern Literary Journal,* 2 (June 1836), 270–71; collected in William Gilmore Simms, *Poems: Descriptive, Dramatic, Legendary, and Contemplative* (Charleston, S.C.: John Russell, 1853), II, pp. 163–165.

[13] In "The Poet," *Russell's Magazine,* 3 (July 1858), 353, Simms called this yoked landscape "psychal" nature.

[14] *Southern Literary Messenger,* 22 (March 1856), 211–13; reprinted in *The Old Guard,* 4 (November 1866), 679–82.

[15] *Godey's Magazine,* 27 (November 1843), 229; collected in Simms's *Sabbath Lyrics: Or, Songs from Scripture* (Charleston, S.C.: Walker and James, 1849), pp. 52–54.

[16] *Letters* II, p. 468.

[17] *Southern Literary Messenger,* 10 (July 1844), 423; collected in Simms, *Poems,* II (1853), p. 11.

[18] Charleston *Mercury* (February 6, 1856).

[19] *The Knickerbocker,* 9 (May 1847), 487; collected in Simms, *Poems,* II (1853), pp. 15–16.

[20] *Southern Literary Gazette,* 1 (February 1829), 280–81; collected in Simms, *Poems,* II (1853), pp. 292–97.

[21] *Southern Literary Gazette,* 1 n.s. (October 1, 1829), 240; reprinted in *Southern Literary Journal,* 3 n.s. (May 1838), 329–333.

[22] *Graham's Illustrated Magazine of Literature, Romance, Art, and Fashion,* 32 (January 1848), 11–12.

[23] *Southern Literary Messenger,* 11 (July 1845), 442; collected in William Gilmore Simms, *Grouped Thoughts and Scattered Fancies; A Collection of Sonnets* (Richmond, Va.: William Macfarlane, 1845), pp. 44–45.

[24] *Southern Literary Messenger,* 10 (August 1844), 484; collected in William Gilmore Simms, *Areytos: Or, Songs of the South* (Charleston, S.C.: John Russell, 1860), p. 412.

[25] In Simms's poetry, the sea is usually a desolate, barren feature of the landscape associated with restlessness, violence, ruin, and loss. Perhaps one clue to this response may be found in "Ashley River," *Southern Literary Gazette,* 1 (October 1828), 108–111, and *The Vision of Cortes, Cain and Other Poems* (Charleston, S.C.: J. S. Burges, 1829), pp. 69–83, in which the poet states that "the Sea hath one I loved"; also, a childhood friend drowned in the Gulf of Mexico.

[26] This and the following quotations come from "Harmonies of Nature," *Southern Literary Messenger,* 22 (March 1856), 211–13; reprinted in *The Old Guard,* 4 (November 1866), 679–682.

[27] Simms, "Poetry and Painting," *Southern Literary Gazette* (February 1829), 301; Simms, *Katharine Walton: or, The Rebel of Dorchester* (Philadelphia: A. Hart, 1851), p. 127.

[28] *Southern Literary Journal,* 3 (December 1836), 277–78; collected in *Poems,* II (1853), 204–206.

[29] James E. Kibler, Jr., *The Poetry of William Gilmore Simms: An Introduction and Bibliography* (Columbia, S.C.: Southern Studies Program, University of South Carolina, 1979), pp. 6–36. This work (p. 13)

also shows Simms's knowledge of Coleridge from as early as 1827, and treats the English poet's influence on him.

[30] Simms, "Grayling," *The Wigwam and the Cabin* (New York: Wiley and Putnam, 1845), p. 1. See also Simms's advertisement to *The Yemassee; A Romance of Carolina* (New York: Harper & Bros., 1835).

[31] Simms, "The Writings of Washington Allston," 378.

[32] Simms, *The Cassique of Accabee* (Charleston, S.C.: John Russell, 1849), pp. 5–38; collected in his *Poems,* I (1853), pp. 204–234. See also, "At every whisper we endow with life . . ." in *Grouped Thoughts,* pp. 56–57.

[33] *Sartain's Union Magazine of Literature and Art,* 10 (May 1852), 414; collected in *Poems,* II (1853), pp. 241–244.

[34] *Southern Literary Messenger,* 22 (March 1856), 211–13; reprinted in *The Old Guard,* 4 (November 1866), 679–682.

[35] *Southern Literary Journal,* 3 n.s. (March 1838), 175. In another poem, also entitled "Ashley River," the river is equated to his sorrow through his stream of tears. Thus, an object in nature mirrors his mental state. Here also his present and mental state is said to "tinge" once lovely waters with "gloom and sorrow." So the process works both ways. See *Southern Literary Gazette,* 1 (October 1828), 108–111, and *Vision of Cortes* (1829), p. 82.

[36] *Southern Literary Journal,* 1 (February 1836), 442; collected in *Areytos* (1846), p. 9.

[37] Charleston, *City Gazette* (October 28, 1831); collected in Simms's *Southern Passages and Pictures* (New York: G. Adlard, 1839), p. 54, and *Poems,* II (1853), pp. 104–107.

[38] Basil Willey, *Nineteenth Century Studies* (New York: Columbia University Press, 1949), pp. 25–30.

[39] First published in Simms's *Vision of Cortes* (1849), pp. 140–141; collected in *Areytos* (1860), p. 416.

[40] William Gilmore Simms, *Lyrical and Other Poems* (Charleston, S.C.: Ellis and Neufville, 1827), pp. 163–166.

[41] The volume was in press no later than September 5, 1826. See Kibler, *Poetry of William Gilmore Simms,* p. 56.

[42] *Southern Literary Gazette,* 1 n.s. (September 15, 1829), 201; reprinted in *Southern Literary Gazette,* 2 n.s. (August 7, 1852), 54.

[43] *Rosebud,* 4 (October 31, 1835), 38; reprinted in Boston *Notion,* 2 (April 10, 1841), 1.

[44] The poem also fits the category of analogy. Actually, analogy is its larger figure, to which the metaphors contribute their part. The poem could thus also be treated in the first section.

[45] *Southern Literary Journal,* 4 n.s. (December 1838), 437; collected

in Simms's *Atalantis: A Story of the Sea* (Philadelphia: Carey and Hart, 1848), p. 142.

[46] *Southern Literary Messenger,* 11 (July 1845), 442; collected in *Areytos* (1860), p. 414.

[47] *Southern Literary Messenger,* 10 (September 1844), 521; collected in *Areytos* (1860), p. 413.

[48] *Southern Literary Messenger,* 10 (August 1844), 484; collected in *Areytos* (1860), p. 412.

[49] Charleston *Courier* (March 25, 1862).

[50] *Southern Literary Messenger,* 22 (March 1856), 211–213; reprinted in *The Old Guard,* 4 (November 1866), 679–682.

Ordered Progress:
The Historical Philosophy of
William Gilmore Simms

DAVID MOLTKE-HANSEN

Progress was a fashionable concept in the nineteenth century. History, the theory was, advanced civilization and human freedom, however fitfully and slowly. That this was the course of history was clear from the spread of western civilization and from the growing success of the political principle of self-determination. William Gilmore Simms fully accepted this whig philosophy of history, as Sir Herbert Butterfield has styled it.[1] He accepted two corollaries as well: one either serves the interest of progress or is left behind by history, and history is the final arbiter of the success of individuals and causes as well as of societies.

Applying this philosophy to the region of his birth and home, Simms treated the American South as a stage where his philosophy was being acted out. In doing so, he took issue with the abolitionist conclusion that Southern retention of slavery made the region anti-progressive. Sharing the abolitionist belief in self-determination, he did not share the complementary belief that men are born equal. Rather, he believed that men earn the right of—evolve into—self-determination. Given this evolutionary model of human socio-political development and the conviction that Afro-Americans and Indians were not as advanced or evolved as European-Americans, Simms saw no inconsistency in embracing slavery and self-determination at the same time, nor any reason to suppose that the region which had produced much of the leadership of the American Revolution had immediately afterwards turned its back on the progressive spirit of the whig cause.

The resulting reading of Southern history as an unfolding of whig philosophy had profound consequences. Self-congratulatory about their inheritance, Simms and the many Southern leaders who shared his application of his philosophy understood that they had a mission: to keep the South on its ascending course. Because charting a course into the unknown is a problematic venture at best, even in the clear light of history, complacency about the past was matched by uncertainty about the future. Heightened by abolitionist attacks, the resulting anxiety ultimately would express itself in secession. Simms's philosophy provided justification for—indeed, seemed to demand—the action and, at the same time, fostered the conviction that the progressive South must win. When the Civil War's outcome contradicted this last assumption, the philosophy provided both an explanation—Southerners' misreading of the course of progress—and a rationale for embracing the New South cause.

Other Southerners wrote on Southern progress in the twenty years before the Civil War—James D. B. De Bow possibly more, and more influentially, than anyone but Simms.[2] Yet only Simms so avidly pursued the history of Southern progress in *belles lettres,* and no author commanded more respectful attention. Despite his position and accomplishment, however, his philosophy has almost entirely escaped commentary.

No doubt it has seemed unrewarding to define carefully the thought of a man who wrote too much to be concise. Moreover, there is a widespread conviction that what is interesting about Simms's thought is not its logic and dynamics, its perimeters and focus, its sources and substance, but rather the ways in which it might serve to illustrate his region's progress to civil war. Much, therefore, has been written about Simms's thinking on slavery and about the changes in his political outlook and the increasing stridency of his writings on sectional issues as the Civil War approached. Much has been made, too, of the aristocratic ideal embodied in Simms's fictional portrayals of planters, although the relationship in Simms's mind between social hierarchy and social evolution has been largely ignored.[3]

This ignorance is not merely the result of prejudice and laziness. Simms by-and-large assumed rather than expounded his philosophy. One needs to read a good deal of him before the repetitions of, and relationships between, ideas begin to suggest patterns of thought. Then one needs to go back and reread with these patterns in mind to test their consistency and persistence and to assess their significance. Given the size of the canon, the task is daunting. Compounding the difficulty for the twentieth-century reader is the fact that not only is much of Simms's work formulaic, but he unthinkingly and fulsomely espoused views on race and other matters which now are reprehensible. Reading Simms in quantity is to evoke negative reactions on several levels, then. In the face of such feelings, scholars have found it difficult to search for the occasional, fine short story or to trace thought.

—

Simms's philosophy of history revolved between two poles: progress and order. In his view, political, social, and cultural progress required political, social, and cultural stability. He held the converse to be true as well: social, cultural, and political stability required social, cultural, and political progress. Revolutions occurred when stability was maintained at the expense of progress or *vice versa*. The American Revolution, like all successful revolutions, resulted in a new harmonizing of the forces of stability and progress. Rather than having been fought out of an unruly love of change, it was, in a sense, what historians are now calling it—a conservative revolution. The war was fought on the battlefield but bore fruit in the Constitution.

These perceptions were not just borrowed baggage. Simms filled them with meaning from his own experience as well as from wide reading, defining both progress and order accordingly. The biography suggests how.

First, there is the fact of Simms's birth in Charleston. The fifth largest city in the United States at the time, it was also by far the wealthiest. Half slave and more than half black, it served as the chief export center for American rice and cotton. Cotton had been introduced as a significant commercial crop in the United States only sixteen years before, in 1790, yet South Carolina was already the world's chief exporter of the commodity. Funded by the profits, conspicuous consumption was becoming habit. Elaborate gardens framed new mansions in town and on the neighboring Sea Islands. Filling these houses were works by local silversmiths, cabinet makers, and visiting portrait painters.[4]

Yet soon the bloom would be off the rose. The West beckoned. Planters began deserting Charleston District for new lands in Georgia, Alabama, and Mississippi. Simms's uncle and widowed father were among them, leaving the boy behind with his grandmother. The embargo of 1807, the War of 1812, the recessions of 1819 and 1824, and the general downward trend of cotton prices under the pressure of a growing supply would take their cumulative toll. Added to these problems was Charleston's inability to access interior markets. Still the sixth largest American city in 1830, by 1861 Charleston would rank only twenty-second—this despite another fifty percent increase in population. As he grew older, then, Simms would see his community's relative fortunes decline.[5]

In good Federalist fashion, he would blame the westward movement. Writing from Mississippi in an April 1831 letter back to the Charleston *City Gazette,* which he was editing at the time, Simms complained: the availability of new lands on the frontier "conflicts with, and prevents the formation of[,] society" at the same time as "it destroys that which is already established." Society requires stability, but "our borderers," he continued, are "mere Ishmaelites. . . . Scarcely have they squatted down in one place, and built up their little 'improvement,' than they hear of a new purchase [from Indians], where corn grows without planting, and cotton comes up five bales to the acre, ready picked and packed. . . . [So] they pull stakes and boom off for the new Canaan."[6]

Simms had an additional reason for lamenting consequences of the western movement. During that same trip to Mississippi in 1831, he wrote of watching "the lingering moiety of a tribe of Indians" near Columbus, Georgia and of seeking "in vain to reconcile . . . the present with the past fortunes and labors of the Indian tribes." His qualified admiration for the "martial, libertine cast of countenance" of Chief Tuskina, "an Indian Mark Anthony," notwithstanding, however, he at the same time was dismissive of the "twiddle-twaddle" and "humbuggery" of the "philanthropists, who . . . would make us believe, and probably believe themselves, that the Indian is a sort of Roman." To the contrary, Simms continued, "We say everything of the North American, and in justice—'nothing extenuate, nor set down in malice,' when we call him a mere savage . . . but a few degrees removed from the condition of the brute." That the Indians themselves recognized this was one possible reason why, Simms theorized, that, "among the Indians, the Negroes [knowing more of white culture] gain caste; acquire authority and certainly great influence."[7]

Behind these conventional Jacksonian era views was the equally common and whiggish assumption that western civilization is the scale against which to measure humanity. Individuals and cultures alike must be judged by the degree to which they approach the norms and mores of leaders in, and leading centers of, Western art, politics, and letters. In short, Simms made of his own aspirations the perspective from which to view others'.

The city was central to that perspective. In Simms's eyes, civilization was an urban-centered phenomenon. Though his mother was a plantation daughter, though his father and uncle became planters, and though he himself would live a planter's life on one of his second wife's father's plantations, Simms never subscribed to the Agrarian vision of Thomas Jefferson. For him, commerce was the foundation of community and culture. Literature, his chosen profession, and the sister arts were the crowning glory, but before one could crown the edifice, one had to erect it. This is what America had been doing in its revolution against Great Britain. Independence meant achieving self-definition and self-determination, preconditions for real artistic expression. Thus this reminder to a Fourth of July audience in 1844:

> It is our common error to regard the close of our revolutionary contest . . . as settling permanently our institutions. This is a

very great mistake. That struggle determined nothing but our independence.[8]

Even before his trips west, Simms learned something else from the Revolution which would become fundamental to his thinking about history. It was at least in part through his grandmother's stories about life when "[t]he next door neighbor of the staunch whig was not unfrequently a furious loyalist." The lesson?: history belongs to the whigs. The corollary was true for Simms as well: history favors progress, or, in other words, progressives deservedly are winners.[9]

This understanding was strengthened by reading. At least as important as Daniel Boone or Cooper's Leatherstocking in shaping Simms's conception of the epic American in the vanguard of history was the Byronic hero. At least as important as the travel accounts by Irving and other visitors to the West in shaping Simms's conception of the impulses leading to the westward movement was his reading of the speculations of Guizot, Michelet, Macaulay, and others on the nature of progress in history.[10]

Underlying and informing Simms's thinking about this eclectic and sometimes hasty reading, in turn, were certain fundamental ambivalences. Many of these were common property in his day. Despite substantial differences in outlook, he shared them, for instance, with Frederick Law Olmsted, the New Yorker who started traveling in and writing about the Old Southwest a generation after Simms did. He also shared them with Augustus Baldwin Longstreet, his contemporary and, like him, a significant early figure in the Southern literary tradition out of which Mark Twain and William Faulkner would later write.

These shared ambivalences were, in part, inherited. Since the Renaissance, Europeans and their American descendents had maintained a double vision of the American frontier. Images of noble primitives and pastoral landscapes had persisted alongside those of filthy savages and impenetrable forests. The West had beckoned as a land of golden opportunity while simultaneously rising up in the mind's eye as a forbidding waste. Often portrayed as the last refuge of the lawless and the barbaric, the frontier had also been heralded again and again as the advance line of civilization.[11]

Not only did Olmsted, Longstreet, and Simms have this common heritage of ambivalence, they had particular knowledge and experiences in common which also fostered mutually contradictory feelings. On the one hand, each had sadly observed the deserted fields and houses left behind by emigrants to the West and the frontier towns which sprang up to flourish one day and turned into ghost towns the next. On the other hand, each had relished the openness and geniality he had met with in Western society, savored the humor and language of backwoodsmen whom he had encountered, and been excited by the vastness and richness of the West.

There was still another reason for ambivalence shared by these three men and the many others of their ilk. Educated in the East, raised on English literary models, writing for largely urban audiences and out of urban backgrounds, they were all, regardless of their places of residence while they were writing, at a great distance—culturally, socially, psychologically— from the backwoods and frontier, which were their frequent subjects. They wrote *about* the West but *as* Easterners. They also wrote *about* untutored frontiersmen and backwoodsmen living in the forests and on the plains but *as* educated professionals living in the ambit of cities.

This common perspective influenced shared attitudes toward political, social, and cultural leadership as well. These men were not democrats. In Simms's words, "Self government does not imply . . . the universal diffusion of a capacity for rule among the great body of a people . . . but simply such a concentration of endowment among individuals rising from their masses as will enable them to carry out the great popular trusts which are to secure the birthright of the race." The equality of the frontier must give way to the hierarchy of evolved society. Illustrating how and why, Simms's fictional heroes are all aristocrats by accomplishment, if not by birth. It was up to them and their spiritual descendents, he argued, to see that the "public mind . . . be awakened, elevated, chastened, nay, goaded and scourged, to its equal duties to patriotism and self." At the same time, leadership was a stabilizing as well as a revolutionary force, for Pope was also right:

Order is heaven's first law, and this confest,
Some are, and *must be,* greater than the rest.

Consequently, the whig *mouvement* (a term Simms borrowed from the French), led as it was by aristocrats, implied not only revolution, but order.[12]

The point had personal meaning. Looking back in 1842, Simms recalled himself as a boy of eighteen, "cumbered by fragmentary materials of thought, . . . choked by the tangled vines of erroneous speculation, and haunted by passions, which, like so many wolves, lurked, in ready waiting, for their unsuspecting prey." During this youthful period, he tried several careers, pharmacy, law, and journalism; experimented with literary forms, styles, and subjects; and embroiled himself in political controversy. Throughout this time he debated with himself about whether or not he should leave Charleston (where he felt himself politically beleaguered and his literary aspirations discouraged) for either the democratic society of the West or the literary society of New York. In the face of such tumult and unhappiness, order became precious.[13]

Simms had three other things to learn or experience before he could begin writing his novels or romances. One was the role of ethnicity in cultural and political life. In the wake of Goethe and the early German cultural nationalists, the French Revolution and the celebration of *la peuple française,* and the surge of nationalist fervor among smaller European ethnic groups in 1814, after the collapse of the Napoleonic Empire, the topic was current and popular. For Simms, the revolutions of 1830, which he celebrated in epic verse, simply drove home the point that culture is an expression of ethnicity and should be developed politically.[14]

Simms's principal teachers in learning the possibilities, purposes, and place of historical fiction were Sir Walter Scott and James Fenimore Cooper. The Scottish border novels and the Leatherstocking tales were never far from his mind when he wrote.[15]

A third lesson came as a bitter experience. Reared without mother or father, a widower at twenty-six, a year after the loss of a house and part of his library in a fire, Simms knew firsthand and poignantly, when he came to write, the meaning of

133

home and family, the value of stability, and the impact of grief. Brought to bear under the tutelage of Cooper and Scott with the ethnic passions of 1830 and repeated trips west in mind, this knowledge helped Simms write fiction which treated Indians, blacks, woodsmen, planters, preachers, conquistadors, and others all as characters with homes, families, and sufferings.[16]

—

Simms's first full-length romance appeared in 1834, *Guy Rivers: A Tale of Georgia.* Two more romances appeared in 1835—*The Yemassee,* the only one of Simms's works that was to be continuously in print up to the present, and *The Partisan: A Tale of the Revolution.* With these works, Simms had launched the three fictional series through which he would explore the South's rise over the next thirty-five years: the Border Series, which treated the region's westward expansion in the nineteenth century; the Colonial Series, which treated the region's European antecedents and settlement, on the one hand, and the resultant destruction of native American cultures, societies, and economies, on the other; and the Revolutionary War Series, which treated the region's wrenching shift from colonialism to independence and, *inter alia,* explored ethnic and social divisions brought out in the war.[17] Though he would grow in technical competence, mature in psychological insight, and add to his historical knowledge as he developed each series, Simms's fundamental understanding of the course and nature of history in the South would remain constant. The American Indians were doomed; the loyalists in the American Revolution were doomed; society was led towards civilization by progressive gentlemen of birth aided by clear-sighted gentlemen of natural talent; the frontier yielded eventually to the farm and, then, to the town.

These conclusions were reflected in both the conceptions and the executions of Simms's fiction. The novels and related short stories share themes and characters despite very different settings. Simms defined the subject of *Guy Rivers* as the formation of a society out of an "incoherent" mixture of people agitated by "strife, discontent, and contention" because of "the

wild condition of the country—the absence of all civil authority, and almost of laws." *The Yemassee* and *The Partisan* would
share this preoccupation with social formation, as would the
later work.[18]

The characters in each novel have common traits as well.
The hero is a cultured man of social standing—a noble, a
planter, or a school teacher. This embodiment of civilization is
aided in most cases by a common man—a woodsman or a comparable incarnation—representing the natural man. Opposed
to these men in their efforts to establish order and advance society are their own wayward passions, a variety of social, psychological, and cultural misfits, and the bovine instincts, short
sightedness, and greed of many of their fellow countrymen.
Together, these opposition forces illustrate what men must
overcome to establish American civilization. Caught in the
middle is often a heroine embodying the beauty of nature, the
refinement of civilization, the sanctity of the home, and the devotion to domestic ideals of her lover, the hero. Frequently
caught as well is a slave, who illustrates Simms's conception of
the role of blacks in Southern culture in general and, more particularly, his conception of the commitment by the slave's master, the hero, to agriculture, a foundation of civilization. These
are the principal characters in the novels. There are many
minor ones.

The reader is never in doubt about who the hero and his
allies are or about the ultimate outcome of the story. Though,
at their best, not without depth and complexity, Simms's characterizations are unambiguous. This is even the case in one of
the last and least typical of his novels, *Joscelyn*. Not only is the
hero of this work, Stephen Joscelyn, crippled, but he suffers un-
requited love and a brooding character; whereas earlier Simms
Revolutionary War heroes, such as Robert Singleton (*The Partisan*) and Willie Sinclair (*The Forayers*), are perfectly formed,
happily in love (despite, in Sinclair's case, parental objections),
and open-natured. These earlier protagonists fight as whigs because they have sound constitutions—politically as well as
physically and emotionally. Joscelyn, however, is less posi-
tively endowed. At the outset of the novel, he is not only physically and emotionally, but also intellectually crippled. He em-

braces war initially to "escape from thought to action." As the narrator observes at the end of the fourth chapter: "Poor Stephen; he was struggling with his demon, and the struggle is not likely to be soon ended." Twenty-five chapters later, Stephen is still brooding.[19]

Throughout, however, Stephen is firm in his adherence to the whig cause. True, in fighting against the crown, he is also fighting to "prove that deformity is not necessarily feebleness." Nevertheless, he is on the right side. Disaffected with himself, he is also disaffected with the crown. His is, according to the narrator, "the full mind, the ardent temperament, and the copious fancy" of the self-tortured and the revolutionary.[20]

The portrayal is sympathetic. The portrayal of Stephen's chief opponent, the tory Thomas Browne, is not. Stephen rises above his deformity through his passionate allegiance to the whig cause, but Browne descends to brutishness through his passionate resistance to that cause. Both men are presented as brave and proud; the passions of both are explained with some psychological subtlety; but one man becomes a hero and the other a villain in the course of the novel.

It can be argued that this character development was inevitable, given the nature of the romance formula Simms was using. Not so. In others of his romances—*The Yemassee*, for instance—the principal antagonist is not a villain. Indeed, Sanutee, "the well-beloved," chief of the Yemassee, is one of the two heroic men in the novel. Like the tory cause, his cause fails, but unlike the tory leaders portrayed by Simms, Sanutee is a man of moral stature.

Simms could accord Sanutee such stature, because, like the whigs, he was fighting out of a patriotic devotion to the good of his people and country. True, his patriotism unfortunately conflicted with the inevitable progress of western civilization into the Carolina woods—the progress represented by Charles Lord Craven, the other man of heroic stature in the novel. This does not mean, however, that Sanutee was wrong to resist the encroaching white man. Given the logic of his situation, a man of his position and character could do nothing other than fight to preserve the integrity of his people and their way of life.[21]

The same could not be said, in Simms's view, of the tories.

Members "of that order which men indulgently call conservative," they were to be damned, he insisted, because of their small-minded resistance to progress, to man's historic pursuit of self-fulfillment through self-realization. Love of country and the public good should have led them to accept the logic and foster the future of the whig cause. "The good citizen," Simms contended, "is bound to his country's progress. It is no excuse for him that he is not sure that proposed events will result in her benefit. He assumes the contrary at his peril."[22]

Given this reasoning, it is no wonder that Simms's tory characters are unsympathetically or, at best, patronizingly (if, sometimes, affectionately) presented. They do not see the justice of the whig cause and, so, are blind. They fight against progress and, so, are backwards. They raise allegiance to private good, to convention, or to a distant king over devotion to country and people and, so, are morally reprehensible.

For Simms, it was unimportant that upcountry South Carolina tories had, as he willingly admitted, legitimate grievances against lowcountry, aristocratic whig pretensions. To his mind, these grievances helped explain the ferociousness of the civil warfare in South Carolina during the Revolution but justified nothing. The tory cause was a historical dead-end. "Unable to lead themselves," he argued, the tories "threw themselves, as so many dead weights, about the car of *mouvement;* and it is no reproach to those who did lead, that they were passed over, or flung off, by the wheels."[23]

Simms's philosophy of history, then, helps explain why he presented his characters as he did. It also helps explain his method of characterization.

As David Potter has pointed out, the historian—and by extension, the historical novelist—has two ways of presenting characters. On the one hand, he can explain characters' behavior in terms of "ideals or interests." On the other hand he can explain behavior in terms of "anxieties and psychological stresses." The choice of method shapes the reader's response. The presentation of characters in terms of ideals

will have the inevitable effect of making the motivation of the participants seem creditable: we tend to sympathize with, or at

least to "understand," a rational position even when we do not
agree with it. But to choose the other [method of presentation]
will have the inevitable effect of making the motivation seem
discreditable: the irrational fear or antagonism of one group toward another partakes of the nature of paranoia, and we are un-
sympathetic toward paranoia.[24]

Simms, because he saw the whigs sympathetically, presented
them in terms of their ideals at the same time that he presented the tories, because he saw them unsympathetically, in
terms of their "irrational fear or antagonism."

This discrimination in his approach to his characters may
seem prejudiced to us, but Simms attempted to be at once fair
and realistic in his portrayals of all his protagonists. As he
noted again and again, a guiding purpose in his romances was to
reveal "the moving impulses of men to action," while still adher-
ing, "as closely as possible, to the features and the attributes of
real life."[25] From his perspective, his fictional treatments of the
loyalists were objective. This is why he could not accept revi-
sionist defences of the loyalists' motives, even though he himself frequently called for further and fairer treatment of the
loyalists by historians of South Carolina. Simms, the historian,
in short, was always Simms, the whig, as well.

Another way of saying that as a historian Simms was always
a whig is to say that for Simms the pursuit of history was a
political pursuit. Not surprisingly, therefore, his political judgments were informed by the same logic as his historical judgments. The language he used to describe the tyranny of the tories in 1780 was the same as he used to describe the tyranny of
the nullifiers in 1832–1833 and the tyranny of Northern interests in the 1850s. Conversely, the language he used to describe
his whig heroes and their cause in the Revolutionary War romances was the same as he used to describe the Unionists and
their cause in 1832–1833 and Southerners and their cause in
the 1850s. In each case, he expressed himself as a partisan convinced of the impartiality and justice of his position.

There was another reason for such continuities. Like many prolific authors, Simms was a formulaic thinker as well as writer. That is why, in part, he was able to write so much and why, too, there is a consistency in the cast and tenor of his political expressions—why, early and late, the same key phrases and the same juxtapositions of ideas occur in his political as well as his historical pronouncements.[26]

This is not to say, however, that Simms did not change his views on specific issues over time. As has been frequently pointed out, Simms's political stances did change, if only because his and his state's and nation's circumstances did. The Unionist resisting proto-secessionist thinking in 1833 was forecasting and supporting his state's secession from the Union fifteen years later. Though historians have been agitated by this apparent inconsistency, there is no sign that the inconsistency (if inconsistency he considered it) caused Simms concern. Given his philosophy, there was no reason that it should have.[27]

Unlike the nullifiers, Simms did not feel that his native state's security and stability were being threatened in such a way or to such a degree in 1828–1834 as to warrant disassociation with the national forces of progress. Fifteen years later, on the other hand, he was beginning to think that secession was not only inevitable but, under the circumstances, desirable. He saw national policy being increasingly influenced by abolitionists and Northern industrialists, and he could no longer equate national progress, as they defined it, with progress for the South. Rather, the contrary: Northern agitators and interests were threatening the very stability of Southern society and culture. Eventually, the South would have either to withdraw from the Union or to undergo a revolution to bring the forces of progress and stability back into harmony again. In Simms's view, as in the view of most of the Southern leadership who considered the problem, secession was the lesser evil. By withdrawing from the Union, they argued, they could direct progress in ways compatible with their society, economy, and culture. This became Simms's hope. Believing it his responsibility to help lead in the realization of this hope, he contributed essays and made speeches, urging his fellow citizens to seize their future. Frequently, he was discouraged, feeling he was

139

not paid enough attention. Still he worked and, his own words to the contrary notwithstanding, with success.[28]

Addressing the South Carolina Historical Society in 1859, Beaufort planter William Henry Trescot, just months away from appointment as Acting Secretary of State in the Buchanan Administration, observed:

> I am young enough to speak from experience, and I am sure that many a boy who is now eagerly following his heroes through the swamps of the Santee, or along the banks of the Ashley, will find his local attachment strengthened and widened into affection for his State, and in the time to come, will do her ready and unselfish service, stimulated by the heroic traditions to which the imagination of [William Gilmore Simms] has imparted a dramatic and living reality.[29]

Another tribute came in the spring of 1862, in the midst of war. It was shortly after Simms had lost his plantation house in a fire. A "plain" farmer came to him and said: "Your house has been a public house, and you are a public man without pay; and you shall have my lumber to rebuild—all that you want,— and you shall *not* pay me." Shortly thereafter, newspapers in Charleston and Columbia printed a public letter to Simms which read in part:

> A few friends, sympathizing deeply with you in your recent losses, and mindful of the important services which, as her novelist, historian, and poet, you have rendered to South Carolina, have subscribed the enclosed sum of $3,600, to aid in rebuilding your hospitable and honored homestead, recently destroyed by fire.[30]

Then came the South's defeat, crushing poverty, the loss of his second wife, the burning of his recently rebuilt plantation home, and debilitating, chronic illness—all in the space of months. Discouraged, Simms even wrote his old Charleston friend and fellow poet, Paul Hamilton Hayne, in 1869: "Let us bury the Past lest it buries us!" Despite such despair and dark predictions of the South being "doomed to be the Ireland of the Union," Simms continued to read about, and work for, civilization's advance.[31] In August 1865, he was announcing to an old friend in New York: "I have schemes for revolutionizing the whole industrial system of our country." Two years later he was asking this same friend, Evert Augustus Duyckinck, to get him a work by Lecky "on the progress of society or civilization," noting that he had been "pleased with the portions [he had] read;" the *History of the Rise and Influence of the Spirit of Rationalism in Europe* has since become a classic of whig philosophy.[32] In December 1869, less than six months before his death, Simms was writing Hayne that, despite lack of pay, he was still willing to help regional literary journals "in order that *the South shall have an organ*," adding, "I am for action to the last."[33]

Simms's commitment to civilization's advance in the South was as strong as ever. It would take on new life after his death. Then another generation of cultural leaders would embrace the cause, arguing for an urban-centered, growth-oriented, educationally advanced, well-ordered, racially stratified, stable South integrated into Western development. At the same time, this new generation drew lessons from the Civil War. One, Henry Grady contended, was that "the old South rested everything on slavery and agriculture, unconscious that these could neither give nor maintain healthy growth," and the old system had been overturned as a result.[34]

Such use of the whig philosophy allowed Southerners to accept defeat and, at the same time, to embrace the future. If they had been wrong, it had been in the right cause. Like Sanutee, the Yemassee chief, they had done what was honorable in the circumstances—fought against overwhelming odds to preserve their homes and way of life from alien influences. However tragic, the war had been necessary, and the future was bright. One honored the dead and got on with living.

The historical philosophy of Simms and Grady was not original or especially subtle, but it was vital. It helped focus energies and give meaning to events. As importantly, it provided a basis for explaining why things happened as they did and for determining how public men as well as private citizens should conduct themselves. In doing so, the philosophy met deep psychological needs and had important ramifications for public discourse and action in the region and the nation. Finally, it provided ideological continuity between Old South and New. Ordered progress was the by-word before as well as after the Civil War.

Notes

[1] Herbert Butterfield, *The Whig Interpretation of History* (London: G. Bell, 1963; first published in 1931). American whig historicism in the eighteenth century is surveyed by H. Trevor Colbourn in his *The Lamp of Experience* (Chapel Hill, N.C.: University of North Carolina Press, 1965). The development of this whig view in the generation before Simms is highlighted by William Raymond Smith in his *History as Argument* (The Hague: Mouton and Company, 1966), and by Charles G. Sellers, Jr., in his bibliographical essay, "The American Revolution: Southern Founders of a National Tradition," Arthur S. Link and Rembert W. Patrick, eds., *Writing Southern History* (Baton Rouge, La.: Louisiana State University Press, 1965), pp. 38–66. The relationship of Simms's views to those of such of his friends in South Carolina and Virginia as James Henry Hammond, Beverly Tucker, Edmund Ruffin, and George F. Holmes is discussed in Drew Gilpin Faust, *A Sacred Circle* (Baltimore: Johns Hopkins University Press, 1977), pp. 73–80 and 168, n.33–39. The whiggishness of many of Simms's contemporaries in the North, Bancroft and Motley among them, is discussed by Harry B. Henderson in his *Versions of the Past* (New York: Oxford University Press, 1974), pp. 16–42. For a discussion of the rationale for approaching writers such as Simms and Bancroft in terms of contemporary idea-complexes, see Arthur O. Lovejoy, *Essays in the History of Ideas* (Baltimore: Johns Hopkins University Press, 1948), pp. xi–xv; and cf. John Higham, *Writing American History* (Bloomington, Ind.: Indiana University Press, 1970), pp. 27–40, 62–63, 70–72.

[2] See Paul F. Paskoff and Daniel J. Wilson, eds., *The Cause of the South: Selections from De Bow's Review, 1846–1867* (Baton Rouge and London: Louisiana State University Press, 1982).

[3] For discussions of Simms, many of them important, in the light of slavery and the Civil War, see John Higham, "The Changing Loyalties of William Gilmore Simms," *Journal of Southern History,* 9 (May 1943), 210–223; Rollin Osterweis, *Romanticism and Nationalism in the Old South* (New Haven, Conn.: Yale University Press,

1949), pp. 113–115; William R. Taylor, *Cavalier and Yankee* (New York: G. Braziller, 1961), pp. 267–297; Clement Eaton, *The Mind of the Old South* (Baton Rouge, La.: Louisiana State University Press, 1964), Chapter X, esp. pp. 187–189 and 193–201; David Donald, "The Pro-Slavery Argument Reconsidered," *Journal of Southern History,* 37 (February 1971), 11, 17–18; Jon L. Wakelyn, *The Politics of a Literary Man* (Westport, Conn.: Greenwood Press, 1973), pp. xi–xiii and *passim;* John Hope Franklin, "The North, the South, and the American Revolution," *Journal of American History,* 62 (June 1975), 11–15; Faust, *A Sacred Circle* (Baltimore, 1977), *passim;* and John McCardell, *The Idea of a Southern Nation* (New York: Norton, 1979), pp. 141–75 and *passim.*

⁴See George C. Rogers, Jr., *Charleston in the Age of the Pinckneys* (Norman, Ok.: University of Oklahoma Press, 1962); David Moltke-Hansen, "The Expansion of Intellectual Life: A Prospectus," in Michael O'Brien and David Moltke-Hansen, eds., *Intellectual Life in Antebellum Charleston* (Knoxville, Tenn.: University of Tennessee Press, 1986), pp. 3–46, esp. 23–31.

⁵See Moltke-Hansen, "The Expansion of Intellectual Life," *passim,* and Alfred Glaze Smith, Jr., *Economic Readjustment of an Old Cotton State* (Columbia, S.C.: University of South Carolina Press, 1958).

⁶Mary C. Simms Oliphant, Alfred T. Odell, and T. C. Duncan Eaves, eds., *The Letters of William Gilmore Simms* (Columbia: University of South Carolina Press, 1952–1956), I, 37–38.

⁷*Letters,* I, 29–31.

⁸*The Sources of American Independence* (Aiken, S.C.: Aiken South Carolina Town Council, 1844), p. 30. Cf. [William Gilmore Simms], "Country Life Incompatible with Literary Labor," *Southern Literary Journal,* 3 (1836–1837), 207–209.

⁹Simms, *The Partisan* (New York: Harper and Brothers, 1835), p. 14.

¹⁰See Henderson, *Versions of the Past,* p. 54 ff.; James O. Hoge, "Byron's Influence on the Poetry of William Gilmore Simms," *Essays in Literature,* 2 (Spring 1975), 87–96; James Everett Kibler, Jr., *The Poetry of William Gilmore Simms:* An Introduction and Bibliography (Columbia, S.C.: Southern Studies Program, University of South Carolina, 1979), pp. 12–16; Lewis M. Bush, "Werther on the Alabama Frontier: A Reinterpretation of Simms's *Confession,*" *Mississippi Quarterly,* 21 (Spring 1968), 119–130; [William Gilmore Simms], "Guizot's Democracy in France," *Southern Quarterly Review,* 15 (April 1849), 114–165. See also *Letters,* I, 387, 425, 430, and II, 417, 507, 540. Michelet's use of the term, *mouvement,* cited in Paul Robert, *Diction-*

naire alphabetique et analogique de la langue française (Paris: Société du Nouveau Littré, 1959), and in the *Grand Larousse de la langue française* (Paris: Librairie Larousse, 1975), postdates Simms's use of the term in 1846.

[11] Among the innumerable reviews of the westward movement and Euro-American perceptions of the frontier are Louise K. Barnett, *The Ignoble Savage* (Westport, Conn.: Greenwood Press, 1975), pp. 21 ff., 197–199; Arthur K. Moore, *The Frontier Mind* (Lexington, Ky.: University of Kentucky Press, 1957), pp. 24–43 and *passim;* Roderick Nash, *Wilderness and the American Mind* (New Haven, Conn.: Yale University Press, 1967), pp. 23–83; Henry Nash Smith, *Virgin Land* (Cambridge, Mass.: Harvard University Press, 1950), pp. 54–87, 138–150; and Ray Allen Billington, *Land of Savagery, Land of Promise* (New York: Norton, 1981), p. 36. Page references are to discussions of Simms and the South and Old Southwest. On Longstreet, see Louis J. Budd, "Gentlemanly Humorists of the Old South," *Southern Folklore Quarterly,* 17 (Summer 1953), 232 ff., a wrongheaded but nonetheless suggestive reading of the ambivalences in which Longstreet was caught. On Olmsted, see Robert Lewis, "Frontier and Civilization in the Thought of Frederick Law Olmstead," *American Quarterly,* 29 (Fall 1977), 385–403, an article which influenced the shape of this discussion of Simms. On Simms in the tradition of the Southwest humorists, see Mary Ann Wimsatt, "Simms and Southwest Humor," *Studies in American Literature,* 3 (November 1976), 118–130, and Edd Winfield Parks, "The Three Streams of Southern Humor," *Georgia Review,* 9 (Summer 1955), 147–159.

[12] Simms, *The Sources of American Independence,* p. 15; Simms, "Southern Literature," *Magnolia,* 3 (February 1841), 71; Simms, "The Morals of Slavery," in William Harper *et al., The Pro-Slavery Argument* (Charleston, S.C.: Walker, Richards and Co., 1852), p. 256. The italics are Simms's.

[13] William Gilmore Simms, *The Social Principle* (Tuscaloosa, Ala.: Erosophic Society of the University of Alabama, 1843); *Letters,* I, 5, 8, 47–49, 51–52, 54.

[14] Simms, *The Tri-Color, or the Three Days of Blood, in Paris with Some Other Pieces* (London: Wigfall and Davis, 1830).

[15] C. Hugh Holman, "The Influence of Scott and Cooper on Simms," *The Roots of Southern Writing* (Athens, Ga.: University of Georgia Press, 1972), pp. 50–60. Cf. Bush, "Werther on the Alabama Frontier;" Floyd H. Dean, "A Comparison of Simms's *Richard Hurdis* with its Sources," *Modern Language Notes,* 60 (June 1954), 406–408; W. B. Gates, "William Gilmore Simms and the Kentucky Tragedy," *Ameri-*

THE HISTORICAL PHILOSOPHY OF WILLIAM GILMORE SIMMS

can Literature, 32 (May 1960), 158–166; James E. Kibler, "Simms' Indebtedness to Folk Tradition in 'Sharp Snaffles,'" *Southern Literary Journal,* 4 (Spring 1972), 55–68; and Miriam Shillingsburg, "From Notes to Novel: Simms's Creative Method," *Southern Literary Journal,* 5 (Fall 1972), 89–107.

¹⁶ See Albert Keiser, *The Indian in American Literature* (New York: Oxford University Press, 1933), pp. 154–174; Roy Harvey Pearce, *The Savages of America,* rev. ed. (Baltimore: Johns Hopkins Press, 1965), pp. 216–220; Alexander Cowie, "Introduction," in William Gilmore Simms, *The Yemassee* (New York: American Book Co., 1937), p. xxvii ff.; William Gilmore Simms, *Views and Reviews in American Literature, History and Fiction* (New York: Wiley and Putnam, 1846–1847), I, 112–147; J. Austin Shelton, "African Realistic Commentary on Culture Hierarchy and Racistic Sentimentalism in *The Yemassee,*" *Phylon,* 25 (Spring 1964), 72–78.

¹⁷ Simms set forth his intentions as an author in prefaces, introductions, or advertisements as well as in more-or-less full dedicatory notes in most of his novels. Discussions of these programmatic statements and the thought behind them include Edd Winfield Parks, *William Gilmore Simms as Literary Critic* (Athens, Ga.: University of Georgia Press, 1961), pp. 10–40; John C. Guilds, "Simms's Views on National and Sectional Literature," *North Carolina Historical Review,* 34 (July 1957), 393–405; John C. Guilds, "Simms's Use of History," *Mississippi Quarterly,* 30 (Fall 1977), 505–511; and Stephen Meats, "Artist or Historian: William Gilmore Simms and the Revolutionary South," Samuel Proctor, ed., *Eighteenth-Century Florida and the Revolutionary South* (Gainesville, Fla.: University Presses of Florida, 1975), pp. 95–108. Simms's eight Revolutionary War romances, annotated and (all but *Joscelyn*) reprinted from the 1855–1866 Redfield edition of Simms's works by The Reprint Company, Publishers, of Spartanburg, in 1976, consist of the following, originally published (sometimes in substantially different versions) on the dates indicated in parentheses after each title: *The Partisan* (1835), *Mellichampe* (1836), *The Kinsman* (1841), *Katherine Walton* (1851), *The Sword and the Distaff* (1852), *The Forayers* (1855), *Eutaw* (1856), and *Joscelyn* (1867 in serial form; 1875 in book form). Simms wrote two romances, *The Damsel of Darien* and *Vasconselos,* and numerous shorter pieces set in French and Spanish America. As Simms makes clear in *The Social Principle,* he felt that the origins and developments of these Latin colonies were fundamentally different in important respects from the origins and developments of the English colonies in America. His sense of those differences is reflected in his fictional treatments of

145

Latin America. His treatments of British America include the following romances: *The Yemassee* (1835) and *The Cassique of Kiawah* (1859). His "border" novels include *Guy Rivers* (1834), *Richard Hurdis* (1838), *Border Beagles* (1840), *Confession* (1841, a novella, rather than a full-fledged romance), *Beauchampe* (1842, later revised and issued as two novels: *Charlemont* [1856] and *Beauchampe* [1856]), *Helen Halsey* (1845), *As Good as a Comedy* (1852, a novella), *The Cub and the Panther* (1869), *Voltmeier* (1869), and *Paddy McGann* (1872, a novella). See also entries 13, 17, 27, 28, 30, 40, 41, 45, 52, 56, 57, 61, 64, 65, 66, 70, 71, 73, 77, 79, 81, 85, 86, 87, 88, 89, 90, 91, 92, 97, 108, and 109 in Betty Jo Strickland, "The Short Fiction of William Gilmore Simms" (Ph.D. dissertation, University of Georgia, 1975) for bibliographic descriptions of short stories by Simms in the same vein as these romances.

[18] *Guy Rivers,* rev. ed. (New York: A. C. Armstrong and Son, 1855), 613. Cf. Simms, "The Civil Warfare in the Carolinas and Georgia, during the Revolution," *Southern Literary Messenger,* 12 (May 1846); Simms, "South Carolina in the Revolution," *Southern Quarterly Review,* 14 (July 1848), 37–77; Simms, *The Social Principle;* Simms, "Our Agricultural Condition," *Southern and Western Monthly Magazine and Review,* 1 (February 1845), 73–84; John A. Welsh, "William Gilmore Simms, Critic of the South," *Journal of Southern History,* 26 (May 1960), 210–211; David Brion Davis, *Homicide in American Fiction, 1798–1860* (Ithaca, N.Y., 1957), pp. 37–43, 185–191 *et passim;* Richard Slotkin, *Regeneration through Violence* (Middletown, Conn.: Wesleyan University Press, 1973), p. 391 ff.; Daniel Joseph Sullivan, "Social Criticism in the Revolutionary Romances of William Gilmore Simms" (Ph.D. dissertation, University of Notre Dame, 1972); C. Hugh Holman, "William Gilmore Simms's Picture of the Revolution as a Civil Conflict," *Journal of Southern History,* 15 (November 1949), 441–462.

[19] Citations are from the 1976 Reprint Company reprint of *Joscelyn,* pp. 37, 49, 251.

[20] *Joscelyn* (1976 rpt.), pp. 44, 46.

[21] See note 16 above; Simms, *The Yemassee,* pp. 102–103 *et passim.*

[22] Simms, "The Civil Warfare in the Carolinas and Georgia," pp. 260–261.

[23] "Civil Warfare."

[24] David M. Potter, "The Tasks of Research in American History," in Don E. Fehrenbacher, ed., *History and American Society: Essays of David M. Potter* (New York: Oxford University Press, 1937), p. 360.

[25] *The Partisan,* (Spartanburg, S.C.: Southern Studies Program,

University of South Carolina, 1976; reprint of 1854 ed.), ix; *Melli-champe* (same as preceding cite), 6. Cf. *Katherine Walton* (same as preceding cite), 3–4; *The Forayers* (same as preceding cite), 3.

[26] Compare the characterizations of abolitionists and nullifiers in *Letters* (consult the general index in vol. V) with discussions of tories, the British, abolitionists, New England intellectuals, French conservatives, etc., in, for instance, Simms's "Miss Martineau on Slavery," *Southern Literary Messenger,* 3 (November 1837): 641–658; his "Mrs. Trollope and the Americans," *American Quarterly Review,* 12 (September 1832), 109–133.

[27] Note 3 above. Cf. Guilds, "Simms's Views on National and Sectional Literature, 1825–45."

[28] Faust, *A Sacred Circle,* pp. 27–30, 112–115, and 176–177; n.5, is the most extended recent discussion of Simms's persistent discouragement. Cf. John McCardell, "Poetry and the Practical: William Gilmore Simms," O'Brien and Moltke-Hansen, eds., *Intellectual Life in Antebellum Charleston,* pp. 186–210.

[29] *Collections of the South Carolina Historical Society,* 3 (1859), 23.

[30] *Letters,* IV, 405 and 409, n.42.

[31] *Letters,* V, 214, 36.

[32] *Letters,* IV, 516; V, 37.

[33] *Letters,* V, 283, 286.

[34] Henry W. Grady, *The New South and Other Addresses,* ed. Henry Lee Turpin (1904; rpt. ed., New York: Haskell House, 1969), pp. 27–34 *et passim.* See Richard N. Current, *Northernizing the South* (Athens, Ga.: University of Georgia Press, 1983), pp. 84–88; and Paul M. Gaston, *The New South Creed: A Study in Southern Mythmaking* (Baton Rouge, La.: Louisiana State University Press, 1976; rpt. 1970 ed.), p. 23 ff.

The Evolution of
Simms's Backwoods Humor

MARY ANN WIMSATT

Gilmore Simms, the foremost man of letters in the antebellum South and the author of many serious romances, is not ordinarily viewed as a humorous writer. Yet he is actually one of the major creators of comedy in the era. His humor springs from a raucous, unbridled streak in his personality, and it was encouraged by his experiences in the same parts of the South that nourished the talents of the antebellum humorists: the Gulf South or Old Southwest of the 1820s and early 1830s and the Piedmont or Mountain South throughout the antebellum period.

Simms apparently inherited his comic sense from his father, and it was also his father who introduced him to the Gulf or lower South. The elder Simms was a playful, mercurial Irishman who had briefly settled in Charleston but who, on the death of his wife after only four years of marriage, had emigrated to Mississippi, where he built up a plantation and remained for the rest of his life. The young Simms, who was reared in Charleston by his grandmother, visited his father in the Gulf South during its primitive Indian phase of the 1820s; he went there again in the 1830s, when he observed the bustle of settlement and expansion that characterized the area in the flush times.[1] On these trips he witnessed the kind of rowdy comic escapades associated with that part of the country, and his experiences led him to write novels about the region that emphasize its danger, humor, and charm. These novels, which he called border romances because they deal with a part of the South that is a border region between civilization and wilderness, began to appear in the middle 1830s at about the same time that major Southern or Southwestern humorists like Augustus Baldwin Longstreet and Davy Crockett began to write, but they are less in debt to these authors than they are to Simms's own experiences and to oral and popular tradition. In the 1850s and 1860s, however, after he had again traveled in backwoods regions and had read widely in Southern humor, he constructed frame narratives portraying rural characters who speak rich dialect, engage in outrageous pranks, or spin marvelous yarns. These narratives—*As Good as a Comedy, Paddy McGann,* "How Sharp Snaffles Got His Capital and Wife," and "Bald-Head Bill Bauldy"—show the direct influence of Southern humor upon the subjects, methods, and concerns of his work.

Simms's writing early and late is linked to that of the humorists in at least three ways that spring from common personal experiences. The first and broadest of these connections inheres in perspective, form, and technique. Like Simms, virtually all of the major humorists came from respectable families in the older, settled parts of the South, and they all, like him, had visited the frontier and surveyed its emerging society. They tended, as he did, to portray the backwoods South from a civilized vantage point by contrasting the language of gentlemen and woodsmen or by using a frame story dominated by a sophisticated observer to introduce an inner narrative in which a rustic speaker takes over. Longstreet, for instance, with his keen eye for social distinctions in rural Georgia, has his narrator Lyman Hall praise the fox-hunt in fulsome language and then makes a plain-spoken servant undercut it. Hall, who has risen before dawn for the hunt, says:

A cloudless sky o'erspread the earth—as rich in beauty as ever won the gaze of mortal. Upon the western verge, in all his martial glory, stood Orion; his burnished epaulets and spangled

149

sash, with unusual brightness glowing . . . "Oh!," exclaimed I,
"how rich, how beautiful, how glorious the firmament! . . . who
shall condemn the chase, when its pleasures are written in characters of deathless fire, upon the face of the heavens!"

I was lost in admiration of the splendors which surrounded me
when . . . my servant announced that my horse was in waiting.
As I approached him for the purpose of mounting, "Master," said
my servant, "you *gwine* fox huntin' on da hoss?"[2]

Simms employs a similar contrast between civilized pom-
posity and backwoods patois when he portrays, in *Guy Rivers*
(1834), an exchange between a fatuous frontier lawyer and
some colorful squatters at the trial of the Yankee peddler Jared
Bunce. The attorney proclaims, "And now, my friends, if I
rightly understand the responsibility and obligations of the
station thus kindly conferred upon me . . . I am required to ar-
raign before you this same pedler . . . on sundry charges of mis-
demeanor, and swindling, and fraud." One of the squatters re-
plies, "Ay, ay, lawyer, that's the how. . . . Put it to the skunk,
let him deny . . . if he can . . . that he doesn't manufacture ma-
ple seeds, and hickory nutmegs, and ground coffee made out of
rotten rye. Answer to that, Jared Bunce, you white-livered
lizard."[3]

The second point of connection between Simms and the humorists is their obvious delight in the coarse or picturesque
types who peopled the backwoods—peddlers like Jared who
sell clocks that run backwards and strike thirty-one times,
itinerant actors who spout passages from Shakespeare to uncomprehending swampsuckers, and brimstone preachers who
tell sinners "how the ole Hell-sarpints wud sarve 'em if they
didn't repent."[4] And the third link between Simms and the humorists is in their use of similar situations and subjects—
hoaxes, pranks, practical jokes; the rough-and-tumble fight,
the horse race, the country frolic, and the shoot for beef.

Simms's first extensive use of Southern humor in his fiction
occurs in *Border Beagles,* a lively novel published in 1840 that
is set in the Yazoo River region of western Mississippi. The
hero of the book is a young man from the civilized South, Harry
Vernon, who has been commissioned by an old friend to pursue
and capture a bank thief and who subsequently runs afoul of

the thugs called the "border beagles," modeled on the John A. Murrell gang. In addition to these criminals, Vernon encounters comic backwoods characters for whom Simms apparently found models in his own experience.[5] Though he probably knew the writing of James Kirke Paulding, Davy Crockett, and a few other precursors of the mode, in *Border Beagles* he anticipates the major humorists in his lavish depiction of types that would shortly become standard in antebellum Southern rustic comedy—a brash backwoodsman, a pompous evangelical preacher, and an itinerant or strolling actor.

Simms's woodsman, Dick Jamison, is a naive and boisterous fellow who defends Vernon when he is captured by the beagles, in the process battling a drunken Irishman on his friend's behalf. The Irishman boasts that he is "Dennis O'Dougherty, of the O'Doughertys of Ballyshannon by the pit of Ballany—a family of the ouldest—there's no telling, indade, when the O'Doughertys were not a family of the ouldest." In the tall language of the backwoods, Jamison retorts, "That accounts for your loss of strength, Mr. O'Dougherty . . . if you hadn't come from so old a family, I should not have tumbled you so easily. . . . But the blood gets mighty thin going through three, or five, or seven generations, unless the breed is crossed mighty often. Now, don't you see the advantage of being of a new family, in my state, all the men are of new families, and we've got the strength in us."[6]

Verbose backwoods preachers would eventually become a target of humorists from Johnson Jones Hooper to George Washington Harris as well as the focus of such fine satiric sketches as "Where the Lion Roareth and the Wang-doodle Mourneth," traditionally ascribed to William Penn Brannan. Simms anticipates this strain in native humor by his clever portrait of a Methodist parson, Billy Badger, a self-important gentleman who is both sensual and sententious. An impatient guest aptly styles the parson's interminable grace before a meal "the dinner cooler" (I, 277), while Simms emphasizes that Badger greedily delights in the dainty victuals he spends such time in blessing. As one of the preacher's acquaintances remarks "[I]t's the most funny thing in the world, to see the pompous old parson, his round, red face looking forth from his white neckcloth, and half fenced in by his high shoulders and black cape, like a terrapin on a wet log, meditating the ways and means for a Sunday dinner" (I, 295).

Perhaps the most amusing aspect of Badger's personality is his prolix speech, which is larded with ornate phrases drawn from the Bible and Christian tradition. Badger likes to dilate on the sinfulness of the world, especially that part of it which is near his home on Zion Hill. When he hears about the crimes of the beagles, he declaims:

> Evil is abroad in the world . . . there is no place altogether se-
> cure from the dominion of Satan; but that here, so nigh unto
> Zion, where I have, for the space of two blessed years, striven to
> uphold the work and the worship of our heavenly father; that
> sin should so boldly demean herself, seems to be as passing
> strange as it is sad. . . . I declare to you that we must all arise
> and put on the armor of strife, yea, the very armor of man, and
> gird upon our thighs the carnal weapons of human wrath. . . .
> We must go forth in seeking for these bloody men; we must put
> them to defiance; and as they have not hearkened to our works
> of prayer . . . we must smite them hip and thigh to their utter
> undoing. (I, 247)

He carries on at such length about crime and criminals, in fact, that one of the beagles who overhears his tirade declares: "By the Dog Shadow of Loosa Chitta . . . Badger deals in no small shot; he's a hundred pounder parson, and I shall owe him large acknowledgements, when next I find it needful to become ghostly and unctuous" (I, 258).

The itinerant or strolling actor would be memorialized in comic backwoods annals primarily through the writings of Solomon Franklin Smith, a New Yorker who acted and managed playhouses in Mobile and New Orleans and who, with his troupes, played in makeshift theaters sprinkled throughout the river towns. In a volume called *Theatrical Apprenticeship* published during 1846, Smith gleefully recounts the way in which unsophisticated rural audiences typically confused life and art. He tells, for instance, how he and his fellow actors put on a play called the *Mock Duke,* in which he took the title role. "When the duke," Smith says, "in answer to a knock at the door, bids his wife to 'see who it is that knocks,' a gentleman who happened to be standing near the stage-door, very composedly opened it, and peeping out, turned to the duke and answered, 'It is nobody but one of the actors; Mr. Tatem, I believe.'"[7]

Several years before Smith's book appeared, Simms had described in *Border Beagles* some equally funny occurrences, dressing them up in dialect for maximum comic effect. The comic heart of the novel is the strolling actor Tom Horsey, a stage-struck youth from the Mississippi backwoods who has played the theaters in New Orleans. Horsey follows Vernon into Yazoo territory, where he meets yokels who do not understand his profession. One such yokel vigorously denounces the scene from a tragedy that Horsey is about to perform:

> "Tragedy be d----d," said he, . . . "tragedy be d----d . . . . 'Taint raal. I was once down in Mobile, when I saw them making tragedies, and, darken my peepers, but the bloody bitches made me mad enough to swallow 'em, they were so cussed rediculous. . . . There was a tragedian that came in looking after his enemy. He had his sword out, and he made a show is if he was mighty angry, but, between you and me, he didn't want to find him, no how. The other fellow was hiding behind a tree, and this chap looked for him every where but there. So, as I wanted to see how they'd fight, I up and told him where to look for him—says I, bung up my peepers, if you don't find him against that rock, squat, jist hiding behind that tree. . . . Well, instead of thanking me, he dropped his jaws and his sword, looked at me as if he'd seed a ghost, mumbled something in his throat, nobody could tell what, and then there was a spree among the people." (II, 131–32)

Shortly after publishing *Border Beagles,* Simms quit writing novels for eight years because the sales of long fiction had been badly harmed by the Panic of 1837 and the popularity of cheap paperbound books. He turned instead to poetry, short fiction, essays, and magazine editing (reading and reviewing important works of Southern humor), which had helped fill the gap created by the decline in long fiction. The books he reviewed in the 1840s and early 1850s, ranging from *Georgia Scenes* and *Major Jones's Courtship* to *The Flush Times of Alabama and Mississippi,* reinforced his interest in the sort of comedy he had created in *Border Beagles* and convinced him that such humor was a saleable commodity in the national marketplace.[8] In some little-known productions after midcentury, therefore, he adopted the short forms the humorists favored and used their typical devices of framing story and tall tale, or outer and inner narratives. The works in question, which are laid in various parts of the rural South, depend heavily for their effect on raucous comic episodes and rustic types.

As Good as a Comedy (1852), the first of these works, has a framing narrative set in a stagecoach, which with the steamboat was an oft-depicted conveyance in antebellum humor and one that made possible a picture of characters from diverse social backgrounds. Like Thomas Bangs Thorpe in the "The Big Bear of Arkansas," Simms shapes his passengers to symbolize different levels of society and various national types—a Yankee schoolmaster, a machinist from Maine, a North Carolina Tar Heel from Tar River, and a Georgian who recounts an amusing yarn about catching alligators in winter with barbed sticks. The central character in the frame, "a broth of a boy in the shape of a huge Tennessean," tells a gentlemanly South Carolinian, who probably represents Simms, "Stranger, ef so be you will only *skrooge* yourself up so as to let me have this arm of mine perfectly free for a swing . . . I'll let out a little upon you in relation to sartain sarcumstances that come pretty much to my own knowledge, a year or two ago, in Florida."[9]

The story that follows, which combines tall-tale elements with a domestic setting, takes place in middle Georgia, the prime territory of both *Georgia Scenes* and *Major Jones's Courtship.* This setting, so evocative of the tradition in Southern humor behind Simms, indicates to the reader that the narrative will have a realistic and comic cast. It also has a fairly complicated formal structure. In *Comedy,* Simms constructs a serious and a comic plot and links them by means of a lively wag aptly named Tom Nettles, who stings or mortifies the pride of pretentious characters in both story lines. In the serious plot, Simms contrasts characters representing the genteel element in Georgia with vulgar nouveau-riche upstarts in order to develop a full picture of Southern society and a criticism of its coarser features. In the comic strand, he involves the pompous gull and

154

dandy Jones Barry in a series of mishaps occurring in those standard settings of backwoods humor, a gander-pulling and a country circus.

When describing the gander-pulling, Simms apparently looks to Longstreet, while in portraying the circus he draws elements from the work of William Tappan Thompson. Longstreet in *Georgia Scenes* conveys his complex attitude toward the barbarous sport of gander-pulling by interweaving lofty authorial language and salty backwoods speech so closely that it is difficult to determine whether genteel revulsion or raw frontier revelry dominates in his presentation. Lyman Hall, the narrator of the sketch, describes how the gander's throat is oiled with grease from his mate's body. As he muses upon this grisly fact, his thoughts take "a melancholy turn":

> They dwelt in sadness upon the many conjugal felicities which had probably been shared between the *greasess* and the *greasee*.—I could see him as he stood by her side, through many a chilly day and cheerless night, when she was warming into life the offspring of their mutual loves. . . . Ye friends of the sacred tie! judge what were my feelings, when in the midst of these reflections, the voice of James Prator thundered on mine ear, "Durn his old dodging soul; brother Med! grease his neck till a fly can't light on it!" (Pp. 122–123)

The brutal game begins, and men on horseback ride in circles around the bird while yanking at its neck. Finally, fat John Fulger bears away the victim's head, and Longstreet (through Hall) indulges in the spiciest language of the sketch as the victor claims his prize. "Come here Naddy Prater," Fulger boasts; "let your Uncle Johnny put his potato stealer [hand], into that hat, and tickle the chins of them *are* shiners a little! Oh you little shining sons o' bitches! walk into your Mas' Johny's pocket" (p. 127).

Simms's feelings about gander-pulling are more negative than Longstreet's, and his authorial disdain for the custom is consequently more pronounced. As a means of implicit protest against the cruelty of the sport, he casts his commentary in the polite language of the well-bred Southerner. He also, like Longstreet, creates humor by contrasting such language with the

155

coarser comments of spectators and participants. After describing the sport in didactic manner—"*Gander-pulling* . . . is one of those sports which a cunning devil has contrived to gratify a human beast"—he shifts into humorous backwoods speech. Jones Barry, thoroughly drunk, rides into the arena, fixes his eyes upon the gander's neck, holds up his outstretched fingers, and cries, in language reminiscent of Longstreet, "Here's the claws that'll have you off, my beauty! You're shining there for me!" (pp. 92, 94). In his excitement Barry grabs the rope by which the gander is suspended, and chaos ensues:

> The horse passed instantly from under him, and, for a moment, he hung in air, the wings of the gander playing the devil's tattoo rather rapidly upon his face, breast, and shoulders. It was but for an instant, however. The cord, calculated to sustain one goose only, broke under double weight, and down came the pair together, the gander uppermost. Never had such a scene been witnessed before, in the whole annals of gander-pulling. . . . The field rang with shouts of merriment; a most royal delirium seized upon the republican. Some rolled on the earth in convulsions; some clapped their hands and shouted; while the boys shot off their guns, to the great confusion and disorder of horseflesh. (Pp. 95–96)

Tom Nettles escorts the stunned, bewildered Barry from the arena, while little Logan Whitesides, a gypsy boy, rides toward the gander. He crouches, leaps upward, and bears aloft, Simms says in pointed reference to the cruelty of the scene, the "head, windpipe, and all of the gander but his body;—the segregated throat continuing to pour scream upon scream, convulsively, as the urchin moved the head of the bird in triumph over his own" (p. 98).

If Simms draws in a general way on Longstreet for the gander-pulling, he draws specifically on Thompson for his sketch of a country circus. Thompson's description of that entertainment in the story "Great Attraction!" (appended to the first edition of *Major Jones's Courtship*) had been perhaps the first full-blown depiction of a circus in Southern humor. In the story, Thompson portrays a dandified physician, Dr. Peter Jones, who, like Simms's Jones Barry, is a fop and a fool. At the circus, the doctor interferes in an exchange between a clown and a star circus performer. The sly performer thrusts his head between the doctor's legs, raises him off the ground, and "dancing once or twice round the ring," tosses him "pell mell" onto the heads of some spectators, who squall "in concert with the general shout."[10]

In the comparable parts of *Comedy,* Jones Barry, a spiritual descendant of Thompson's Peter Jones, staggers into a circus where he meets a clown who throws a drink in his face. Barry tears away the clown's false head, but the "mountebank, squatting low," darts between the fop's legs, hoists him off the ground, carries him around the ring, and pitches him into the audience as the pavilion rings with "delirious shouts" (pp. 103–104). The similarities between Simms's presentation and Thompson's, which include the circus performer, the shoulder ride, and the presence in each account of the name "Jones," suggest that Simms in *Comedy* profited from Thompson's example in *Great Attraction!*

After *Comedy,* Simms published several works that reveal his growing interest in the humorous potentialities of tall talk. For example, a character from Alabama in *Southward Ho!* (1854) declares, in language reminiscent of Davy Crockett, "I was born in a cloud and suckled by the east wind," while a servant in *The Forayers* (1855) tells his friends that in their new home, "De cawn grus jis' at de bery sigh ob de hoe; de chicken crow jis' as he shak' off de shell; de 'simmon . . . so tick, dat you kin catch twenty-seben and fifteen 'possum and coon a' night on de same tree; and der's no eend to sich eatable leetle varmints as de squirrll and rabbit. Dem you knocks ober wid little stick when you is walking 'bout in de sunset."[11] But in the evolution of Simms's backwoods humor, the real successor to *As Good as a Comedy* is *Paddy McGann* (1863), a remarkable book in several respects and perhaps the most fruitful work in Simms's canon for a study of his comic talent. *Paddy* is that rare thing in Southern humor, a novel (as opposed to a story or sketch) told almost entirely in dialect. In both the manner of its telling and in specific episodes like a long sequence on a raft, it looks forward to Mark Twain's masterpiece, *Huckle-berry Finn;* and there is some indication that Twain may have imitated certain passages from Simms for his own book.[12]

At the beginning of *Paddy McGann,* Simms establishes the contrast between the civilized and the rural South through a framing narrative in which planters from his own part of South Carolina drink and spin stories with their rustic companion Paddy, a rollicking Irish backwoodsman who boasts that he was "nursed on whiskey, weaned on whiskey, and vaccinated with whiskey."[13] The story he tells is a comic devil yarn with similarities to other antebellum stories of that type such as James Hall's "Pete Featherton" and John Pendleton Kennedy's "Mike Brown." It shows some equally interesting connections to mid-century tales of the supernatural by Poe and Hawthorne—notably "Ligeia," "The Fall of the House of Usher," and "Young Goodman Brown." In these works, as in *Paddy,* the vividness and credibility of the story, achieved in part by the way it is told, make it hard for the reader to decide whether the narrative is a product of a deluded imagination or whether it describes an actual occurrence.

Paddy, who owns a small cabin in the woods and makes his living by farming and hunting, tells the planters that some years back he found that his gun was apparently bewitched and that he was no longer able to kill any game. For this dilemma he blames the devil, whom he thinks is haunting the woods. The ensuing episodes in his story of tribulations demonstrate Simms's familiarity with the standard materials of Southern humor as well as with the oral folklore of the South. These materials include the shoot for beef and the rough-and-tumble fight, which had been described by humorists from Longstreet and Davy Crockett onward. They also include freshly used folk motifs that show Simms mining veins of orally transmitted lore—a bewitched gun, a devil in animal form, and a demon that inhabits a tree.

As can be seen in his depiction of a shooting match and in hunting sequences, Simms moves between scenes grounded in printed Southern humor and those derived from folklore. At the shooting match, Paddy says, his friends had heard that his gun was bewitched, "and they came about me, several of 'em, and begun to ax questions, and to worry me." His chief heckler is Isaac Clymes, a loud-mouthed, drunken bully of the rough-and-tumble school. When Paddy prays before the match begins, Clymes sneers, "[D]o you calkilate that praying will take the witch pison off your rifle?" and he also mutters, "I wonder if in getting religion, he's left off whiskey!" After praying, Paddy calmly fires at the target, an ace of hearts nailed on a pine tree. But he misses the tree altogether, and says, "Jest as if there had been no bullet in the gun!" (pp. 273–276).

When Paddy fails, there is a "most infarnal yelling, and whooping, and shouting, and hallobalooing, from all the fellows that run up to look for the shot." In a rage, he smashes his rifle; Clymes bedevils him; Paddy calls the bully "a d----d dirty beast . . . something of a cross between a polecat and a skunk"; and the two square off for a fight. Paddy pitches Clymes over an ugly stump and breaks his leg; but "it was all the Devil's doings, gentlemen," he tells his hearers; "he caused me to miss the tree; he put the ugly stump in the way that broke Clymes' thigh bone, and 'twas him that worked me up to smash the poor we'pon that had sarved me, like a most faithful sarvant, now going on twenty years. It was the Devil that had the strong gripe of me through all that season!" (pp. 277–280).

Paddy's next major brush with the devil occurs when he hunts a magnificent buck that comes thundering down upon him through the woods. The sequence shows Simms drawing on folk material about invincible supernatural animals that was widespread in both serious and comic antebellum literature. Foremost among such serious literature, of course, is *Moby-Dick,* but perhaps more directly pertinent for *Paddy* is Thomas Bangs Thorpe's account of the Big Bear of Arkansas, "*an unhuntable bar*" that "*died when his time come.*"[14] At one point in Thorpe's story, narrator Jim Doggett thinks the bear may be an incarnation of the devil; and Paddy likewise assumes that the devil has come to taunt him in "the innocent figger of the buck." He shoots both barrels of his gun at the deer, but the creature seems to feel nothing, and it torments Paddy and his friend Sam Hartley, neither of whom can bring it down. As if to trick and annoy them, it doubles back and forth between them, swipes a hunting dog with its antlers, and leads Paddy across a railroad track directly in front of a speeding train. The next day Paddy and Sam go after the buck with more than fifteen dogs at their heels, but Paddy concludes that the dogs "might jest as well been at home in the kennel, for the good they waur in the chase of that devil buck." Even Sam, he sadly concludes, began "to feel shy of keeping company with a man so onfortynit as me . . . and I didn't blame him; for who could blame a man who wanted to eat his hominy in peace, without the human sartinty of finding the Devil, all the time, dipping his spoon into the dish!" (pp. 288–293).

The apparent meaning of these strange episodes emerges after Paddy has killed a string of partridges feeding on the ground and the devil has rebuked him for his unsportsmanlike behavior: "Murder, I call it . . . to take 'em in a line upon the ground! To give 'em not the shadow of a chaince! . . . But I'll punish you for your murdering acts, you dirty villain. I'll see that you get no more meat!" Paddy then sees the devil in the shape of "a big red eye" looking out from a "big, ugly, black stump." Enraged, he shoots his gun "pint-blank" at the eye, and the devil shouts, "You've burned my eyebrow, you buzzard!" Paddy fires again, and the devil cries, "[Y]ou've only shet up my front window, you blackguard!" (pp. 315–316). The contest concludes when Paddy grabs the stump, uproots it, and rolls with it down a hill, but it turns into a great bird and flaps away. The devil is obviously punishing Paddy for his heedless destruction of forest game; and through the sequence Simms has therefore voiced a concern about the proper treatment of the wilderness that would preoccupy later Southern writers such as William Faulkner.[15]

Despite the verisimilitude of Paddy's tale, his gentlemanly listeners suspect that it is old demon rum rather than any real devil that has caused the torments that afflict him while he is hunting. Because of his own ardent belief in what he is telling, however, it is finally impossible to determine whether his story is veracious or (in Huck Finn's terms) a "stretcher." What does seem clear is that throughout the narrative Simms is probing what the Vanderbilt Agrarians would later call the poetic supernaturalism of the South, and it is also apparent that to some degree he intends Paddy's tale as a rebuke to the sophisticated skepticism of his educated hearers. For, as Paddy tells his planter friends, "[E]f you were able to find out the raison of everything, you would niver be seeking God at all—you wouldn't belave in God, and, what's more, you wouldn't need a God!" (p. 321). However one is finally inclined to interpret the story Paddy spins, it is a fine narrative of the supernatural and a splendid example of the tall tale rolled onto one; and it draws directly and ingeniously on both oral and written strains of humorous backwoods material.

The fruition of Simms's backwoods comedy comes in two tall tales apparently written during the last decade of his life— "How Sharp Snaffles Got His Capital and Wife," which has been widely praised by critics,[16] and its companion piece "Bald-Head Bill Bauldy," which has largely been ignored. Like the much earlier *Border Beagles,* these tales originated in Simms's travels through the backwoods or frontier South, particularly in a trip to the Appalachian mountains he had made in 1847, where he spent two weeks hunting and camping with mountaineers.[17] Several elements in the stories show that Simms, by this point in his career, felt comfortable enough with the material of Southern humor to manipulate freely the stock elements of the genre—copious bouts of drinking, heavy dialect, and scenes of wild adventures. His familiarity with these devices is particularly obvious in the framing narrative for the tales, where he draws on his mountain experiences while carefully preparing for the account that is to follow.

The frame for both stories is set on Saturday night, which is "dedicated among the professional hunters to what is called 'The Lying Camp!'"[18] At this function, Simms says, "The hunter who actually inclines to exaggerate is, at such a period, privileged to do so! To be literal, or confine himself to the bald and naked truth, is not only discreditable, but a *finable* offense!" (p. 423). The situation gives birth to incredible stories, of which Sharp Snaffles's is the better-known but Bill Bauldy's is perhaps the more fantastic. Certainly it is unique in humor annals, for while Sharp tells a fairly familiar, if wonderfully embroidered, yarn of a fabulous hunt, Bill produces a story that draws on elements ranging from the Indian captivity narrative and the Florida Seminole wars to underwater adventures with an Indian lady who is a sinister blend of mermaid and alligator.

Like other tellers of antebellum tall tales, Bill Bauldy is a fantastic figure, with "a head as clean as the palm of a damsel's hand and . . . shining bright in the sun." To disguise his baldness, he wears a ridiculous wig, "a great shaggy mass of reddish brown hair"; and it is "only as a favor to the amateurs of the party" that he shows his naked skull. Just as liquor acted as the stimulant for Paddy's imagination, so smoking, loafing, and drinking operate comparably on Bill. The chief cook of a regiment in the Second Seminole War, he insists that, when off duty, he was captured by an Indian, taken to camp, and forced to tote a "cussed leetle dirty wretch of a red skin papoose, from daylight to dark." He is then carried by an alligator to the bottom of a lake, where he is made captive by a woman he calls "the Calypso of Flurriday; a Type Unknown to Ulysses." [19]

The vision that ensues is a blend of paradise and Tartarus, with elements looking back to the Book of Revelation and forward to the Wizard of Oz. Bill enters an enchanted realm where "the pathway was wide and spread with white sand"; he sees hills "stuck full of shiny shells"; and he finds himself "in a most tremendous big hall, all kivered over with shells and chrystals" where alligator courtiers are coming and going (p. 498). The queen of the fabulous realm, who is half Indian and half alligator, has floating black hair, "bright . . . lightning-like eyes," and teeth "sharp as a dog's grinder" (p. 502). When she grows amorous toward Bill, she flings out from her body some twenty feet of tail, catches him around the waist, pulls him into her lap, and kisses him until the blood comes. He finally realizes that he is being fattened for the kill—for, he says, when kissing him, "[t]he infarnal critter was a-tasting me all the time, and calculating the meal she was to make of me!" (p. 508). When he sees "a whole pile of skillytons, more than a hundred" (p. 507), he knows that the queen has killed and eaten a host of men before him.

Bill eventually gets away from the alligator queen, who is a darkly comic version of La Belle Dame Sans Merci. But he falls into the hands of his regiment, whose members charge him with desertion and maintain that the wild experiences he recounts derive from a drunken dream. Yet they forgive him, for reasons that their leader makes clear: "Who kin fry a trout, a pairch, or a bream, with Bill Bauldy? Who kin bile a bluecat, to

make it eat hafe so sweet? . . . A great sodger, Gentlemens, is
one thing, and a great thing; but a great cook is a greater;—
he's sort of life-preserver, and comforter, and saviour of the
body, which, you know, is next to being the saviour of the soul!"
(p. 519).

In depicting comic woodsmen, actors, and brawlers along
with such customs as the gander-pulling and the shoot for beef,
Simms and the Southern humorists were drawing upon a vast
and fluid body of material emanating from the rural portions of
the South. When he used this material for early novels such as
Border Beagles, Simms was working slightly in advance of the
humorists; and as a widely known popular author he may actually have influenced their descriptions of strolling thespians or
bombastic backwoods preachers. On the other hand, in his mature fiction he himself was influenced by the work of established writers like Longstreet and Thompson, and he drew
upon their sketches in order to enhance the energetic, inventive strain of humor that animates his own books. The flights
of his comic imagination in *As Good As a Comedy, Paddy
McGann,* and "Bald-Head Bill Bauldy" demonstrate beyond
much doubt that he was a major creator of backwoods humor in
the antebellum period. He should take rank with Longstreet,
Thorpe, and Thompson in future studies of this intriguing
branch of Southern comic art.

Notes

[1]These events of Simms's childhood and adolescence are described
by William P. Trent, *William Gilmore Simms* (Boston: Houghton
Mifflin, 1892), pp. [1]–18, and Alexander S. Salley, "William Gilmore
Simms," in *The Letters of William Gilmore Simms,* eds. Mary C.
Simms Oliphant, Alfred Taylor Odell, and T. C. Duncan Eaves (Columbia, S.C.: University of South Carolina Press, 1952–1956), I, lix–
lxi (hereinafter cited as *Letters*). Two important series of letters de-
riving from Simms's trips to the Gulf South are "Notes of a Small
Tourist," published in 1831 in the Charleston *City Gazette* and reprinted in *Letters,* I, 10–38, and "Letters from the West," published in
1826 in *The Album* and edited by James E. Kibler, Jr., in "The First

Simms Letters: 'Letters from the West (1826),'" *Southern Literary Journal,* 19 (Spring 1987): 81–91. Professor Kibler has also studied Simms's travels of 1826 in the deep South in "*The Album* (1826): The Significance of the Recently Discovered Second Volume," *Studies in Bibliography,* 39 (1986), 62–78.

[2] Augustus Baldwin Longstreet, *Georgia Scenes, Characters, Incidents &c. in the First Half Century of the Republic* (Augusta, Ga.: S. R. Sentinel Office, 1835), pp. 183–184. Further references to this work are to this edition, cited within the text.

[3] William Gilmore Simms, *Guy Rivers: A Tale of Georgia* (New York: Harper and Brothers, 1834), I, 71–72.

[4] The quotation is from George Washington Harris, *Sut Lovingood. Yarns Spun by a "Nat'ral Born Durn'd Fool["]* (New York: Dick and Fitzgerald, 1867), p. 52.

[5] In the Advertisement to the revised edition of *Border Beagles* (New York: J. S. Redfield, 1855), Simms insists that all the leading characters in the novel, including Horsey, are "drawn from the life."

[6] Simms, *Border Beagles; A Tale of Mississippi* (Philadelphia: Carey and Hart, 1840), II, 17–18. Further references to this work are to this edition, cited within the text.

[7] Solomon Franklin Smith, *The Theatrical Apprenticeship and Anecdotical Recollections of Sol. Smith* (Philadelphia: Carey and Hart, 1846), pp. 119–120.

[8] Simms praised the rare, racy, articulate, native humor of *Georgia Scenes* in *Views and Reviews in American Literature, History and Fiction, Second Series* (New York: Wiley and Putnam, 1845), p. 178; he reviewed *Major Jones's Courtship* in *The Magnolia; or, Southern Apalachian* n.s., 2 (June 1843), 399; he commended *Flush Times* in the *Southern Quarterly Review,* 25 (April 1854), 555. That he wrote most of the reviews for the two periodicals during the time he edited them is indicated by his comments in his correspondence; see, for example, *Letters,* III, 120.

[9] Simms, *As Good as a Comedy: or, The Tennesseean's Story,* in *The Writings of William Gilmore Simms, Centennial Edition,* ed. James B. Meriwether, Introduction and Explanatory Notes by Robert Bush (Columbia, S.C.: University of South Carolina Press, 1972), III, 11. Further references to this novel are to this edition, cited within the text.

[10] [William Tappan Thompson], *Major Jones's Courtship* (Madison, Ga.: C. R. Hanleiter, 1843), p. 74.

[11] *Southward Ho! or A Spell of Sunshine* (New York: J. S. Redfield, 1854), p. 328; *The Forayers: or The Raid of the Dog-Days* (New York: J. S. Redfield, 1855), p. 456.

[12] On this point, see Robert Bush, "*Paddy McGann,* William Gilmore Simms's Devil Story," *Bulletin of the New York Public Library,* 69 (March 1965), 200.

[13] Simms, *Paddy McGann; or, The Demon of the Stump,* in *The Writings of William Gilmore Simms, Centennial Edition,* ed. James B. Meriwether, Introduction and Explanatory Notes by Robert Bush (Columbia, S.C.: University of South Carolina Press, 1972), III, 254. Further references to this novel are to this edition, cited within the text.

[14] Thomas Bangs Thorpe, *The Big Bear of Arkansas, and Other/ Sketches, Illustrative of Character and Incidents in the South and South-West,* ed. W. T. Porter (Philadelphia: Carey and Hart, 1845), p. 31.

[15] For a similar point, see Robert Bush's Introduction to *Paddy McGann,* p. xxiii.

[16] In his *William Gilmore Simms as Literary Critic* (Athens, Ga.: University of Georgia Press, 1961), p. 9, Edd Winfield Parks called "Sharp Snaffles" "one of the finest tall tales ever written by a Southern humorist"; in the Introduction to *Letters* I, lii, Donald Davidson said it "stands almost without a peer, surely," among American tall tales; and in the Explanatory Notes to *Stories and Tales* in *The Writings of William Gilmore Simms,* ed. John Caldwell Guilds (Columbia: University of South Carolina Press, 1974), V, 804, Guilds remarked that it and its companion piece "Bald-Head Bill Bauldy" show "Simms's excellence in the genre of Southern and Southwestern humor." Recent studies of the story include James B. Meriwether, "Simms' 'Sharp Snaffles' and 'Bald-Head Bill Bauldy': Two Views of Men—And of Women," *South Carolina Review,* 16 (Spring 1984), 66–71, and Ian Marshall, "The American Dreams of Sam Snaffles," *Southern Literary Journal,* 18 (Spring 1985), [9.]–107.

[17] For a treatment of the various literary uses Simms made of his 1847 travels, see Miriam J. Shillingsburg, "From Notes to Novel: Simms's Creative Method," *Southern Literary Journal,* 5 (Fall 1972), 89–107.

[18] "How Sharp Snaffles Got His Capital and Wife" in *Stories and Tales,* in *The Writings of William Gilmore Simms,* V, 423. Further references to this work are to this edition, cited within the text.

[19] "'Bald-Head Bill Bauldy,' and How He Went Through the Flurriday Campaign!—A Legend of the Hunter's Camp" in *Stories and Tales,* V, 467.

Paul Hamilton Hayne and William Gilmore Simms: Friends, Colleagues, and Members of the Guild

RAYBURN S. MOORE

As a schoolboy, Paul Hamilton Hayne read William Gilmore Simms's romances, heard Simms make a political speech in 1847, and reviewed his work as early as 1852. In turn, Simms encouraged the young poet, wrote a letter of introduction to a Northern publisher in his behalf in 1853, and helped to install Hayne as editor of *Russell's Magazine* in 1856.[1] The two men subsequently got along well together; the editors of *The Letters of Simms* in fact maintained in 1952 that a "tender relation" "without one cloud" existed between them (I, cxiii). This may be expecting too much from writers whose constitutions, temperaments, and ages were so different, but over the twenty years of their friendship, cut short only by Simms's death in 1870, it may also approximate the truth. It is certainly true that Simms considered Hayne his favorite among his younger colleagues in Carolina and that Hayne admired and respected Simms both as man and author. Despite the well-known outline of their friendship and the central importance of each writer as a spokesman for the South over a period covering fifty years (1835–1886), the literary relationship between the two has never been fully elaborated. Though I shall examine the relationship primarily from Hayne's angle of vision in this essay, I shall offer an account balanced throughout by Simms's views.

166

Hayne, to be sure, had enjoyed Simms's work since his school-days. He read his poems and romances, and when he began to review books and write criticism in the 1850s, Simms's writings were among the first to receive his attention. In 1852, for example, Hayne lauded Simms's *Norman Maurice* in the *Southern Literary Gazette,* and, as editor of the journal, "re-published" the play with Simms's "consent."[2] He also praised the *Golden Christmas* and *The Wigwam and the Cabin* when Walker, Richards and Company brought them out in August of the same year. Moreover, *The Sword and the Distaff,* certainly one of Simms's best novels, appeared in the *Gazette* while Hayne was assistant editor.[3]

In turn, Simms encouraged Hayne, and when the budding writer contemplated collecting his verse for his first volume, Simms wrote a letter on August 12 [1853] to James T. Fields, the Boston publisher, introducing Hayne and characterizing him as a "young Poet & the Editor of a Literary Weekly . . . [and] one of the most amiable of Gentlemen, intelligent and modest."[4] Hayne, accordingly, met Fields a few weeks later, arranging with him to bring out his volume, and *Poems* appeared in Boston a year later.

Hayne's response to Simms was more fully revealed later in the decade in *Russell's Magazine.* As editor for most of the journal's three-year run, Hayne not only listened to Simms's advice and printed his contributions (over sixty poems and six essays), but he also reviewed his works when they appeared and commented on Simms as poet and author in editorials and essays. In examining Simms's latest collection of poems in 1857, for example, Hayne considers Simms's overall situation.

> In fiction, historical, or purely imaginative, in criticism of every kind and degree, from the piquant newspaper notice to the profound analysis of Hamlet, in the delicate labor of annotation, in essays upon every variety of topic, . . . in the editorship of reviews and journals, in history proper, even in geography, he has worked with singular energy and success. No American writer has covered so extensive a ground. His versatility and facile command of resources are astonishing. Indeed, in copiousness of thought, and instantaneous grasp of expression, we have not met his superior. (II, 153)

In considering Simms as poet, Hayne sees him as Elizabethan in style, "in richness and force of thought, affluence
of expression, [and in] comprehensive imagination" (II, 154).
Nevertheless Simms's poems are not without their faults—
"improvisation" that leads to "an exceeding diffuseness," for
instance—"blemishes the more annoying as they might frequently be rectified by a mere dash of the pen" (II, 159).[5] Still,
Hayne concludes that "we of the South should be proud of our
Poet." To the South, he adds, Simms "has devoted with patriotic singleness of purpose, the noblest of his endowments—
the first and last fruits of his intellectual manhood" (II, 159).
Then Hayne develops this theme—one that will recur subsequently in his work, as it had already appeared from time to
time in Simms's own criticism. He continues:

> Surely this union of genius and patriotism *should* receive our
> sympathy. But we fear that *it is not so.* Something we ourselves
> have seen and heard—enough to convince us that Mr. Simms is
> scarcely an exception to the mournful adage interwoven more or
> less with all intellectual history, that a prophet is not without
> honor, save by his own hearthstone.
>
> Nowhere, probably, in the Union has he been honored with
> less of encouragement and appreciation, than in the city of his
> birth, and among the people of the very State whose traditional
> and revolutionary annals, whose society, institutions, scenery
> and peculiar phases of life, and character, he has done more
> than any other, to describe, perpetuate, and defend. (II, 160)

Two years later upon the appearance of the *Cassique of
Kiawah* Hayne turns to Simms's novels, praises them, and
later quotes at length from a favorable essay in the *North
American Review.*

> Were this tale destined to be Mr. Simms' last [he writes in June,
> 1859], we scarcely think that it would be possible for him to
> produce a work which more fittingly closes, in a high artistic
> sense, the brilliant series of his Carolina Novels. All of the au-
> thor's characteristic powers of invention, narrative, dramatic
> effect and picturesque description, are happily combined in this
> story, the action of which is wonderfully vivid, whilst the chief
> personages introduced possess an individual charm that greatly
> adds to the interest of the romance. (V, 287)

Moreover, in the following December he maintains that the article on *Cassique* in the *North American Review* (October 1859) demonstrates, among other things, that "the North" could appreciate Simms's "genius and his works" while in the South some could carp that his fame was "ephemeral" and "hemmed in by mere State or City limits."

Thus, early in his career Hayne announces and examines several of the basic premises of his criticism of Simms's work. He praises the poetry's Elizabethan vigor, invention, and imagination, but acknowledges its weaknesses of diffuseness, too ready facility, and lack of the "distasteful duty of correction." He prefers the fiction, the Colonial and Revolutionary novels in particular, for its narrative, character, dramatic effect, and scenery. Eventually, after Simms's death (and perhaps even following Simms's own conclusion), he will sound another note—that the man was greater than the work.

In the meantime the friendship blossomed, and the two writers met frequently in Charleston to discuss *Russell's* and other literary matters at "petit soupirs" at Simms's home on Society Street and at John Russell's bookstore on King Street.[6] Hayne was invited to Simms's plantation home, Woodlands, where he enjoyed hunting partridges and wild ducks, "luxuriated on country fare," and reveled in the bountiful reception which led him to characterize the place as "Hospitality Hall." There he also could watch his friend at work (*Man of Letters*, pp. 53–54). Admitted to Simms's "*sanctum sanctorum*" as only a "few sympathetic friends were," Hayne has left us a picture of the author at his desk wielding "for hours"

the indomitable pen across page after page—a pen that rarely paused to erase, correct, or modify. At last, when the eternal scratch, scratch became a trifle irritating, and this exhaustless labor a reproach to one's semi-idleness, Simms would suddenly turn, exclaiming "Near dinner time, my boy; come, let's take a modest appetizer in the shape of sherry and bitters."

At dinner he talked a great deal, joked, jested, and punned, like a school-boy freed from his tasks; or if a graver theme arose, he would often declaim a little too dogmatically and persistently, perhaps, to please those who liked to have the chance of wagging their own tongues occasionally. At such periods it was im-

possible to edge in the most modest of "caveats." Still, Simms
could be a charming host, and was, *au fond,* thoroughly genial
and kind-hearted.("A–B C," n.s. I, 265–266)

Concurrently, Simms was reviewing Hayne's work, especially *Avolio: A Legend of the Island of Cos. With Poems, Lyrical, Miscellaneous, and Dramatic* (c. 1859), Hayne's most important collection of poems published during Simms's lifetime,
but still, of course, a gathering of his early verse. In a full-
length review in three issues of *The Mercury* (July 31, August 1
and 2, 1860), Simms examines all aspects of Hayne's poetic nature and production, praises his fancy and his passion, likes
some of his sonnets and dramatic sketches, compliments his
blank verse, but warns him that his poetry's "defects result
from the over-exercise of the faculties in which he is most rich,
tending naturally to the sensuous and erring in the use of superlatives and compound epithets" (July 31, p. 2) and urges
him to write fewer sonnets, particularly those based upon the
Italian form. At the end he lectures Hayne on the "lack of care
and finish" in some of the shorter pieces and for "common-
places of thought and fancy," but he acknowledges that Hayne
has "relieved his portfolio of his early productions" and is now
ready for "better things," for art worthy of his "best talents"
and "most exquisite care" (August 2, p. 1).

Though Hayne apparently did not react irascibly to this
criticism, he could, on occasion in private, be irritated by the
older writer's "crotchets" and "bullying" manner. On September 29, 1864, for example, Hayne notes in his diary that he has
just received a "fretful and impertinent" letter from Simms
and has replied in a "rather peremptory fashion." "He deserves
it," Hayne adds, "& I care not what he may think. These bullying fellows . . . *must* receive a Roland for an Oliver sometimes,
or they'll ride rough-shod over everybody." Six weeks earlier
Hayne had acknowledged that his "venerable critic (whom I
love & respect) is full of *crotchets;* if his criticisms are now &
then profound & suggestive, they are more frequently distinguished by principles partial & one-sided; nay! sometimes
absolutely *puerile!* It is certainly strange, for S. does possess
brilliant talent—talent barely stopping short of genius" (Au-

gust 15, 1864). And, in October, Hayne comments on another letter from Simms: "Old fellow on his high horse! but I don't mind him in the least; he means well" (October 5, 1864).[7] But, in his own letters, Hayne expresses even more directly his admiration for Simms's achievement under adverse conditions of health and poverty and acknowledges his affection for the man.

Indeed, the exchange of letters between the friends during the war and the remaining years of Simms's life provides clear evidence of the strength of their friendship and of the depth of their care for each other, separated as they were by distance and difficulty (Simms in Charleston and Woodlands and Hayne in up-country towns and in Georgia after July, 1865, both impoverished by the war, and both grubbing for the bare necessities of life during its aftermath). When, for instance, Chevillette Roach Simms died September 10, 1863, Simms poured out his heart to Hayne on September 23:

> . . . I have been ill, my friend, I may say dangerously ill, from the moment when I was struck down by the heaviest bolt of all that ever shattered my roof-tree. I was, I think, insane. I neither slept nor ate for four days and nights. Fever seized me, and I should have gone mad but for the administration of timely opiates. I am once more on my legs, but very weak. Today is the first that I have given to the desk, and this I could do only in scratches of brief period. I move about the house & try to see to things. But every thing seems blank, & waste, & cheerless. I am alone! Alone! For near 30 years, I had one companion in whose perfect fidelity, I felt sure. . . . Your eulogy is not mere varnish & gilding. She was all that you describe,—a dutiful wife, a devoted mother, and the most guileless of women. Ah! God! And I am lone! . . .
>
> Write me, my young friend. The old man has grown much older—much feebler—& it is becoming, the ministration of you, the younger brother of his guild, to assist his palsying eyelids, and point his sight and say—here place your staff—set your foot here, & now—sit. (*Letters,* IV, 437–38)

They saw each other rarely, though Simms visited Copse Hill in December, 1866, after receiving an invitation from Hayne in the form of a sonnet addressed to his "Old Friend" and urging him to come "while our woods are grand."

I yearn once more to clasp thy cordial hand,
To hear thy voice, to feel thy kindling eye
So clear with spiritual light, that will not die
Nor veil its luster at dull Time's command.

("A–B C," n.s. I, 267)

They had no Madeira and few amenities (the "mermaid measure of rare wine" mentioned in the sonnet turned out to be
"'middling Monongehela'" in a pewter cup!), but, as Hayne remembered almost two decades later, they "were only too thank-
ful to see each other after the lapse of a *lustrum;* and the hours
flew in the exchange of mutual confidences" ("A–B C," n.s. I,
267). Hayne was touched also by the signs of aging in Simms
suggested by his white hair, his grizzled beard, his forehead
"scored with wrinkles," and his eyes covered by a "film . . . of
unshed tears." "Five years of 'hope deferred' and of final de-
spairing agony" over the struggle of the South, Hayne concluded, "had done the work of half a lifetime" ("A–B C," n.s.
I, 267).

In the correspondence, each describes his living and working
conditions, and Simms frequently offers avuncular advice about
what to write and what to plant in gardens, among other topics. On May 13, 1869, for example, he urges Hayne to devote
himself to "prose writing as that province alone which might
properly compensate you." Poetry, he continues,

holds forth no attractions to the Magazine publisher in America,
unless coupled with some notorious name. But if you would
write a series of sketches like your Skepter Jogul (?) or rewrite
that, you could sell to Putnam, Lippincott & Harper very readily.[8] Short tales, & sketches of that class are always popular.
Verb. sap. For myself, I barely live, & to do so, have not an hour
to spare in any aside from my daily tasks. I have rebuilt one
wing of my house . . . & I have so far resumed planting as to
take 2 acres under my charge for gardening purposes. I have
probably the finest garden in all this precinct. I have set out
1200 cabbage plants, have been eating radishes, lettuces, green
peas, snap beans &c. have squashes beginning to bear, corn in
tassel, beans in any quantity, sweet corn for the table, tomato,
cucumbers, Irish potatoes, okra, onions, white & red, eschelots,
turnips, beets, carrots, parsnips, and most of the herbs, most of

these in large quantities, as I hope to supply the table of my daughter in town, as well as our table here, where we never seat less than 10 persons, 3 times per diem. With these vegetable supplies, a little meat will suffice. I hope you are pressing your labours in the same direction. Potatoes will pay better than poetry. I have four large beds of them, planted at different periods. You could also find a market in Augusta doubtless for much that you can raise. But if you will write for the magazines try the prose. Your prose is fully as fine as your verse. (*Letters*, VI, 274–75)

Hayne attempted to follow his friend's advice about gardening and on April 25, 1869, acknowledged that he was writing prose for as many periodicals as possible, "composing a story or essay to day for the full-blown adult monthlies, and to morrow entering the lists of fancy for the benefit of the Juveniles, thro the medium of Burke's 'Weekly' at Macon, or Scudder's 'Riverside' in Cambridge (Mass.). Only by becoming an absolute *free Lance,* or a *Bohemian* of Letters, can a man of my *light calibre,* make his bread now-a-days" (*CHL*, pp. 213–14).

Acknowledging Simms's "indissoluble connections" with "the brighest hopes of [his] youth, no less than the few humble successes of manhood" (*CHL*, p. 210), Hayne expresses his affection for the man and his admiration for the author. "Years, my *friend,* misfortune, sickness—, all the ills to which our So. 'flesh' has especially fallen 'heir,'" he writes in the letter of February 23 already referred to, "cannot weaken my affection for the 'old man eloquent,' my literary father, & patron" (*CHL*, p. 210). Two months later on April 25 he characterizes Simms as "the last,—*ultimus Romanorum*—, of those vigorous *Literati,* who thro much travail, laid the corner stone of the temple of American art in fiction" (*CHL*, p. 214).

After Simms's death in 1870, Hayne published an essay on his life and work in *Appletons' Journal,* composed an elegy in his honor in 1877, and in 1885–1886 penned two more sketches of his friend for the *Southern Bivouac* and *Youth's Companion.*[9] These works offer his mature critical opinions of Simms's work, and though he occasionally expresses himself more forthrightly in letters to close friends like Margaret Preston, a fellow poet and long-time correspondent, or to Charles Gayarré, the well-known Louisiana historian, Hayne usually delivers his opinions with some degree of objectivity. Indeed, shortly after Simms's death in 1870, Hayne wrote two letters to Francis Peyre Porcher, a mutual friend, in which he refers to the essay he is writing for *Appletons'*, says he is not writing a "mere *eulogy*" but a "critical article," maintains that Simms "*emphatically was not* . . . a really *great author*" and doubts that his "works will endure" because of "careless" composition and the lack of "*labor limäe*," but unabashedly acknowledges his love for the "gallant old man . . . whatever his faults" and asserts that Simms's "genius *never had fair play*," that the "*man* was greater than his *works*," and that he was "worthy of *all honor*." [10]

The piece for *Appletons' Journal* appeared in the issue of July 30, 1870, six weeks after Simms's death and is mainly a "brief sketch of the character, intellect, and achievements of this remarkable man," as Hayne indicates.[11] Simms's poetry, as before, is too diffuse, depends too much on improvisation, and buries its "gems" under a "large mass of mediocre versification" (p. 138). The fiction receives higher marks, and the "colonial or ante-Revolutionary tales are fairer and fuller exponents of their writer's ability than any other of his works of fiction" (p. 138). *The Yemassee* and *The Cassique of Kiawah* receive special mention, and Hayne concludes, for the first time in public, that the man is "far greater than his works" (p. 138).

The "Monody" on Simms, composed seven years later, is a tribute to the man and patriot, the "vanished genius" who "lavished freely" "all that he was, all that he owned" "on the sacred shrine . . . of home and country." Written to be read on the occasion of a program at the Charleston Academy of Music to seek funds for a monument in honor of Simms, this elegy characterizes the late poet as Viking in mien, as Falstaff in jollity, one whose "fluent talk/Roved thro' all topics, vivifying all," whose nature was magnanimous and "generous withal" and whose soul, now "exalted, nobler," "*dwells forever individualized*" in heaven. Possessed of "all pregnant powers that wait/ On intellectual state" (imagination, fancy, "bluff humor true"), Simms devoted himself and his genius to the "one glorious goal" of defending his country and its "noble people." Such a man and artist deserves homage

Large as that splendid prodigality
Of force and love, wherewith he staunchly wrought
Out from the quarries of his own deep thought,
Unnumbered shapes; whether of good or ill,
No puny puppets whose false action frets
On a false stage, like feeble Marionettes;
   But life-like, human still;
Types of a by-gone age of crime and lust;
Or, grand historic forms, in whom we view
   Re-vivified, and re-created stand
The braves who strove through cloud-encompassed ways,
Infinite travail, and malign dispraise,
To guard, to save, to wrench from tyrant hordes,
By the pen's virtue, or the lordlier sword's
   Unravished Liberty,
The virgin huntress on a virgin strand![12]

True "homage" from one son of Carolina to another.

Five years later Hayne reviewed a new reprint of the Redfield edition of Simms's work being published by Armstrong & Son, in which he considers, especially, the fiction, centering on the Revolutionary Romances, the Border Romances, *The Yemassee, The Wigwam and the Cabin,* and *Vasconselos.* He praises its characters who, though "often of the rudest sort . . . because of the time and people," represent nevertheless "genuine flesh and blood, [and are] thoroughly and essentially human." He adds,

> They are entirely too active and busy as the agents of a great cause; too absorbed in matters of paramount importance to indulge in morbid humors of any kind, such as a minute examination of their own spiritual and intellectual condition, a dissection of each emotion, or sentiment, as it chanced to arise—in a word, that species of nauseous self-study which makes the men and women of the new analytical school of novelists a plague and weariness to themselves and to most persons, we venture to say, outside the charmed circle of its fastidious adherents.[13]

Such a view he maintains at greater length two years later in an essay on Simms in the *Southern Bivouac.* Here he repeats and sums up his criticism of Simms's poetry:

That Simms was essentially a poet, that he possessed force, feeling, imagination, an active fancy, and a not unmusical ear, I hold to be unquestionable, but his prodigious faculty of verse-making, amounting to improvisation, led to great diffuseness, and a fatal neglect of "labor limäe." (n.s. I, 262)

At the same time, Hayne praises much of Simms's fiction, particularly the Revolutionary Romances, the Colonial Romances, and such other novels as *Beauchampe* and *Vasconselos* while concurrently taking pot shots at "aesthetic realism," the special preserve of those he had earlier called "adherents of the analytical school," i.e., Henry James and William Dean Howells and their followers. Hitting directly at their disdain for story, plot, character (all intrinsic to Simms's fiction) and their predilection for style and analysis, he imagines a conversation between James and Howells in which they scoff at Poe and Cooper, and Howells needs to be informed about Simms by James who notes that such a "literary Goth" could only "have lived in the South" and written such things as "'The Game Chicken'" or "'The Sucker of the Swamps'" (n.s. I, 264). Simms, indeed, Hayne acknowledges, "worshiped the *genius loci,* as an old Greek might have done. . . ." "As Scott loved the heather, as Whittier loves the mountains, the lakes, . . . the green meadows of New England, so with as deep, unfaltering a passion, Simms adored the sultry pine barrens, the luxuriant swamps, the desolate sea-side solitudes of the State of his nativity. And, as he loved her scenery, he upheld and vindicated her historic fame" (n.s. I, 266). Such interests, he points out, led Simms to "the fertile field of Revolutionary history and legend in the Southern States, . . . then veritable virgin soil, and he proceeded to cultivate it with singular vigor and perseverance" (n.s. I, 263). Simms was, Hayne concludes, "a typical Southerner of the ante-bellum period, . . . a virile and upright spirit, constitutionally incapable of fraud or meanness, and chastened, at last, into pathetic gentleness: a man greater than his works, produced, as they had been, under circumstances of peculiar trial, but of which, nevertheless, it may be predicted, 'NON OMNEM MORITURAM'" (n.s. I, 268).

In his final sketch of Simms, written for *Youth's Companion* in the last six months of his life, Hayne offers an essay on Simms's life and career based upon personal knowledge and reminiscence.[14] He makes some of the old points of diffuseness and lack of "*labor limäe*," though he admits Simms possesses the "instinct and endowments of the true poet" (p. 19). Simms's reputation must rest, Hayne maintains, "upon his prose works chiefly" (p. 19), and he focuses upon the so-called Revolutionary Romances, particularly *Katharine Walton,* and comments briefly upon the merits of *Beauchampe, The Yemassee,* and *Cassique.* The best of his books, he concludes, "have taken their place in the permanent literature of America, nor are they unknown in Europe" where "several of his romances" have been translated into German, and the *London Quarterly* in 1883 lauded him as a writer of "powerful sketches of genuine American incident" and as one of a few "imaginative authors" of great desert produced in America (p. 20). He does not here assert that Simms the man is greater than Simms the author, but the sketch stresses his courage, his integrity, and the nobility of his character.

Hayne's general criticism of Simms as artist and man has of late occasioned some discussion of his influence on the views of Simms expressed by William Peterfield Trent in his study for the American Men of Letters series in 1892.[15] John McCardell, for example, maintains that Trent's "sentiments" coincided with Haynes "barbed references to the Charleston elite that he believed had snubbed men of literary leanings" and with "the poet's candid, though confidential, assessment of Simms and his work," especially the opinion he expressed in his letters to Porcher in 1870 shortly after Simms's death, i.e., that Simms's "genius *never had fair play*," that the "*man* was greater than his *works*," that Simms "*emphatically was not . . .* a really *great author . . .*" (pp. 189–90). Hayne's reaction to Charleston's treatment of Simms, it should be noted, follows Simms's own response to what he considered to be the failure of his city to support him adequately.[16] As for Hayne's "private" view of Simms, the record needs to be modified by his opinions expressed in the 1880s, especially in 1885–1886, the last year of

Hayne's life. And, of course, the point about Simms the man being greater than Simms the author was suggested by the "old man eloquent" himself in a projected epitaph: "'Here lies one who, after a reasonably long life, distinguished chiefly by unceasing labor, has left all his better work undone'" (Trent, pp. 323–324).[17]

With regard to Trent's view of Simms as a poet, he seems to have agreed with Hayne, though it is not clear that Trent read all of Hayne's essays on and reviews of Simms's poetry. He presumably read Hayne's reviews in *Russell's* and possibly the piece in the *Southern Bivouac* (Mary Middleton Hayne apparently sent him a copy), but it is not clear that he read Hayne's essays in *Appletons'* and *Youth's Companion* or his review of the reprint of the Redfield edition in the *Sunday Argus*. At any rate, though Hayne and Trent agreed that Simms's best work was in the Colonial and Revolutionary Romances, they did not agree about its lasting value. Trent concluded from Hayne's letters to Porcher in 1870 that he thought Simms's work would not live (pp. 321–322, 331). This is hardly an accurate conclusion, for Hayne indicated in a number of places after 1870, including the essays in the *Bivouac* and the *Companion,* that Simms's work would not die. Moreover, Trent decided that Simms's fiction will live because boys will read it (p. 331), a view Hayne never intimated. Nor would Hayne have agreed with Trent that the Border Romances should be "omitted from consideration [because] they never should have been written, since they have nothing ennobling in them" (p. 328). Hayne thought well of *Beauchampe,* for example, as he observed in "Ante-Bellum Charleston" (p. 263), and elsewhere. Least of all would Hayne have accepted Trent's premise that intellectual life in the South in general and Simms's "development" in particular had been hampered by feudalism and slavery. Hayne, indeed, would in all likelihood have been appalled by Trent's views. Anyone who has read his letters of 1885–1886 to Gayarré about the prospect of a book on Simms by George Washington Cable can only conclude that Trent's opinions would have upset him and that he would have been particularly irate that Trent selected his comments from Hayne's own private letters to Porcher in 1870 (letters Trent did *not* have permission to quote) to serve as Hayne's final judgment of Simms as man and author.

Hayne's view of Simms the man, it is true, did not change. He loved and honored his old friend and, despite his "crotchets," defended him against all comers and would doubtlessly have written in his behalf against Trent had he been alive when Trent's book appeared. "Whatever his faults," Hayne wrote Porcher, "I—for one—loved him with all my heart." As for Simms the author, Hayne's opinion also remained consistent. He thought Simms was a "skillful versifier" and not an important poet, but he early concluded that Simms was a significant writer of fiction in the tradition of Scott and Cooper and maintained this view until he died. The only time he ever acknowledged that Simms's work would not "endure" was in his letter of August 4, 1870, to Porcher, and Trent, unfortunately, chose this letter and one other to represent Hayne's final judgment of Simms's work, a judgment much less representative of Hayne's critical thought than of Trent's or of the views expressed either in "Ante-Bellum Charleston" or in the essay in *Youth's Companion,* for as Hayne concludes in the first of these: Simms was "greater than his works, produced, as they had been, under circumstances of peculiar trial," but, nevertheless, regarding these works, "it may be predicted, 'NON OMNEM MORITURAM!'" It seems, then, that Trent, through ignorance, inadvertence, or design, selected from Hayne's critical comment what suited his own interpretation of Simms.[18]

It is ironic, to be sure, that Hayne may have been echoing Simms in expressing such a view of his work and perhaps even more ironic that Trent may have followed what he considered to be Hayne's judgment in the matter. The final irony is, of course, that Trent's view, in the absence of book-length challenges, has influenced Simms criticism and scholarship to the present. If Hayne was ready in 1885 to "*break every bone* in [Cable's] (intellectual) carcass" if he wronged "Simms' memory" (*Man of Letters,* p. 276), what would he have done to Trent? The reader of Hayne's letters, reviews, and essays regarding Simms can be in little doubt, for Hayne loved and admired the man and considered the author to be a pioneer in "the art of American fiction."

Notes

[1] For relations between Hayne and Simms, see William P. Trent, *William Gilmore Simms* (Boston: Houghton, Mifflin and Company, 1892); Rayburn S. Moore, *Paul Hamilton Hayne* (Boston: Twayne Publishers, Inc., 1972) and "Paul Hamilton Hayne as Editor, 1852–1860," *South Carolina Journals and Journalists,* ed. James B. Meriwether (Columbia: Southern Studies Program, University of South Carolina, 1975), pp. 91–108; *A Collection of Hayne Letters,* ed. D. M. McKeithan (Austin: University of Texas Press, 1944), referred to hereinafter as *CHL; The Letters of William Gilmore Simms,* eds. Mary C. Simms Oliphant, Alfred Taylor Odell, and T. C. Duncan Eaves (Columbia: University of South Carolina Press, 1952–56, 1982), 6 vols., referred to subsequently as *Letters;* and *A Man of Letters in the Nineteenth-Century South: Selected Letters of Paul Hamilton Hayne,* ed. Rayburn S. Moore (Baton Rouge: Louisiana State University Press, 1982), referred to below as *Man of Letters.*

[2] N.s. II (June 19, 1852), 296.

[3] Later called *Woodcraft,* this novel first appeared on February 28, 1852, and completed its run on November 6. The reception of *Woodcraft* is discussed in my paper on the novel read at the conference on Simms's Revolutionary Romances sponsored by the College of Charleston and the University of South Carolina in Charleston, May 7–8, 1976.

[4] *Letters,* VI, 141. The periodical referred to is the *Weekly News and Southern Literary Gazette,* Charleston.

[5] For Simms's comments on similar flaws in Hayne's poems, see p. 170 and in his own poems, see his letter to Rufus W. Griswold, June 20 [1841], South Caroliniana Library, University of South Carolina. "I am conscious too that there are very few of my pieces not impaired by blots, deficiencies, crudities. . . . My verses have usually been overflowings rather than workings. Like all overflowings they bear in their passage a great deal that is unseemly,—they are themselves too frequently turbid." I am grateful to Allen Stokes, librarian, and Henry Fulmer, manuscripts, for allowing me to quote from this letter.

[6] See Hayne's "Ante-Bellum Charleston," *Southern Bivouac,* n.s. I (November 1885), 327–336. Published in three parts, this essay also appeared in the September and October issues. The sketch of Simms came out in the October number. Referred to hereinafter as "A–B C" by volume and page.

[7] Hayne's diaries are in the Hayne Papers, Perkins Library, Duke University, and I am grateful to Mattie Russell and Robert Byrd, Curators of Manuscripts past and present, for allowing me to use and to quote from these and other papers. All manuscripts not otherwise identified as to location are in this indispensable collection.

[8] "The Skaptar Yokul," a Poesque story, had appeared in *Russell's,* I (April, 1857), 55–63. Hayne subsequently took Simms's suggestion and revised the story; it came out in *Appletons' Journal,* 8 (November 23, 1872), 567–570.

[9] Hayne also wrote a "memoir" of Simms intended for publication in *Harper's Weekly.* See S. S. Conant's letter to Hayne of August 4, 1877. Six months later J. W. Harper, Jr., of the publishing firm, wrote Hayne that the "biography" would appear in "book form with sketches & personal recollections of American and English authors by various hands." "We have withheld the volume," he explained, "on account of the depressed condition of the times, but we have not lost sight of it" (January 30, 1878). Hayne still hoped, as late as November 29, 1881, that the sketch would eventually appear, as he indicated in a letter of that date to E. L. Didier, currently a member of the editorial staff of *The American* in Philadelphia.

[10] These letters are dated July 9 and August 4 and are in the Paul Hamilton Hayne Papers, South Caroliniana Library, University of South Carolina, and I am grateful to E. L. Inabinett and Allen Stokes, librarians, for permission to quote from them.

[11] *Appletons' Journal,* 4 (July 30, 1870), 136–140.

[12] *Poems of Paul Hamilton Hayne.* Complete Edition. (Boston: D. Lothrop and Company, 1882), pp. 315–20. The poem first appeared in the Charleston *News and Courier,* December 18, 1877, p. 3, was reprinted by William Cullen Bryant, Simms's old friend, in the New York *Evening Post* on January 14, 1878, and came out in pamphlet form in February, 1878. Mrs. Augusta Simms Roach, Simms's eldest daughter, wrote Hayne on December 19: "You are the only one who could have written the 'Ode,' and you have done it well & with a heart full of love & a just appreciation of the genius of him you loved."

[13] Louisville, Kentucky *Sunday Argus,* January 7, 1883.

[14] Youth's Companion, 59 (January 21, 1886), 19–20.

[15] See, for example, Franklin T. Walker, "W. P. Trent: A Critical Bi-

ography" diss., George Peabody College, 1943, chapter 6, and John McCardell, "Trent's *Simms:* The Making of a Biography," *A Master's Due: Essays in Honor of David Herbert Donald,* ed. William J. Cooper, Jr., and others (Baton Rouge: Louisiana State University Press, 1985), 179–203.

[16] See Jay B. Hubbell, *The South in American Literature, 1607–1900* (Durham: Duke University Press, 1954), pp. 576–578, 579–582. Though Hubbell does not maintain that Hayne follows Simms on this point, his discussion of the matter clearly establishes Simms's priority. Hubbell's treatment of Charleston's response to Simms and Hayne is still the best available.

[17] It should also be noted that in the nineteenth century such verdicts were not necessarily meant to be unfavorable. See, for example, John Greenleaf Whittier's birthday tribute to Oliver Wendell Holmes in 1884: "To those who have enjoyed the privilege of his intimate acquaintance, the man himself is more than the author" (*The Critic,* n.s. II, [August 30, 1884], 108). Hayne's own tribute to Holmes appears on p. 104.

[18] For similar conclusions, see McCardell, pp. 189–190.

Simms's Failed Lecture Tour of 1856:
The Mind of the North

MIRIAM J. SHILLINGSBURG

On August 30, 1856, six weeks before he departed on his lecture tour in the North, Simms wrote to Senator James Orr referring to making his proposed trip, unless "the dissolution takes place before we look for it." Asking Orr to send him news of Washington, Simms alluded to the immediate reason for this regional devisiveness, for "between Butler's and Keitt's interest in cudgellings & courtships, I have not received a single public document from either of them this session."[1] Three months earlier Senator Butler's kinsman had caned the Senator from Massachusetts, and the sectional repercussions were felt all over the country. Simms advised Orr to shore up his sectional image, for his stand as a "national" man was being charged against him in South Carolina. Well before he left for this tour, then, Simms was aware of the potentially explosive character of the lectures he planned to deliver.

Simms had been an occasional lecturer in the South for many years and in early 1856 he was lecturing regularly in South Carolina. The first allusion to taking his lectures to the North appears in a letter to young Mary Lawson, daughter of his New York business manager, James Lawson. Simms casually remarked that "I think of trying a course of lectures at the North this coming winter. My own health requires that I should be less at the desk, & Augusta's [his daughter's] may be im-

183

proved by a Northern winter" (*Letters,* III, 423–424). The very next day, April 18, he mentioned to his long-time literary friend E. A. Duyckinck, who had just published the *Cyclopaedia of American Literature,* that he was "thinking seriously of preparing a couple or more of lectures suitable for the North" and asked Duyckinck's help in promoting such a scheme (*Letters,* III, 425). By the third day Simms had determined his subject matter: "I design one or two Lectures touching the scenery, the society, habits[,] manners, of the South, especially for your people & to establish better relations between North & South respectively. May this not be done," he wrote to Boston publisher J. T. Fields on April 19. Simms evidently wrote to his own publisher, J. S. Redfield, requesting advice on the tour, and Redfield must have offered to act as agent, for in a reply Simms thanked him for his "suggestion" and told Redfield that he had met "one Geo. Peckham . . . [who] broached the subject of Lectures to me, and gave me to understand that he was the Ruling Spirit for all such matters for the good city of Gotham," and would see that Simms received invitations (*Letters,* III, 430–431). On May 20, Simms wrote to J. R. Thompson, editor of the *Southern Literary Messenger,* asking his help in scheduling lectures in Virginia, for he was "called on several hands" to go north. In this letter to Thompson, Simms first suggested that the Northern lecture tour would be a welcome source of much-needed money: "I need to earn $3,000 per ann. apart from the plantation, to live decently in broadcloth."

It was on May 19 and 20, 1856, that Charles Sumner, Senator from Massachusetts, delivered to the Senate his speech, "The Crime against Kansas." On the first day, in an aside admittedly "not belonging to the argument," Sumner had likened the absent Senator Andrew P. Butler of South Carolina to Don Quixote whose chosen mistress, "though ugly to others, is always lovely to him; though polluted in the sight of the world, is chaste in his sight . . . the harlot of Slavery." Senator Stephen A. Douglas of Illinois whom Sumner called slavery's Sancho Panza[2] was reported to have muttered, "That damn fool will get himself killed by some other damn fool."[3] On the second day Sumner concluded his speech with allusions to Butler, Douglas, and Senator James Mason of Virginia. "Uncharitably referring to the effects of the slight labial paralysis from which the elderly South Carolina senator suffered," Sumner charged that "with incoherent phrases [he] discharged the loose expectoration of his speech, now upon her representative, and then upon her people." Without using the word, Sumner called a Butler a liar who "cannot ope his mouth, but out there flies a blunder."[4]

Then Sumner turned to South Carolina, rhetorically asking whether Butler had read the history of "its shameful imbecility from Slavery, confessed throughout the Revolution, followed by its more shameful assumptions for Slavery since. . . . It will be difficult to find any thing in the history of South Carolina [to compare with Kansas' fight for freedom.]. . . . Were the whole history of South Carolina blotted out of existence, from its very beginning down to the day of the last election of the senator to his present seat on this floor, civilization might lose—I do not say how little; but surely less than it has already gained by the example of Kansas. . . ."[5] Sumner then implied that South Carolina lacked scholarship, education, and even newspapers. His remarks made that state out to be unpatriotic and un-American, not only in 1856 but at least as far back as the Revolutionary War. It would be these charges that Simms would address in New York State, not the specific political bitternesses occurring in the Congress over whether Kansas should be slave or free.

By May 21, newspapers all over the country carried excerpts of the speech and editorial commentary on it, and South Carolina representative Preston S. Brooks studied the published version on May 21 before avenging his cousin, Senator Butler. But Simms, still at his plantation at Midway, seems not yet to have been aware of the speech, for on May 22 he replied to Northern historian Ben Lossing about his lecturing schedule, requesting "any hints in regard to this Lecturing business, which is new to me *as a business*. . . . My object," Simms explained, "will be to economize time and travel, & realize the largest possible pecuniary results. . . . But, as I am a man of large family, and so large needs, and 'one who has had losses,' I cannot merely travel. The Lecturing business seems to promise me that respite from the desk which I so much require, while affording me as liberal an income as I could possible acquire at the desk" (*Letters,* III, 434–435). Simms asked Lossing to inform him about fees, expenses, "and especially, what subjects would be most likely to please the Northern ear, from Southern lips. I propose to write two or three Lectures this summer. . . . I desire to select topics for these which will be fresh, suitable & within my range. You can enlighten me in this respect" (*Letters,* III, 435).

Meanwhile in Washington, Representative Brooks meditated his "punishment" of the Senator, and after the close of session in the early afternoon of May 22, Brooks addressed Sumner at his Senate desk: "I have read your speech twice over carefully. It is a libel on South Carolina, and Mr. Butler, who is a relative of mine."[6] The beating, which occurred in less than a minute, was so severe that the one-inch gold-headed gutta percha walking cane broke, and the Senator was "senseless as a corpse for several minutes, his head bleeding copiously from the frightful wounds, and the blood saturating his clothes."[7] Sumner soon regained consciousness, but he was so severely injured in the attack, especially psychically, that, although re-elected to the Senate, he never was able to return effectively to his regular work, either for Massachusetts or for the Republican party.[8]

Both Brooks and Sumner were hailed heroes by their respective constituents; "Bleeding Sumner" and "Bully Brooks" became rallying cries, while "fragments of [Brooks's] stick [were] begged for as *sacred relicts.*"[9] The New York *Tribune* sold Sumner's speech at twenty dollars a thousand, and perhaps a million copies were distributed.[10] It was practically impossible for any public figure, North or South, to remain aloof from the prevailing opinion in his region. Bostonian Edward Everett's refusal to serve as vice-president of a rally was considered approval of Brooks's action, and Everett's lecture invitations were withdrawn. Is it any wonder, then, that a South Carolinian would not be listened to in New York State?

There are no known Simms letters from the day of Brooks's attack until he wrote author and publisher William Carey Richards asking for suggestions on "some topics, such as you may suppose would be tolerable to Northern ears" including "moral, political, social, historial or what?" (*Letters,* VI, 163).

On June 27 Simms did not yet have enough invitations to "justify me in the enterprise," but he suggested to Ben Lossing the topics he had been using in his Southern tour: Poetry and the Practical, The Ideal and the Real, The Moral Character of Hamlet, The Ante-colonial History of the South, and The Choice of a Profession. (*Letters*, III, 437). Evidently Lossing did not encourage him in these topics, although Simms must have taken at least some of them to the North along with the three especially written for audiences there, for in Syracuse he was required to make a substitution.

Exactly what Simms thought of the Brooks-Sumner affair when it occurred in May is not known. But in September Simms wrote to his friend James H. Hammond complaining that

> Butler and Evans are flooding me with the attacks of the Northern Press on South Carolina. Butler says, "I have no time to answer them. It is the business of the Historian." But his blunderings have provoked them, & he is one of the victims in all the attacks. In brief he wants me to take up the cudgels and fight his battles. It is a pretty thing that one who has fed all his life at the treasury bowls, who is still feeding,—who is chosen for this very sort of warfare—should call upon me to do the business, whom he & and his fraternity have always contrived to keep without feed at all. (*Letters*, III, 446–447)

Simms's own poor health and family cares turned the proposed Northern jaunt into a "considerable sacrifice," as he wrote to James Lawson (*Letters,* III, 451). But his financial situation had become desperate, and "my earnings, rated at about $2000 per ann. are now beginning to be consumed for the support of the plantation" (*Letters,* III, 452).

Although some letters must be missing, and although it is clear that Simms was perfectly aware of the Brooks-Sumner attacks and the Northern newspaper opinion, it is also clear that he looked forward to seeing his friends in the North. He went with no overly patriotic Southern mission, and particularly not as the "fire-eater" of the Bully Brooks school, as he was called by certain newspapers. His intention was to inform Northerners about the Revolutionary War history of South Carolina in a lucrative forum, whose change of scene would be healthful to himself. He also believed that he would receive a fair hearing in New York, if not in Boston, and he wrote to historian George Bancroft, poet William Cullen Bryant, and others on his lecture committee, "I trust, I shall be able to disabuse the public of the North of many mistaken impressions which do us wrong. You will, I doubt not, be pleased if I shall succeed in this, since it is always grateful to the just and magnanimous nature to witness the ultimate ascendency of Truth" (*Letters,* III, 454). As a means of doing this, he officially offered two lectures on Marion, The Carolina Partisan, two lectures on the Appalachians, and one on South Carolina in the Revolution. The New York Committee selected the latter three.

The outlines of the failure of his tour have been readily available in the Simms *Letters* for thirty years, and some examination of the tour has been made by a few scholars in recent years.[11] In brief, Simms read "South Carolina in the Revolution" in Buffalo, Rochester, and New York, and a substitute in Syracuse, but over the Thanksgiving weekend he cancelled all further appearances, refunded his fees, and lost about $2,500. He returned to Midway, and confided in only a few friends until he was "specially requested" the following spring (1857) to explain the animosity between the two regions and to account for the early abandonment of his tour.

Simms's response was a lecture, "Antagonisms of the Social Moral. North and South," now housed still unpublished in the Charles Carroll Simms Collection. In addition to chronicling the failure of his trip, Simms, on the eve of the Civil War analyzed, for a Southern audience, the "mind of the North," the "moral" which made Northerners, he believed, unable to listen to the Southern viewpoint as it concerned both the present and the interpretation of the past. He used his personal history as a parable for the "politico-social relations of the two great sections . . . , now in absolute and direct antagonism. . . . As straws may . . . show the direction of the winds," he said, "so the simple career of an individual, may . . . indicate the courses of the political currents . . . which affect human communities."[12] His narrative would be, he said, instructive and profitable, and he warned of impending "mortal crisis," perhaps "the fiery furnace of . . . civil war" ("Antagonisms," p. 2). He admonished auditors "calmly and resolute [to] prepare" and "study all signs . . . which seem to be the harbingers of convulsion" (p. 2). To that end Simms promised them "no flourishes of rhetoric, [only] . . . a simple, plain, unvarnished tale of experience"; no "amusement," no "wit or fancy," no "gaudy declamations" (p. 2).

For thirty years, Simms had been an almost annual visitor to New York. His daughter Augusta had been educated intermittently in Massachusetts. His books were, since 1830, nearly all published in Philadelphia, and, when the publishing center shifted to New York about 1840, they were published there. He counted among his close long-time friends William Cullen Bryant, James Kirke Paulding, and James Lawson, as well as less intimate acquaintance with highly influential men in literature, history, theatre, and business. Now he went to take part in lecturing which was, to use Simms's words, "the popular mode of education at the North" which "exercises a vast influence upon the popular mind."[13] Believing that "the people of the North are surely not all hostile," and "thousands . . . will gladly listen to the truth" ("Antagonisms," pp. 3–4), he hoped to correct among the populace mistaken notions they had acquired from a few radical newspapers and politicians. He believed their "thousand mistakes & misrepresentations" to be "the result of mere ignorance" ("Antagonisms," pp. 5, 7), for the standard United States histories were written by New Englanders. Clearly Simms took his key word from Sumner's speech when he told Southerners:

It was especially important that the North should be disabused of the notion that the South *is imbecile*—imbecile because of her slave institutions—imbecile in war—unproductive in letters—deficient in all the proper agencies of civilization,—and so, incapable of defence against assaults. Upon these notions our enemies very strenuously insist, & every form of phrase, & through every popular medium—the press, the pulpit, the Poet and the Politician. A miserable paragraphist will prate of the intellectual, moral and military deficiencies of a region . . . whose wisdom, virtue, valour, eloquence, have established the government. . . . This babble about our imbecility . . . will be uttered every where, by the most miserable scribblers of a venal press, & fanatic pulpit—by flatulent orators & trading politicians. ("Antagonisms," pp. 7–8)

But in the autumn of 1856 what Simms had encountered, and was warning Southerners about, was hostility from the masses previously unimagined as he travelled in intellectual circles. He found that this "jealous, grasping, arrogant race" now had "every motive for aggression and assault" ("Antagonisms," p. 8) because it had been taught that the South "is at once rich in wealth and poor in spirit, . . . feeble of will; wanting in energy and courage; . . . & timid of resolve." Besides correcting mistaken ideas about the past, Simms also hoped to define present resources and "to disabuse our neighbors of the notion that the South was imbecile" ("Antagonisms," p. 10). Simms particularly avoided the topic of slavery because, he explained, people could no longer discuss the issue rationally. But the very avoidance evoked abuse from some newsmen who said Simms omitted it "because it exposed our asserted imbecility" ("Antagonisms," p. 12), a charge Simms refuted to Southerners by a long digression on the relationship between slaves, masters, and crop-growing during the Revolution.[14]

Three days after Sumner was first caned, his physician had testified that he suffered "nothing but flesh wounds," and now six months later his political opponents still "found something suspicious about his invalidism," since he was able at strategic moments to give a speech or attend a parade.[15] Simms, for his part, admitted both privately and on the platform that he had alluded to "Sumner's attack on S.C. as that of a deliberate & wanton malignant" in his November lectures (*Letters,* III, 474). He asked his Southern audience, "Was he not himself a wanton assailant? Did not his coldblooded, venomous, deliberate assault upon our State, so entirely gratuitous, invite and justify retort?" ("Antagonisms," p. 21). Simm's allusions to Sumner (he did not mention Brooks) were partially extemporaneous, and only an imperfect account can be deduced, but the language is heated. He did say Sumner's only purpose in maligning South Carolina was "to goad and mortify . . . a hated party!" He wondered whether the "same malignity which made the assault . . . so wholly gratuitous" might also have "darkened the moral vision . . . , obscured his perceptions;—made obtuse his faculty for discrimination between fact and falsehood" (*Letters,* III, 522). Even though Sumner's colleagues had counselled against it, Simms now told his Southern audience, "Having sharpened his javelin, and anointed it with venom from his concoction, no human argument, no social scruples, no Christian virtue, could keep his vanity from launching his bolt at the bosom of his victim. . . . Why should I forbear him? Because he had been cudgelled?" ("Antagonisms," p. 22).

Simms reported a mixed reception in Buffalo, his first stop, where he spoke to about twelve hundred. Simms thought that his committee's having chosen "South Carolina in the Revolution," under the "warm & vexing excitements" caused by Sumner's speech and Brooks's retaliation, "argued favorably for the public mind" ("Antagonisms," p. 18). Yet even the moderate press objected to Simms's comparisons, which, he said, were made only to answer false impressions. For instance, historians had claimed that beleaguered Charlestonians had failed to defend their city, to which Simms answered that "they had done much more than Boston, New York or Philadelphia," all of which were "seized & held by the British, without standing siege at all" ("Antagonisms," p. 20). The more radical papers, however, employed "beastly language" for which Simms was totally unprepared. He was described "as a Southern pauper, 'seeking cold charity in Northern lecture rooms'" (*Letters,* III, 472, 462) and called in as a "foreign fiddler, with his dancing dogs & monkey, to amuse them" ("Antagonisms," p. 23).

In Rochester, Simms found his committee "laboring under considerable uneasiness" at the Buffalo reports, and some wanted to change the topic. Simms reluctantly offered, but, because the history "has been so shamefully misrepresented," he wanted to "set some matters right . . . which have been grossly perverted . . . [by] malignant misrepresentations. . . . I deny the claims set up for Massachusetts as more pure, or true, loyal & valiant than other colonies, in the great struggle of the Revolution. But what of that? Is Massachusetts to be held more sacred from assault in N.Y. than South Carolina? . . . Surely, New York, at least, should be an open arena, as between Massachusetts & South Carolina" ("Antagonisms", pp. 26–27). This last appeal—that New York was neutral territory and fair-minded—seems to have struck home, for one of the editors present agreed and threatened to denounce the whole procedure if the lecture were changed. Some reviewers in Rochester (no doubt also at this meeting) suggested the same thing: "As we should listen to a Parker, a Sumner or a Phillips, if they chose to lecture upon Massachusetts and the Revolution, so should we listen to Simms."[16]

Simms admitted to warm extemporaneous remarks about the "false relations" between North and South, asking his audience to assure the continuation of the Union by "truth & justice & magnanimity," maintaining "sacred social sympathies, founded upon faith, good feeling & real kindnesses" ("Antagonisms," p. 28). These sentiments were intermittently applauded by the crowd of about a thousand. However, Simms warned Southerners, most of Northern society is "warped & tortured . . . wild, disordered, anarchical, ready for chaos and disruption, . . . marked by a frivolity, a levity, which makes it reluctant to grapple seriously, with serious things . . ." ("Antagonisms," p. 29). This he attributed to their "great & sudden prosperity," "lack of veneration," "refusing to recognize anything as sacred," "morbid self esteem," "trampling upon all authority"; they had become a people who live "wholly for show & appearances [and] lack individuality." ("Antagonisms," pp. 29–30). After the lecture, Simms was entertained by a "large & intelligent [party], consisting mostly of clever active, young men . . . desirous of the truth, . . . progress, proper performance, and free from the malignant impulses of fanaticism" ("Antagonisms," p. 29). These gentlemen possessed "intelligence, good sense, and good feeling," and Simms "spoke frankly of our issues, North and South, . . . more freely . . . than . . . with [the] audience" ("Antagonisms," p. 30).

The Buffalo papers preceded Simms also to Syracuse where his local committee refused to allow the South Carolina lecture.[17] In Syracuse Simms first encountered the Underground Railroad: while conversing with a man who assured him that Northerners "*loved* the South, . . . its generosity, hospitality and other vulgar domestic virtues," someone approached with the news that several fugitive slaves had arrived just that night. Simms warned Southerners that this was an "institution, openly avowed and existing, for carrying on a regular warfare" against other states in the Union, in spite of the "most sacred bonds of law." He called it a "monstrous anomaly . . . which beholds, without rebuke or remedy, the perpetual warfare of one section upon the rights of another" ("Antagonisms," p. 31). From here on Simms stressed the theme (as he had done to some extent in "South Carolina in the Revolution") that Southerners tolerate from the North transgressions which "would be cause of war between nations living under independent dynasties" ("Antagonisms," p. 32). And, he warned, it is not a despicable minority of fanatics, as the North would have Southerners believe; rather they "rule the country, and these virtuous lovers of the South have neither the courage nor the will to oppose them." The North cherishes the Union only because the South contributes to its material prosperity.

New York City, which he knew well, Simms believed "should naturally afford a sufficient body of highminded people, solicitous of right & justice; calm and judicious; thoughtful and earnest; who will confer upon it tone & character, and interpose, to prevent fanaticism" ("Antagonisms," p. 33). He believed that the intellectual men who had invited him presaged the tone of his reception; but he was wrong. Letter-writers had commented on Buffalo's reports of offense and had employed a "common method of assault . . . to describe [Southerners] as an insolent & haughty aristocracy, who show themselves especially scornful of all the *working* classes" ("Antagonisms," pp. 36–37). His committee requested that he edit his lecture, and he satisfied them by "striking out something, here & there, which prejudice and suspicion might construe into gratuitous sarcasm" ("Antagonisms," p. 38). He insisted that the content was nothing but "proper Historical criticism" although delivered with an "occasional sharpness in the tone" and that it "*was* warmly Southron" ("Antagonisms," p. 38).

But by evening only about 150 people could be found who were willing to listen to Simms. The "vigorous, powerful, concentrated party, fanatical of mood, despotic of will" had cowed the people. Simms's own analysis was that his great mistake was failing to take account of the election which the Republicans had lost (*Letters,* III, 467). However, he did not intend to "engage in . . . the miserable politics of today. I know no subject so little calculated to provoke my consideration, as the small traffic of politics, in the hands of hireling partisans. It is an outrage upon sacred histories which I resent" (*Letters,* III, 522–523). A "philosophical view of the facts based upon a knowledge of military as well as civil affairs" would correct the mistaken impression most Northerners had of South Carolinians' role in the Revolution, Simms believed.[18]

Papers the following day repeated the "brutal assaults" of the Buffalo reports, and claimed Simms was "seeking to do, in the historical field, what Brooks had done in the physical. I was only another sort of bully, dispatched to hector the Northern People in their own homes" ("Antagonisms," p. 41). Horace Greeley's *New York Daily Tribune* was particularly vituperative, referring to South Carolina as "the richest of all the colonies" and calling Simms's interpretation "misapprehension or misrepresentation" filled with "simply ridiculous . . . misstatements."[19] Elsewhere in the same issue editors sarcastically printed an article "for the benefit of the public, and the special edification of Mr. W. Gilmore Simms." It included some passages from the Secret Journals of the Congress of the Confederation which suggested the British were attempting to incite the slaves to "revolt or desert." A proposal (which was not adopted) to reimburse owners, then emancipate and give fifty dollars to "every negro who shall well and faithfully serve as a soldier to the end" of the Revolution was put forward by Governor John Rutledge, General Isaac Huger, and the Southern delegates to the convention.[20] The *Tribune* editorial then suggested that Simms should "henceforth include those gentlemen among the 'ignorant maligners' of his State, to whom he refers in his lecture." In truth, however, Simms had, as he explained to his Southern audience, specifically avoided the issue of slavery, a claim corroborated by the report of the New York lecture in the *Tribune,* the *Herald,* and the manuscript preserved by A. S. Salley and printed as an Appendix to Volume 3 of Simms's *Letters.*[21] It was only Senator Sumner who had brought up slavery as the mark of South Carolina's "imbecility." The *Tribune* was correct when it wrote that this was "the head and front" of Mr. Sumner's offense against South Carolina, and was malicious when it implied that Simms was dishonest in omitting a plan which was not adopted, and which, as Rutledge proposed it, would have given arms to the blacks so that they would not revolt at British instigation, thus becoming allies with the enemy.

The next afternoon Simms's committee informed him that "such was the public hostility, such the rancour occasioned by my revelations, and by what they held to be my attacks on the North, that they—the Committee—could neither sell nor give away the Tickets;—the common answer to all their attempts . . . being . . . a wholesale imprecation on S.C. and all that comes from her" (*Letters,* III, 472). On November 21 Simms wrote some fifty official letters cancelling the remainder of the tour. The papers of November 22 claimed that the second lecture was not delivered because "thirteen gentlemen and four ladies" including reporters comprised the whole audience."[22] But Simms pointed out to his Southern listeners, as he had written to James Henry Hammond, that the *Herald* was "a budget of the most foul & reckless lies." As Simms said, the lectures were indeed "badly advertised," the second "not advertised at all in a single paper. . . . The night was one of storm & rain," and "the church was unopened" (*Letters,* III, 467–468). "Invention was thus coerced in aid of the fact. . . . and there was quite a howl of triumph over the event!" Simms warned Southerners that one could "only obtain a hearing through means of your own party, and *the South has no party in the North!*" The papers "denounc[ed Simms] as a Southern bully, [and] insult[ed] the very people who c[a]me to hear" ("Antagonisms," p. 45).

As he explained to a Boston correspondent, "My subjects, and birthplace, seem to have been so sufficiently provocative in themselves, as to establish prejudices in advance of my appearance, which are utterly hostile to any idea of successful usefulness" (*Letters,* VI, 168). While still in New York he wrote to a friend in Mobile that he was "driven away . . . in consequence of the deep & bitter hostility expressed here, in regard to the very subjects of my Lectures" (*Letters,* VI, 171). When

195

pressured to keep an engagement, he insisted that his topics were "unseasonably brought before a Northern audience," although "at another period, perhaps" he would return with a different program (*Letters,* VI, 173). "As a gentleman, they left me hardly any choice, I had simply to button my coat, close my portfolio, and quietly withdraw" (*Letters,* VI, 175). A measure of the vitriol and distortion may be seen after Simms was in South Carolina, when the "family magazine of literature and news," the *New York Weekly Times,* reported the stale news that Simms "complains that 'prejudice has preceded his lectures'" and "he does not wish to address 'unruly audiences or empty benches'. . . ." Their answer was that "he has been heard with attention and respect. . . . If he enters the lists he must be prepared to receive the blows, as well as give them. . . . Senator Sumner took one side of the question which Mr. Simms presents, and was savagely beaten. . . . Mr. Simms takes the other side, and talks to empty benches . . . the more civil of the two."[23]

Simms knew that if he stuck to his "Southern" material he was merely a "new brand of pitch pine to fling into the [party] furnace" (*Letters,* III, 467) so that "the fires by which they keep the party warm, may not burn down" ("Antagonisms," p. 47). Even when the Young Men's Institute in New Haven, "by a decided vote of an intelligent auditory," pledged to give Simms "a candid hearing,"[24] he declined; for he did not wish to do what others did: "seize upon some of the popularized topics, in the hope of making a little capital for himself" ("Antagonisms," p. 47). Besides, it had become clear that the "little societies . . . can in no way determine for their audiences" ("Antagonisms," p. 46). In a second letter to the Young Men's Institute, Simms again declined to be "brutally described . . . as a Southern pauper, 'seeking cold charity in Northern lecture rooms'" and could therefore accept no pay for his services. Furthermore, he was "not a politician, not familiar with the weapons used by this class of people, and my self-respect forbids me to enter a field in which I am utterly weaponless."[25] But by then Simms's "blood was in a ferment," his "*heart* . . . was *slavishly* in these topics of S.C." and his "mind followed [his] heart" (*Letters,* III, 469). His withdrawal was deliberate. As he told his Southern friends, "Though wanting in riches, I had never in all my life, surrendered a single sentiment of my soul, a single conviction of my mind, a single feeling of my heart, in the pursuit of gain. . . . why should I now, at the mellow [age] of fifty . . . ?" ("Antagonisms," p. 48).

On November 24 the *Herald* carried a long diatribe against "itinerant" lecturers who "make out a very good living . . . upon the fruits of other men's labors." They give "but little in return for the harvests which they make," by writing "the two or three lectures which are to form their stock in trade . . . , compiled from elementary scientific treatises, the reviews . . . in the periodicals, or the reports of [other] lecturers. . . . In vain," the *Herald* opined, "we look for an original idea or a little novelty in the language. . . . Both ideas and forms of expression are plundered by wholesale. . . . Where they find that they cannot control the action of the press they resort to the expedient of reading them in so hurried and indistinct a manner that neither reporters nor audience can make anything out of them." After another paragraph of general complaint, the *Herald* suggested that "whilst on this subject, we must not omit a passing allusion to the lecture lately delivered in this city by Mr. Gilmore Simms." [26]

For Southerners, Simms interpreted the treatment he had received from the Northern press as similar to the gratuitous maligning which his home state had received from Sumner. At first, reviewers attacked his topic as unsuitable; but he felt they should not have censored him, even if just to keep up appearances. Then, seeing their error, they decided the lecture was inferior because he had only put together a lot of commonly known information. No doubt he was thinking of the skewed implication in the *Herald*. But Simms rightly pointed out that if his material were so familiar, why was it so different from Sumner's, and furthermore, if so common, why did it enrage them so? As he began to analyze the misrepresentations in the newspaper reviews, Simms's Southron temperature rose, and almost for the first time he resorted to metaphoric language. The North loves the South "as the tick, the cow;—as the leech the vein" ("Antagonisms," p. 52). Simms insisted that "as I forebore politics, I fancied that I should have toleration"

("Antagonisms," p. 55). But Simms discovered that Northerners were "the most intolerant people in the world, and have been so from the days of Cotton Mather" ("Antagonisms," p. 53).

Simms concluded his explanation to his fellow Southerners by drawing out the moral of his personal history. He had learned first-hand what his compatriots did not know—that "all classes are united against you" by newspapers and pulpits, schoolrooms and parlors ("Antagonisms," p. 58). "Millions of desperate men, whom a grinding daily necessity, makes reckless of every consideration of law, justice and the constitution" ("Antagonisms," p. 58), are taught to believe that the abolition of slavery will open "boundless" employment for them. To create sectional parties would sunder the Union, but the national parties lied to the people. While his compatriots believed the politicians who told them that the North was only having fun with the South, Simms believed the abolitionists and counselled destroying them. If he should be wrong, he advised Southerners, they should certainly "make . . . a very neat apology, in the best English;—but, be sure, that you have first knock'd [them] down!" ("Antagonisms," p. 61).

This long unpublished lecture, "Antagonism of the Social Moral. North and South" is an important document especially for two reasons. First, it contains the observations of a respected and influential Southerner who was not a politician concerning the hostility developing between the regions a half decade before the Civil War. Simms's main conclusion was that the general public in New York was materialistic, intolerant, and unwilling to think for themselves. This was an unexpected insight because his personal friends among New Yorkers were, like Simms himself, generous and open-minded. Simms wished to awaken his Southern acquaintances to this overwhelming intolerance, and, since it now seemed to him that reconciliation through truth, justice, and magnanimity was not possible, he advised aggressive propaganda and preparation for armed conflict. Partisan politics was the mode of the day, and Simms had not realized that.

The lecture also is important for information which can help in understanding Simms's later works, written during the most obscure portion of his career. His new awareness that audiences were most content in hearing "popularized topics"—not in receiving information or interpretations which might cause them to rethink—confirmed him in his convictions and sentiments, in short, in guarding his personal integrity. This refusal to give pre-digested lectures caused his immediate rejection by the Northerners and had repercussions through the remainder of his writings. It is interesting that, although Simms stuck to his Southern subjects, he seems to have turned away from romance after the war and toward more "realistic" stories, including greater use of the lower-classes as central characters. Yet even then he found himself in the uncomfortable position of having to write for magazines like *The Old Guard,* whose audience he found to be low-toned. Possibly even after the War his Southern subjects, like his Northern lectures, provoked enough prejudice that he could scarcely find other publishers. Though Simms did not know it in 1856, attitudes in the press about his lectures would also be applied to his fiction. But he was correct in understanding that his personal experience in the North was a precursor of the ominous events of the next decade.

Notes

[1]Mary C. Simms Oliphant, Alfred Taylor Odell, and T. C. Duncan Eaves, eds., *The Letters of William Gilmore Simms* (Columbia, S.C.: University of South Carolina Press, 1952–1956, 1982), III, 440–441. Hereinafter referred to as *Letters.*

[2]Charles Sumner, "The Crime against Kansas," D. A. Harsha, *The Life of Charles Sumner* (New York: Dayton and Burdick, 1856), p. 170.

[3]David Donald, *Charles Sumner and the Coming of the Civil War* (New York: Knopf, 1965), p. 286.

[4]Donald, pp. 286–287.

[5]Donald, pp. 288–291.

[6]Donald, p. 294.

[7]Donald, pp. 296–297. This information comes from House of Representatives records.

[8]His symptoms recurred mainly when he turned his attention to public responsibilities. Modern diagnosis of his lingering mala-

dies suggests that, although his suffering was genuine, it was post-traumatic syndrome of "psychogenic" origin. Donald, p. 336.

[9] Donald, p. 304.

[10] Donald, p. 302.

[11] Merrill Christopherson, "Simms's Northern Lecture Tour: A Tragedy," *Southern Speech Journal,* 36 (Winter, 1970), 139–51; Miriam J. Shillingsburg, "The Southron as American: William Gilmore Simms," *Studies in the American Renaissance,* ed. Joel C. Myerson, (Boston: Twayne Publishers, 1980), 409–23.

[12] Simms, "Antagonisms of the Social Moral. North and South." Unpublished Lecture in the Charles Carroll Simms Collection of the South Caroliniana Library, University of South Carolina; hereinafter referred to as "Antagonisms."

My especial thanks are extended to the Editorial Board of the Writings of William Gilmore Simms for permission to quote from this manuscript.

[13] *Letters,* VI, 161.

[14] In "The Crime Against Kansas" Sumner had asked whether Senator Butler had "forgotten [South Carolina's] shameful imbecility from Slavery, confessed throughout the Revolution" (Harsha, p. 288). Halfway through "South Carolina in the Revolution" Simms echoed Sumner's "imbecility" twice; and he concluded by repeating "imbecile" five times in the last paragraph, threatening, "We scorn the imbecile; we do not contend with them! We crush them under foot. . . ." (*Letters,* III, 548).

[15] Donald, pp. 313, 322.

[16] Rochester *Evening Union,* November 14, 1856.

[17] Although it is not known which lecture he read, the "wholly innocuous" substitute ("Antagonisms," p. 31) may have been "The Choice of a Profession," which he had called "a favorite with me" when he had offered it to a Boston contact as late as November 4 (*Letters,* VI, 167).

[18] *Morning Courier and New-York Enquirer,* November 19, 1856.

[19] *New York Daily Tribune,* November 19, 1856.

[20] *New York Daily Tribune,* November 20, 1856.

[21] Further, the *Tribune* of November 24 charged Simms for making "no mention whatever of her negroes, who, after all, were her greatest drawback. . . . This is the more noticeable on the part of Mr. Simms, since it was this particular drawback of Slavery, alluded to in the speech of Mr. Sumner, which drew down upon him the ferocious attack of Bully Brooks . . . to which Mr. Simms also saw fit to allude . . . in terms reproachful to Mr. Sumner, and, we must be allowed to say, very

little creditable either to the head, the heart, or the taste of Simms." In the Charles Carroll Simms Collection is a lengthy addendum, apparently for the Southern auditors of "South Carolina in the Revolution," explaining the role of the slaves in the war—the great "omission" from his Northern version of the lecture.

[22] *New York Herald,* November 22, 1856.

[23] *New York Weekly Times,* November 29, 1856.

[24] *New York Herald,* November 29, 1856; rpt. from New Haven *Paladium.*

[25] *New York Herald,* November 29, 1859; rpt. from New Haven *Paladium.*

[26] *New York Herald,* November 24, 1856.

Biography and the Southern Mind: William Gilmore Simms

JOHN McCARDELL

"In general," wrote W. J. Cash in his influential *The Mind of the South,* "the intellectual and aesthetic culture of the Old South was a superficial and jejune thing, borrowed from without and worn as a political armor and badge of rank; and hence (I call the authority of old Matthew Arnold to bear me witness) not a true culture at all."[1] This governing premise, or something very much like it, has long shaped what passes for the conventional wisdom on the subject of intellectual life in the nineteenth-century South. The story of the Southern mind between the Revolution and the Civil War, according to this view, is simple and sad. It is a narrative road that leads from the heights of Monticello, across the black belt, to the lowlands of Red River, from elevated discussions of the rights of man to nattering over the rights of states to, finally, the perverse exertions of proslavery polemicists. Isolated on his plantation, the Southerner lacked the stimulation afforded by urban life. Enervated by leisure, he consumed second-rate literature and half-baked ideas indiscriminately. Smothered by the ethos of slavery, he turned from thinking to mere feeling. His mind grew narrowed, his emotions more sensitive, and his intellectual endeavors, such as they were, became hopelessly, embarrassingly limited to illogical defenses of immoral, anachronistic institutions and values. Having thus tidily disposed of what one recent critic has called "a region of literary reaction,"[2] the scholar of ideas may then feel free to take his readers and listeners to places where American literature was being produced and American ideas were being promulgated and refined— anywhere, that is, except the South.

The persistence of this conventional wisdom has a variety of explanations, perhaps the most significant resulting from the vicissitudes of geography. This particular problem has had manifold consequences for the development and treatment of Southern literature. Unlike compact New England, the South sprawls across 1,500 miles of varied terrain. The region has never possessed a single urban center or cultural marketplace but rather a number of smaller such settings. In other words, where nineteenth-century New England had Boston, the South had Baltimore, Richmond, Charleston, New Orleans, Mobile, and Memphis. The potential for competition, and diffusion, was thus markedly greater. The home market, problem enough in matters economic, had its intellectual equivalent. There was no single publishing center, no single literary community to which the aspiring Southern writer or thinker might turn for the sort of automatic exposure and visibility that New England provided. Nor was there a sizable, concentrated market for published material. For these reasons, ironically, though Southern literary output was probably as varied in type as it was in quality (and in both cases more so than in other regions), it had constantly to struggle for recognition. Some writers, resigning themselves to this reality, cultivated Northern audiences and publishers. Most of William Gilmore Simms's best known fiction, most of Paul Hamilton Hayne's best verse, to cite but two examples, were published in Boston or New York. Perhaps it is only coincidental that these two men were generally recognized as the South's leading literary lights.

To considerations of geography might be added those of historical accident. The first serious attempts to write the history of American literature occurred in the latter stages of the nineteenth century. Triumphant nationalism produced a steady stream of work seeking to define an American literary tradition and set critical standards for evaluating past and present American authors. Inevitably the Civil War and its outcome influenced these activities. One side had won the war, one had lost. And to the victor went the spoils, not the least of which was the assumption of the rightness of its cause. Nation had triumphed over section, equality over slavery, light over darkness, North over South. It was easy enough to make this neat equation. What came before the war must surely have foreordained its outcome, and, that being so, Southerners, like Tories ("whig" historians often made this linkage), must have possessed some fundamental flaw, which made the outcome of this irrepressible conflict inevitable. Southerners, groping for an explanation of defeat, were as inclined to seek flaws in their past, which had so violently disrupted their natural evolution as a society (this was the age of Social Darwinism after all). As a result, the definition of American literature, and the terms by which the stature of individual writers and works were to be determined, fell into the hands of scholars and publishers in a particular section of the country possessing a distinct and at times parochial point of view, which, in heady triumph, assumed without dispute the mantle of nationalism. As a further result, the term "literature," which might more properly have been broadly understood, came instead to mean a particular kind of literature, which, not surprisingly, had flourished in that part of the country that was defining the critical standards. The imaginative writer became the quintessential American writer. The writer of social or political commentary, the critical reviewer, the teller of frontier tales, the polemicist, received brief, barely polite, attention.

This development put Southern writers in the late nineteenth century in an awkward position. To have their work accepted by the now dominant Northern publishing houses, Southern writers were forbidden, according to one influential editor, "any expression of the old hostility."[3] A whole generation, grateful for an outlet, accepted the terms, received encouragement, and prospered. Whether the abandonment of a distinctive sectionalism was motivated by circumstance or conviction matters less than the result, which witnessed some of the most withering criticism of the antebellum South flowing from the pens of young, fully reconstructed Southerners. George W. Cable, for instance, wrote not so subtle works critical of antebellum race relations. And William Peterfield Trent's first book was a biography of Simms, which summarized the debilitating effect that life in the Old South had upon the mind: "It was a life affording few opportunities to talents that did not lie in certain beaten grooves. It was a life gaining its intellectual nourishment largely from abroad [hence in some way un-American],—a life that choked all investigation that did not tend to conserve existing institutions and opinions."[4] Both Cable and Trent soon removed to the North, where their views were warmly received.

By about 1900, then, treatments of Southern intellectual activity, colored by the outcome of the war, came to form a logical circle around a critical consensus summed up by the Brahmin scholar Barrett Wendell: "Up to the Civil War, the South had produced hardly any writing which expressed more than a pleasant sense that standard models are excellent."[5] Dissenters from this opinion who might not have viewed the South as intellectually barren, because their work was outside popular late-nineteenth-century critical thought, found this occasionally hostile circle impenetrable.

Once critics, editors, and publishers had defined the terms, texts that did not fit dropped from sight. One by one even those few imaginative writers from outside New England went out of print, joining those of their contemporaries whose better work had been done in other fields of literary endeavor. By century's end one sought in vain for readily available editions of John P. Kennedy or A. B. Longstreet. Even the works of the prolific Simms were published from aging plates that soon were no longer usable. Relegated to the dustbin of American literary history, antebellum Southern writers (the term "antebellum" was in its own way damning) became, at best, quaint relics given passing reference in textbooks or perhaps half a class lecture in survey courses, accompanied by much hand wringing and moralizing about the fate of societies who would not keep abreast of truth.

Succeeding generations, increasingly preoccupied with literature distinctively American, treated the south no differently. Summarizing a life's work given to arguing the South's place in American literary history, Jay B. Hubbell, trained by

Trent, remarked in 1954 that "if circumstances had been more propitious, the literary achievement of the Southern states would have been greater."[6] Capping the thought of this generation was, of course, Cash's classic, published in 1941. Clearly the reigning cultural mores, in the heyday of New Deal liberalism, which tended to view the South as a persistent "problem," limited consideration of nineteenth-century writers. Meanwhile the historians of the period, for the most part, accepted the verdict pronounced by Cash and others, repeated it, and hurried on to other subjects, such as slavery (bad), plantations (debilitating), and the absence of dissent (lamentable). As Michael O'Brien has aptly put it, the South continued to function as "an excluding system of discourse."[7]

Perhaps for these reasons, the study of nineteenth-century Southern intellectual history is still in its infancy. A long and robust life lies ahead. The evidence seems to confirm O'Brien's recent prediction that the field now stands where Puritan studies stood at the advent of Perry Miller. Numerous recent forays—biographies of James Henry Hammond, Nathaniel Beverley Tucker, George Frederick Holmes, and Hugh Swinton Legaré, Edmund Ruffin's diary, and assorted monographs on theology, education, and social thought—suggest that within another generation our thinking will have been transformed.[8]

This latest scholarship makes a series of simple suggestions that are nonetheless, in the context of the past century, audacious. Let us consider, it urges, seriously and at face value, what Southerners had to say about themselves and their world. Let us reconsider, it continues, our understanding of what constitutes literature. Let us then try to grasp anew what the texture of Southern intellectual life may have been. Let us dare to discover, finally, that that life may have had a great deal more complexity, vitality, and substance than has been previously supposed. Then and only then might we make intelligent and informed judgments concerning the stature of individual writers and the importance of Southern intellectual achievement.

Until the texts themselves have been resurrected and disseminated and until the social and economic context has been reassembled and analyzed, such judgments regarding stature or significance would obviously be premature. That work is now going forward and, though it is still far from complete, contributes to and draws from such speculation as constitutes the remainder of this essay.

—

And what remains is perhaps best understood as a prospectus, not unlike the exercise in which graduate students must engage before commencing a major writing project. One is permitted in such an exercise, I trust, a certain degree of latitude so long as he remains mindful of one of William Gilmore Simms's favorite literary citations, from Book III of Spenser's *Faerie Queene:* "Be bold, be bold, be bold—be not TOO bold."[9] It is timely and appropriate as well to recall David Herbert Donald's admonition of twenty-five years ago in the preface to his biography of Charles Sumner: "If biography is to have a useful function in the historical craft, perhaps it is to steer us away from cosmic and unanswerable questions to the intricacies of reality."[10] The central questions are thus framed: why study the life of William Gilmore Simms? what might the study of this "intricate reality" tell us in response to the "cosmic and unanswerable" questions of intellectual life in the Old South?

To begin, though it may go without saying, the historian of cultural, intellectual, and political life in mid-nineteenth-century America might profitably study the career of William Gilmore Simms. On virtually every issue of the period, Simms, the South Carolina novelist, poet, historian, critic, editor, and man of affairs, ventured an influential opinion. His astonishing productivity was unmatched—at least one volume a year, and frequently more, every year from 1832 to 1860—and won him acclaim as the South's leading man of letters.

Generations of Simms scholars have subjected this enormous output to intense and illuminating critical scrutiny. These students, mostly concerned about Simms's literary stature, have focused mainly on the relationship between the author's South Carolina residence and the quality of his writing. Trent, Simms's only biographer, contended in 1892 that the stifling intellectual atmosphere in aristocratic South Carolina prohibited Simms from ever producing a major work of American literature. Subsequent shorter studies by Vernon Louis Parrington (1926), John Higham (1943), and William R. Taylor (1961) have been in essential agreement with Trent, adding that Simms's humble social origins forced him to prostitute his artistic talents in order to win acceptance by the Charleston elite. In numerous essays, C. Hugh Holman and Louis Rubin, though denying the status argument, have concurred that there was something about life in the South that kept Simms from fulfilling his literary potential.[11]

Recently, more attention has been paid to Simms's other writings and activities. Jon L. Wakelyn (1973) ignores the fiction to concentrate instead on the writer's public political role. Wakelyn emphasizes Simms's apparent conviction that he must give repeated public expression to the values and political beliefs of his native region. That task became ever more demanding as a distinct sense of Southern nationalism developed during the 1850s. As a result, concludes Wakelyn, "Simms sacrificed his art willfully to an active public career. His best work of art was his own public life."[12] Drew Gilpin Faust (1979) places Simms in the context of a small "sacred circle" of Virginia and Carolina intellectuals seeking a proper role for the man of mind in a world that paid him little heed.[13]

Any biographer of Simms must of course take this extensive bibliography into account. At the same time we must, as the most recent scholarship has, take the man and his times as they were rather than as we might wish them to have been. I would offer three propositions, in the form of chronological subsections in a proposed biography, as a way of shedding new light on the life and times of William Gilmore Simms. These titles are drawn from lectures Simms frequently delivered and they suggest the central themes in the intricate reality of Simms's life.

1. The Choice of a Profession (1806–1836).

Simms's decision to try to make his living as a professional writer was crucial. No other American, with the possible exception of Irving, had attempted it when Simms made his decision to try. The publishing industry, like the profession of writer, like the nation itself, was not at all well defined in the 1820s and 1830s. The idea of being a professional writer in Jacksonian America was novel indeed, partly because the work itself did not pay regularly, partly too because social convention required that a man "DO" something with his life. In a world on the move and on the make with an emphasis on getting ahead and producing more, a professional writer was a rare, irrelevant being. Yet Simms rejected the law and fulltime journalism to take that chance, and throughout his life the choice of a profession was a recurring theme in his writing. Several examples illustrate the point. On June 11, 1830, coincidentally forty years to the day from his death, Simms composed a possible epitaph:

> We sometimes since considered the great mistake of men, in the pursuit of happiness, of which pleasure may be held subsidiary, to consist generally in their proposing to themselves at an early stage in life, the attainment of some one single object, upon which the acquirement of this imaginary state of felicity was supposed to depend. They set out with a determination to reach a certain point. They place happiness as they do pleasure, at the termination of a certain distance. Some are more liberal than others in fixing this distance . . . and all arrive in time at the goal not to find the object they have sought for, but in her place the awful sentence "you have employed a long life in seeking that which at its termination you discover to have been elusive and unreal." There is no further time for search—the golden round has eluded the clutch of the wretch, to whose hopes and fears alike, death puts a common termination.[14]

Simms believed that the proper vocation was one that chose the man. Writing of the Chevalier Bayard's choice of a profession, Simms noted, "He obeyed an instinct. It was not that he chose war as his vocation—the vocation had chosen him. His natural endowments required him to go and be a soldier."[15] And so the artist pursued his vocation, however unconventional or unrewarding it might be. In 1849 Simms observed, "Nay, what were the real value of the tribute of acknowledgment, were the world to make free and full confession of the benefits received? Would that be sufficiently compensative for the performance? It is not intended that it should be. The essence of compensation to man, for good and great works upon earth, is to be found in the performance itself. It is in the feeling that he does, is doing, and has done, that the worker finds his reward."[16] Simms recognized that those who chose the profession of artist chose also work that brought little material compensation or public acclaim. This knowledge must be weighed against his frequent laments that neither Charleston nor South Carolina appreciated him or his work. The evidence seems to indicate that much of this protestation, accepted literally by his descendants and those scholars in whom they confided (chiefly Trent), reflected neither the reality nor Simms's perception of the reality but rather the pose of a man who saw himself as an intellectual and sought to distance himself by adopting the language and outlook of the detached artist, which, in point of fact, he emphatically was not.

2. Poetry and the Practical (1836–1850s).

But the choice of a profession eased neither the internal nor the external pressures upon Simms. Externally he remained obsessed by society's demands that a man be "useful," a word that repeatedly turns up in his work of the 1840s. "Usefulness, understood in its enlarged, and proper sense," Simms wrote in 1849, "covers the entire tract of Christian obligation. I am not arguing for the vulgar doctrine of utilitarianism. I said usefulness, in its enlarged and proper sense, in which the Poet, in all probability, occupies the highest position as social benefactor. He is the father of the profoundest philosophy. He speaks for our noblest nature. His very language belongs to a condition which humanity may understand and feel, but cannot ordinarily use."[17]

Simms argued repeatedly that the artist could also be useful, a position indicated by the title of a favorite public lecture, "Poetry and the Practical." Much of Simms's activity during this middle third of his life may be viewed best within this context. For it is during this period that Simms takes up the cause of American literary nationalism (which, in his view, is the sum of its sectional parts); that he undertakes a series of unsuccessful editorial ventures in order to promote the development of this national literature (*Southern and Western Monthly Magazine and Review, Magnolia,* and the *Southern Quarterly Review*); that he launches a short-lived political career; and that he turns away from fiction and toward history and biography. In the preface to his 1840 edition of the *History of South Carolina,* Simms wrote, "I have sought rather to be useful than original, and I have never suffered myself to be excursive" (p. vi). His choice of biographical subjects—Captain John Smith, Francis Marion, Nathanael Greene, and the Chevalier Bayard—further illustrates the combination of poetry and the practical. There is at least a touch of self-assessment in Simms's description of Bayard: "Never was hero more unselfish. His generosity and disinterestedness, struggling steadily against his successful valor, left him always poor while in the constant acquisition of money." [18] Simms may well have had in mind his own modest ancestry in describing the early years of Greene, whose father was a blacksmith: "In new settlements, which suffer from a thousand influences of which a high condition of civilization affords no just idea, the distinguishing merit of the citizen must necessarily be his usefulness. He who, in such a condition of society, is prepared to meet and overcome even its meanest necessities, is a benefactor, and in just degree with the importance of his service will be his social distinctions. Nathanael Greene the sire suffered accordingly no diminution of rank when he graced his arms with a sledge-hammer; and it is one of the honorable distinctions in the descendant that he was duly taught to wield it also." [19]

During this same period Simms also experienced intense private pressures. His plantation at Woodlands was constantly unprofitable and thus added to the pressures upon him to compose hastily and often for cash to meet debts. He borrowed from his friend and neighbor James H. Hammond, whose admonitions on how to run a plantation efficiently tell us, as Professor Faust has shown, not only about Hammond, the brutal taskmaster, but also about Simms, the quintessential benevolent patriarch who knew nothing and cared less about soil types, fertilizing, or labor management. Repeatedly he contemplates removal to the North, where he thinks he might be more useful, more appreciated, and less burdened by the demands of his plantation. Public role and private necessity thus combine to bring Simms to the third, climactic phase of his career.

3. *South Carolina and the Revolution (1850s–1870).*

The title of this section, too, is taken from that of an aborted lecture series undertaken by Simms in New York in December, 1856. Both his fiction and his public pronouncements provide him opportunities to attack abolitionism and New England, to justify the role of South Carolina in the war for independence and to claim for his native region a prominent place in the nation's history. As these efforts to align section and nation proved increasingly futile, Simms became, by the end of the 1850s, a strong advocate of secession. Like many Southerners, Simms viewed the Civil War as a reenactment of that earlier Revolution. He offered strategic and tactical advice to South Carolina officials. But this Revolution—like almost everything else in Simms's life—did not turn out as he had hoped. His plantation house was twice burned, the second time, by Sherman. In that conflagration he lost virtually all of an 11,000-volume library, acquired over a lifetime, much of it irreplaceable. After the war, an ailing shell of a man, he took on more work than he could physically manage, including several romances and a Southern Mother Goose. Bitter and broken, he died in June 1870.

~

These general topics, then, will constitute both the divisions within the work and provide a thematic unity to each subsection. Though all deal in some way with Simms's public life, they have their counterpart in his private life as well. For one brief, specific example, we might look in some detail at his formative years as a young boy in Charleston. With this shift we become tempted, as I am sure all biographers are, to become instant psychoanalysts. Those sorts of conclusions may be drawn from the following description of a childhood that surely was father of the man.

Simms was born in Charleston in 1806. His mother died in childbirth when young William was an infant. His father simultaneously went bankrupt and moved west, first to Tennessee then to Mississippi, where he established a plantation. Simms was left in the care of his maternal grandmother, who had remarried a local grocer. The young boy was sickly, lonely, and an omnivorous reader. The evidence seems to indicate that his grandmother mismanaged the small inheritance so that her son-in-law was forced to sell off a parcel of land in 1818. That same year, 1818, Simms's father returned from the west to claim his son. In what must have been a bizarre custody trial, a judge who was terribly hard of hearing and had a reputation for being sympathetic to feminine entreaties (and also for making wrong decisions) left the matter up to the twelve-year-old boy. In the biggest decision of his life, the boy chose Charleston (as he would again and again throughout his life). He did visit his father in the 1820s and learned much about backwoods life in the western South, much of which he later incorporated into a series of "border tales."

Two points, one solid, one speculative, might be made from this brief episode. First, one may discern the beginning of an ambivalent attitude toward Charleston and South Carolina that persists throughout Simms's life. Later in life he would claim that "the old man was right," that he ought to have gone west.[20] Again and again he would give expression to the issue of removal, always returning, with maternal allusions, to advising the prospective emigrant to stay put.

The speculative point is closely related. The maternal/paternal split might be related to Simms's desire to reconcile poetry and the practical. The mother he never knew is idealized in feminine references to his native land and in feminine characters (such as Singleton, the hero of *The Partisan*, who bears his mother's maiden name). The fatherly images, by contrast, are rough and rugged, the basis of his backwoods characters, equally virtuous but less attractive. It is more complicated than a mere juxtaposition of mother-poetry-Charleston-romance-section on the one hand and father-practical-west-realism-nation on the other might suggest. At the same time, these relationships do appear meaningful.

In summary, then, the question remains, at this stage of the project, what do these random observations appear to add up to? It would not be especially daring or original to observe that many of the tensions experienced by Simms were also being experienced by many other Americans in the first half of the nineteenth century. Choosing a profession, needing affection and appreciation, desiring to put down roots in a supportive community, coping with incomprehensible changes, all are part of the human condition at any time in any place. Nor would it be particularly original or useful to claim for Simms a preeminent position in Southern or American letters. Those arguments have already gone on far too long. It would furthermore be tiresome and obscurant to advance a case for Simms's supposed representativeness of that ever elusive "Southern mind."

To study Simms as exemplary of anything more than his own life and his own experience is therefore to miss the mark. That life, I submit, is intrinsically interesting, and those experiences, I contend, are worthy of recounting, but less for what they may tell us of cosmic and unanswerable questions than for what they may suggest about a particular human being in a particular time and place. In the case of Simms we have an abundance of evidence from which the life can be reconstructed, and that evidence, imaginatively used, ought to produce a story worth telling. "A modest claim," you may politely say; "rather trite and obvious," you may, less politely, think. But do remember, there has been no biography since 1892, largely because of both the historiographical context I have described and the specific concerns of individuals and groups who have since 1892 studied the subject. My immodest aim is to bring this man and his career to life, for I believe that a letter of introduction written for Simms by a friend in 1832 speaks at least one volume. It was the young Charlestonian's first trip to the big city, New York, and the letter he bore would determine his acceptance in the highly competitive publishing world of that day. "His mind is seemingly ever on the wing," the letter said, "and his heart, unless I greatly mistake it, is full of good feelings, genial juices, and the milk of human kindness."[21] I also hope, by the time I have completed this project, to have persuaded others, as the writer of this same letter of introduction—and my own study of Simms—has persuaded me: "The bearer is W. G. Simms, Esq. That is enough to say. If you come to know him as well as I do, you will regret that you did not know him sooner."

Notes

[1] W. J. Cash, *The Mind of the South* (New York: Alfred A. Knopf, 1941), p. 96.

[2] Larzer Ziff, *Literary Democracy: The Declaration of Cultural Independence in America* (New York: The Viking Press, 1981), p. 182.

[3] Paul H. Buck, *The Road to Reunion* (Boston: Little, Brown, 1937), p. 222.

[4] William Peterfield Trent, *William Gilmore Simms* (Boston: Houghton, Mifflin, 1892), p. 7.

[5] Barrett Wendell, *A Literary History of America* (New York: Charles Scribner's Sons, 1901), p. 480.

[6] Jay B. Hubbell, *The South in American Literature, 1607–1900* (Durham: Duke University Press, 1954), p. xiii.

[7] Michael O'Brien, ed., *All Clever Men, Who Make Their Way* (Fayetteville: University of Arkansas Press, 1982), p. 15.

[8] Drew Gilpin Faust, *James Henry Hammond* (Baton Rouge: Louisiana State University Press, 1982); Robert J. Brugger, *Beverley Tucker: Heart Over Head in the Old South* (Baltimore: The Johns Hopkins University Press, 1977); Neal C. Gillespie, *The Collapse of Orthodoxy: The Intellectual Ordeal of George Frederick Holmes* (Charlottesville: University of Virginia Press, 1972); Michael O'Brien, *A Character of Hugh Swinton Legaré* (Knoxville: University of Tennessee Press, 1985); William K. Scarborough, ed., *The Diary of Edmund Ruffin*, 2 vols. (Baton Rouge: Louisiana State University Press, 1972–1976); E. Brooks Holifield, *The Gentleman Theologians* (Durham: Duke University Press, 1978).

[9] William Gilmore Simms to William Porcher Miles, April 12, 1858, in *The Letters of William Gilmore Simms,* Mary C. Simms Oliphant, Alfred Taylor Odell, and T. C. Duncan Eaves, eds. (Columbia: University of South Carolina Press, 1952–1956, 1982), IV, 52.

[10] David Donald, *Charles Sumner and the Coming of the Civil War* (New York: Alfred A. Knopf, 1960), p. x.

[11] See, for example, C. Hugh Holman, *The Roots of Southern Writing* (Athens: University of Georgia Press, 1972), pp. 16–86; and Louis D. Rubin, *William Elliott Shoots A Bear* (Baton Rouge: Louisiana State University Press, 1975), pp. 17–26.

[12] Jon Wakelyn, *The Politics of a Literary Man* (Westport, Conn.: Greenwood Press, 1973), p. 264.

[13] Drew Gilpin Faust, *A Sacred Circle* (Baltimore: The Johns Hopkins University Press, 1977).

[14] [William Gilmore Simms], "Pleasure and What Pleases," *Charleston City Gazette,* June 11, 1830.

[15] William Gilmore Simms, *Life of the Chevalier Bayard* (New York: Harper Brothers, 1847), p. 8.

[16] William Gilmore Simms, *Father Abbot, or, The Home Tourist* (Charleston: Miller and Browne, 1849), p. 98.

[17] *Father Abott,* p. 99.

[18] Simms, *Life of Bayard,* p. 3.

[19] William Gilmore Simms, *Life of Nathanael Greene* (New York: G. F. Cooledge, 1849), pp. 11–12.

[20] Quoted in Trent, *Simms,* pp. 238–239.

[21] Willis Gaylord Clark to James Lawson, August 13, 1832, William Gilmore Simms Papers, South Caroliniana Library, University of South Carolina.

Simms, Charleston, and the Profession of Letters

LOUIS D. RUBIN, JR.

In the year 1845, under the aegis of William Gilmore Simms (though his name is nowhere mentioned), there was published an annual, *The Charleston Book: A Miscellany in Prose and Verse*. Pleased with the idea of displaying in the pages of a single volume the numerous writings of his fellow Charlestonians, Simms had scurried about seeking subscriptions to help pay the cost of having Samuel Hart of Charleston print and bind the book. The "Advertisement" preceding the table of contents noted that enough material had been collected to fill several *volumes*, and that if the present edition met with success, a second would be published for the next holiday season. Apparently it did not, for a sequel never appeared.

Simms was careful to point out that none of the contributors whose work appeared in the *The Charleston Book* was a professional author. The names of a few of them are still remembered by students of nineteenth-century Southern culture. There was Washington Allston, the Charleston-born painter and poet who had studied painting abroad and then settled in Massachusetts, where he published verse and worked for years on a never-to-be-completed painting entitled "Belshazzar's Feast." There was Hugh Swinton Legaré, lawyer, antiquarian scholar, editor of the *Southern Review* for several years, and former attorney general and acting secretary of state in President

Tyler's cabinet. There were the playwrights John Blake White and Isaac Harby. There was Joel Roberts Poinsett, stalwart Jacksonian during the nullification crisis of the previous decade, former ambassador to Mexico and secretary of war, and best known today for having a Christmas flower named after him. There were the Gilmans, Samuel and Caroline, transplanted New England Unitarians; he is remembered principally for having written the words to "Fair Harvard," and she for her several books and editorship of *The Southern Rose.* There was J. D. B. De Bow, soon to leave for New Orleans and for the editorship of the pro-slavery *De Bow's Review.* There was Penina Moise, the blind Jewish poetess, and William Crafts, pet and socialite of the early decades of the century whose dilettantism H. S. Legaré had savaged so masterfully in the *Southern Review.* (Oddly, Crafts' contributions include a paean to the Pilgrim Fathers and the pride they would feel if they could see the New England that they founded in its present glory; it would not be long before no Southern publication would want to praise anything having to do with that.) There were John Bachman, the naturalist; Stephen Elliot, the botanist; Charles Fraser, the miniaturist; and William Henry Timrod, father of the poet Henry Timrod. Two of the elder Timrod's poems are the best by far in the collection. There was the poet James Mathewes Legaré—and so on. The table of contents is not exactly a roster of literary or intellectual greatness, but *The Charleston Book* was a respectable showing for a small Southern city whose reading public all told was probably no more than a few thousand persons. If none of the contents of the annual seems worth reading today, that is because literary and journalistic fashions have changed so utterly since the 1830s. Surely the average was about as good as any American community of the size of Charleston could have produced at the time.

In pointing out that all the contributors were amateur authors, Simms, who was no amateur but a thoroughgoing professional, noted:

> What is done among us, in a literary point of view, is the work of the amateur, a labor of stealth or recreation, employed as a re-

218

lief from other tasks and duties. From this fact the reader will be able to account for that air of didactic gravity, that absence of variety, and of the study of artistic attributes, which would not strike him so obviously had the sources of the collection been found in the more various fields of a national literature. He will discover, however, that in most of the pieces which follow, there is a liveliness of fancy, a fluency of expression, and a general readiness of resource, indicating such a presence of the imaginative faculty, as leaves no doubt of the capacity of the community, from which the work is drawn, to engage with great success in the active pursuits of literature. Should this little miscellany contribute, in any degree, to bring about a result so very desirable the reward of the publisher will be ample.[1]

One might wonder why an author such as Simms, busy with his professional commitments, involved in South Carolina politics, and with an enormous correspondence to take care of, would expend so much time and labor on a project such as this, which could scarcely benefit either his literary reputation or be of political gain. If one knows very much about Simms and his relationship to the city of Charleston, however, there can be little doubt about what was involved.

What Simms craved most of all was to be recognized and honored as an outstanding man of letters, a distinguished literary personage in a city-state (as was often said) in which literature, culture, and learning were strongly allied with wealth and position. By the early 1800s the city had already developed the peculiar combination of civic pride, hedonism, gentility, and self-sufficiency that has characterized it. The powerful lure of membership and status within the community that it offered its citizenry went along with a complacent self-congratulation that permeated a fairly active cultural life. What galled Simms was that his own fame as a nationally-distinguished author, surpassing by far that of any other author in the South, seemed to mean little more in Charleston than that of any locally-prominent poetaster, and that in the final reckoning political and social distinction counted for more than artistic renown. No matter how great his reputation might be elsewhere, in Charleston there was a sense in which he was and always

would be the talented but rough-edged youth who had once delivered drugs about the city, and whose subsequent attainment
might mitigate but never completely cancel out that fact. Indeed, in some ways his success as an author seemed to be resented by local citizens; in addition to the Lord Morpeth episode, we have the incontrovertible testimony of both Hayne
and Timrod to that effect.[2] It was almost is if the fact that he
had shown himself unwilling to be content with local renown,
and had advanced far beyond the limited literary horizons of
amateur status, was actively resented. (One thinks of Poe in
Richmond.)

The opportunity to preside as editor over publication of such
a project as *The Charleston Book,* in which dozens of locally-
prominent littérateurs were participants, thus gave him considerable satisfaction. No one knew better than he the limitations of almost all of the work being anthologized; nor was
anyone more aware of the fact that Charlestonians not only
could not distinguish between such work and writings of genuine distinction, but did not care. He recognized all too well the
self-congratulatory nature of such civic cultural enterprises;
that Charleston's literary life was in the nature of a mutual admiration society was quite evident to him.[3]

For all that, he still liked to be part of it. Moreover, the very
self-sufficiency and self-satisfaction were attributes of the community's solidarity, emblematic of the powerful sense of community identity that had so attracted him as a young man
struggling to be accepted. In a very real sense he had never put
it aside; it had shaped his life, made him into the kind of writer
that he was. The old-time Charleston Federalist aristocracy of
wealth and social distinction, with its plantations and town
houses, its pleasant if amateur concern for literature and culture, became and remained his ideal—an ideal he pursued,
however, with an ardency of spirit and a professional skill and
boldness that in themselves prevented his ever fully being part
of the circles he so admired.

The "Advertisement" to *The Charleston Book* embodies the
ambivalence of his emotions. If only there could be, within and
as part of the Charleston community, a professional literary
situation, one that would be free of the dilettantism and com-

placency of the community identity. What he could not see was that the two goals were contradictory. The professional literary environment he craved could have been achieved only at the cost of setting aside the intellectual and artistic limitations that enabled the literary activity to conform to the standards and expectations of the social community.

Yet in the early 1850s it did begin to look as if Simms's wish were coming true, and that a genuine professional literary community might be forming in Charleston. Two young poets, Henry Timrod and Paul Hayne, were now active and both made it very clear that they had no intention of settling for a genteel amateur standing. Other promising young men began gathering about them. It was Simms's pleasure, as distinguished elder, to play host (at his home in the city) to Hayne, Timrod, and certain of the mostly young Charlestonians of intellect and promise. It was there that the idea to publish a literary magazine of their own was hatched. Simms had been in on the birth and death throes of not a few previous such ventures, but he was always game for another try.

Realizing that the venture would require for its success considerably more in the way of both literary and financial resources than were available to them, they joined with a larger, older, and generally more influential group of citizenry: the lawyers, physicians, clergymen and others who convened regularly in the "sanctum," the back room of John Russell's bookstore, to discuss matters of cultural and civic import. "Lord" John Russell, the bookstore proprietor—so called because he was so very pleased at his fancied resemblance to the English statesman—agreed to finance the enterprise until it reached self-sufficiency.

Russell's Magazine published its first issue in 1856 and its last in early 1860.[4] For most of the period Hayne served as editor, which soon turned out to be, in his estimation, a thankless task, for few of the gentlemen amateurs of the group produced the material that had been counted on to fill its pages. Hayne, Timrod, and Simms, however, wrote regularly for it. *Russell's* might have succeeded, had it not been for the intensifying sectional crisis, which not only meant that the magazine failed to win the interest of an increasingly distracted public, but also

221

obviously diverted the attentions of the contributors, including Simms, who by this time was so caught up in the political conflict over slavery that he was giving less and less attention to matters of literature.

During its brief existence, however, the magazine did become the occasion for several of Henry Timrod's essays on poetry. It seems clear that Timrod was the most genuinely gifted member of the group, who in other circumstances might have developed into an important poet. But it is also evident, if one reads his essays on poetry carefully, that what the *Russell's* writers suffered most from was a political situation that prevented them from doing what similar literary groups customarily do—grounding their literary interests in a cultural and social position that placed them in a quasi-adversarial relationship with the larger community. Timrod's exchange with William J. Grayson on the nature of poetry, in which he championed the modern poetry of Tennyson and Wordsworth against the eighteenth-century neoclassical writers, was implicitly political, in that the younger man was attacking an attitude toward poetry which held it to be the considered utterance in rhymed metric feet of a general community wisdom, asserting a settled truth past argument.[5]

In his several *Russell's* essays, Timrod wrote in glowing terms of the Romantic movement as a much-needed revolution in sensibility; and he raged at Southern patriotism for its insistence upon viewing all literary utterance in terms of sectionalism. It is true that he suggested that one value of good literature, as opposed to mediocre work, is its ability to report to the world the "truths underlying the relations of master and slave,"[6] but in context the statement seems in the nature of an afterthought, as if it were expected of him to make clear that his claims for literature posed no threat to the community's political and social arrangements.

What seems obvious in almost everything that Timrod wrote for *Russell's* is his general dissatisfaction with the attitudes and tastes of the community. But if so, it does not carry over into a criticism of the social and political arrangements of Charleston and the South. One can only speculate on the extent to which, in a politically less volatile and militant atmosphere, the young professional writers of *Russell's* might have been emboldened, through mutual encouragement, to undertake the radical critique of Southern institutions that, in the situation in which they found themselves, they showed no sign whatever of wanting to make. In any event, the coming of secession and civil war ended not only the magazine but the very existence of the group.

The historical fiction that Simms himself wrote, and which is by all odds his best work, has been interpreted, by Jon Wakelyn and others, in terms of its relevance to contemporary political issues. Thus Wakelyn remarks that in the Revolutionary fiction the author's

> themes were shaped less by class conflict or by his view of status in South Carolina society than by his interpretation of the need for unity in the state after the Revolutionary War. To build its power inside or outside the Union, South Carolina had to demonstrate that the Revolution had unified the state. Simms felt that it was particularly important for the average citizen to accept the leadership of the conservative and privileged elite in tumultous times.[7]

And he notes that the Charleston newspapers were quick to recognize that message.

Certainly when Simms wrote about the South, whether in fiction or non fiction, he was aware of contemporary political needs. But Wakelyn's approach —fiction as political persuasion—entails some serious handicaps. Wakelyn is unable to take account of the ways in which artistic necessity can modify, distort, and even contradict conscious political purpose, for he does not see that Simms the literary artist is at least as important a storytelling presence within the fiction as is Simms the political propagandist, and that it is the storytelling artist who confers importance upon the political commentator, not the other way around. Wakelyn's approach cannot distinguish between the fiction of Simms and that of someone such as his friend Nathaniel Beverly Tucker, whose fiction *was* not only shaped purely as political statement but possesses almost no artistic dimensions whatever.

Specifically, the approach overlooks or neglects one of the

most important ties between the author and his work: the personal, emotional needs out of which its composition arose. It has room for no curiosity about any dimension other than conscious political intention. Yet Simms's extraordinary zeal for Southern and particularly South Carolina history grows in intense ways out of his wish to identify himself with his community's past. It is an act of possession, a way of asserting his claims, as a Charlestonian and a South Carolinian, to full-fledged membership in the community. His father was a latecomer on the scene, but his mother's family, specifically his great-grandfather, did play a role in Charleston's life during the Revolutionary War era. Simms not only described an incident involving his ancestor in his novel *Katherine Walton,* but he gave the family name, Singleton, to the well-born hero of his first Revolutionary War novel, *The Partisan* (1835). In *The Yemassee* (1835), his first venture into South Carolina history, is an episode—a tribute to his father—in which an Irish settler bravely defies the torture of the Indians.

In becoming an expert on his community's past, Simms was able to instruct Charlestonians on their own history—and be it remembered that it was in part because his own family ties to that past were oblique that he was not himself a member of the Charleston gentry. To say this is not to portray Simms as a sycophant or a social climber; in no important way was he either, which is one of the reasons why he had failed, where someone such as James Louis Petigru had succeeded, in securing full social acceptance. But the impassioned fascination with his community's past is testimony to the hold that Charleston had on Simms's affections and the force that the ideal of membership in the community exerted upon his imagination throughout his life. It helps us to understand, for example, why he became so enraged when Petigru and not he was chosen the first president of the South Carolina Historical Society.

When one examines the zeal that men such as Simms and his friend James Henry Hammond displayed in the defense of slavery during the period of rising sectional tensions, it is important to bear in mind the fascination which that ideal of the aristocratic gentleman-planter held for them. For someone like

Hammond it was intricately involved with dreams of wealth and power. In Simms's instance the wealth and power would seem to have been less important than the public acclaim. But in both cases the enormous amount of imaginative abstraction involved in the transaction must be recognized.

It is a mistake, I think, to approach the views that these men, and others like them, expressed about the Peculiar Institution principally as ideology, in the sense that any logical and coherent exposition of ideas is what was at issue. Visionary theorizing, the reification of emotional longing even, is a better way to look at their utterances. That they believed, like most ante-bellum Americans, in the congenital inferiority of black people is undeniable; that both Hammond and Simms thought that the condition of chattel slavery constituted no unwarranted hardship for the chattels is likewise beyond question. But when one reflects on the extravagant theorizing about mudsills and slave empires, it seems obvious that what is involved is not calculating, realistic political and social thinking, as some would have it, but passionate hyperbole, rhapsodic conceptualizing of abstractions, a sometimes giddy and often self-contradictory mingling and extending of thought and fancy. Like Thomas Browne, each loved to pursue reason "to an *O altitudo*."

Consider, for example, Simms writing to Hammond in 1847 about proper Southern political strategy. The time is that of the dispute over whether the territories of the far Southwest were to be admitted into the Union as slave states:

> *At all events, the slave interest must be held intact without reference to the soil upon which it happens to labor now.* Remember that! It is one inevitable necessity with slavery that it must accommodate its habitation to its profits—in other words that slave labor will only be continued where it yields an adequate profit. Slavery will be the medium & great agent for rescuing and recovering to freedom and civilization all the vast tracts of Texas, Mexico, &c., and our sons ought to be fitted out as fast as they are ready to take the field, with an adequate provision in slaves, and find their way in the yet unopened regions. The interest is one which must be maintained without reference to places.[8]

225

Did Simms really believe all this? Only in the sense of a political abstraction. In actuality it goes against everything that most characterizes his life and work. He wanted most of all to be a South Carolina landed gentleman, if not in the area adjoining Charleston then in the Barnwell district, and to enjoy a position and public renown in his native state. At least twice he had turned down attractive invitations to move southwestward in search of greater opportunities. Imaginatively and zealously he sought to establish his antecedents and sink his art deeply in his community's past. To belong, to be part of a stable, rooted, social community steeped in history and memory, was his consuming passion. What, then, could *his* life and work possibly have to do with an economic interest "without reference to" place? Or Hammond's, for whom a "well educated and wellbred *independent* So. Carolina *country*" gentleman represented a status "the nearest to nobleman of any possible in America"[9]—and who summoned the slave children to sing outside the window of his deathbed?

Clearly the cause of expansion of the slaveholding South was being made into a shibboleth that bore little or no logical relationship to the deepest personal concerns and objectives of either man's life and career. Yet so thoroughly had Simms and Hammond identified themselves and their dreams of status with the political rhetoric of their community, and so histrionic was Simms's response to the growing criticism of the South during the dispute over the annexation of Texas and the Wilmot Proviso, that he sounds like a fire-eater such as William Lowndes Yancey at his most hyperbolic. He and his friend Hammond obviously derived much satisfaction from demonstrating rhetorically to each other just how intransigent and uncompromising a Southron each was, and they did so with a zeal that only two self-made men, not born into the planter gentry, could muster. One is reminded of Samuel Johnson displaying his Toryism. The passage, with its mixture of Manifest Destiny, sectional bellicosity, and dogmatic generalization, is as truly and as extravagantly Romantic as anything to be found in Emerson or Victor Hugo.

It should be pointed out that this seemingly "pragmatic" and "practical" approach to the practice of slavery as a labor and social system devoid of attachment to a time and place is in almost ludicrous contrast to the practice of the Peculiar Institution as observable on Simms's own plantation. Simms's inability and unwillingness to make his slaves work at the customary rate kept the annual agricultural yield so low that he was in constant debt. Hammond, who was considerably more realistic about the function of slavery as a system of forced labor, chided him for the lamentable inefficiency at Woodlands. Visitors there recorded their astonishment at the exorbitant prices that Simms paid for the produce that his slaves grew in their own gardens. Some of the slaves at Woodlands were even permitted to own firearms. The novelist blamed his father-in-law for the failure of Woodlands to produce profitable crops, but there is little evidence that the situation improved after he took personal charge. The incompetence of the slave labor at Woodlands was apparently a source of amusement among his friends. It was Simms's literary earnings that kept the plantation going. When William Cullen Bryant came to visit Simms, he did not change his opposition to slavery, but his description of it as practiced at Woodlands depicts it in terms that are about as innocuous as could ever be managed by an avowed opponent of the Peculiar Institution.

To say all this is not to excuse slavery in the Old South, either on Simms's plantation or anywhere else. Rather it is to indicate that Simms's insensitivity toward its evils, one that he shared with his neighbors, was not hypocritical. The fervor with which he defended it against hostile criticism, the ferocity with which he spun out his theories for its perpetuation and expansion, can be viewed most usefully neither as defensive rationalization nor as abiding philosophical conviction, though certainly both were involved. Instead, such all-out enthusiasm might best be understood as the product of his lifelong effort to demonstrate his orthodoxy as a Charlestonian and a South Carolinian, a way of gaining the respect he coveted in a community that, as he constantly complained, was less than passionately committed to the fine arts, and that was also under relentless ideological and political attack, even while its economic and political power within the Union was steadily ebbing.

Simms and Hammond provided what each other needed: a

companion in ambition and sensibility who could understand the intensity of the other's desire to achieve status and distinction within the South Carolina establishment and who could recognize, too, that there was so much more to that ambition than materialistic achievement. Like almost every other important figure in the political and cultural life of the antebellum South, both were outsiders, not to the establishment born, and the status which both had managed to secure had come in spite of and not because of the early attitude of the dominant community leadership toward them. Unlike Simms, Hammond had achieved a college education, at South Carolina College—and one can imagine that checks and rebuffs had not been unknown for a youth whose father was in charge of provisioning the school's dining hall and the proprietor of an open-air market in Columbia. But a onetime apothecary's apprentice and delivery boy could be trusted to understand. If Simms had the finer sensibility of the two, and seems so much more attractive a figure, less self-centered, gentler, and certainly far less ruthless in pursuit of his ambition, even so their common bond of high intelligence, depth of emotional hunger, powerful ambition, great energy and self-made status were sufficient to bind them closely together.

It is Simms's friendship with Hammond that makes one realize what the absence of any real literary community, or "clerisy" as Lewis Simpson calls it,[10] in the South of Simms's upbringing meant for him. Had there been companions who could share and understand his literary ambitions and imaginative gifts when he was a youth, it is quite possible that his efforts would have been directed more firmly and exclusively toward literature in its own right, rather than toward fulfillment within and on behalf of the political and social community. Had there been anyone to be for the young Simms what a generation later the youthful Hayne and Timrod were for each other, or for that matter what the older Simms himself was for both of them, the achievement of William Gilmore Simms might have been a different and, from a literary standpoint, more enduring affair than it turned out to be. All such speculation, of course, is moot; but with Simms's drive, talent, and ambition, there is no telling what might have resulted. In any event, it was not to be.

Paul Hamilton Hayne, in a memoir written after the novelist's death, described the first time he saw Simms. It was during the period of the Mexican War, and Hayne was attending a meeting in a Charleston theater. There was a series of speeches, and then, as some in the audience began to leave, "there was a cry, at first somewhat faint, but rapidly taken up, until it was earnest, even vociferous, for Simms, Gilmore Simms!" As a fledgling poet Hayne had long wished to see the great man. "He now came forward with a slow, stately step, under the full blaze of the chandeliers, a man in the prime of life, tall, vigorous, and symmetrically formed."

He began his speech, Hayne says, with a "bold startling paradox," thereby gaining the full attention of his audience.

> An extraordinary speaker, certainly. For some time his manner was measured and deliberate; but once plunged *in medias res* he became passionately eager. His gesticulation was frequent, unrestrained, now and then almost grotesquely emphatic . . .
> His peroration I vividly recall. It was a scathing rebuke of the selfish, time-serving politicians who sacrificed to personal and party ends the interests of their people and the dignity of their country.[11]

The occasion Hayne describes, which took place at about the same time that Simms wrote the letter to Hammond about the need for slavery to "accommodate its habituation to its profits," was probably a Democratic party rally attendant to the forthcoming political campaign of 1848, and it is likely that the call, "at first somewhat faint, but rapidly taken up," for "Simms, Gilmore Simms!" was a deliberately planned maneuver of the Young Charleston group, with whom Simms was at the time busily engaged in promoting the candidacy of Zachary Taylor and the return of Hammond to office. Taylor was a Whig, and the dominant Democratic organization and newspapers in Charleston were reluctant to join in a move in which open sectionalism—Taylor was a slave-owner and a Southerner, while the Democratic candidate, Lewis Cass, was neither—would for the first time take precedence over national party allegiance. What the Young Charleston faction was doing was attempting to take over control of the local party, and late that summer a convention of Charleston Whigs, independents, and Democrats did formally endorse Taylor's candidacy. Thus one may assume that what the seventeen-year-old Paul Hayne may have thought was a spontaneous outcry and an impromptu oration had been carefully arranged in advance of the meeting.

What is important, however, is that it was through political activity, not literary achievement, that Simms could experience exhilarating moments like that, with enthusiasts shouting for "Simms, Gilmore Simms!" and partisan audiences listening eagerly as he denounced time-serving politicos and called for the conquest of Mexico and the annexation of new territories for slavery. Such a condition was hardly peculiar to the state of South Carolina, of course. But the inescapable fact is that it was because William Gilmore Simms was a South Carolinian, and because as the son of an Irish-born father he craved the status and recognition that in ante-bellum Charleston could never be his as a result of cultural distinction alone, that he sought the limelight and rewards that public politics could afford him.

Nathaniel Hawthorne of Massachusetts was also involved in Democratic politics. It was his party affiliation that secured for him the consulate at Liverpool. Herman Melville of New York was likewise a Democrat; and his brother was President James Knox Polk's selection for secretary of the American legation in London. Can anyone, however, imagine either Hawthorne or Melville engaged in active politics, in the way that Simms was, or delivering a stump speech such as that described by Paul Hayne?

One may readily concede that Simms was no Hawthorne and no Melville. Yet to say that is to beg the issue, for we do not know the form or the range that Simms's talents might have assumed had he grown up in New England or the Northeast under circumstances different from those he knew in Charleston. What we do know is that through the sheer force and persistence of his character and will, Simms had all but *created* a professional literary association in Charleston in the early

230

1850s. He had assembled and encouraged a group of gifted young men, who were learning to view the writing of literature as something other than a pleasant amateur diversion. In particular his two young poet friends Henry Timrod and Paul Hamilton Hayne were showing themselves ready for truly whole-souled engagement with literature. The founding of *Russell's Magazine,* beginning in 1857, not only gave Simms's circle an organ but touched off critical discourse that resulted in Timrod's writing several important documents about the nature and role of literature.

From the standpoint of nineteenth-century Southern letters, the situation with the *Russell's* group is the great might-have-been. If what Lewis Simpson has *pointed out* is true concerning the role of a "clerisy," the group of writers, intellectuals, and informed readers who constitute a genuine artistic and cultural constituency to which the writer can belong in contradistinction to the social and economic community in which it exists, one can only say that this is what *seemed* to be developing in Charleston in the 1840s and 1850s. If so, the war destroyed it utterly. There are few more melancholy documents in American literary history than the sketches that Paul Hamilton Hayne wrote for the *Southern Bivouac* in the late 1870s, describing what had been and now was gone for good. Not until the 1910s and 1920s would another such condition begin to exist anywhere in the South again.

If we read the frantic, sometimes inchoate correspondence that Simms was scribbling at exorbitant length to his friends during the late 1850s and early 1860s, given over almost wholly as it is to politics, secession, and the coming of the war, we see the collapse of his literary vocation taking place right in front of our eyes. Repeatedly he quotes to his New York friends the Latin tag, *Quem Deus vult perdere, prius dementat;* "whom the Gods would destroy, they first make mad."[12] He meant it to apply to Northern political opinion, but he was really writing about himself. Some of Simms's friends even suggested that he seemed to have gone quite mad. He was witnessing the utter collapse of the equilibrium that Simms had managed, however unevenly, to maintain between his literary interests and ambitions and his involvement in the political and social life of his

231

community. It was no longer possible to be a professional Man of Letters in the South; henceforth he must put aside his artistic vocation and sink his entire hopes into his indentification with the secular, political Southern community.

Not given overmuch to introspection as he was, it is impossible to say whether he realized what he had done to himself, by virtue of his involvement in his politically-obsessed community. Yet it had not really been a matter of choice on his part. He could not have done otherwise, being the man he was and in his time and place. For the gifted young parvenu in Charleston in the 1810s and 1820s, the dream of the planter-statesman-author had proved irresistible; who had there been, in the South Carolina he so loved, to help him resist it? Surely not his friend Hammond. The public goal had become irretrievably entangled with the artistic vocation. He had sought valiantly and bravely to weave them into the single harmonious entity: to be a *Southern* writer, to create a *Southern* literature. But in the ante-bellum South of slavery and the plantation, that was more than any man could bring off—even one with his energy, his willpower, and his integrity. He was too close to his subject matter to be able to discipline his Romantic passion for it through a detachment that would enable him to see himself and his experience with the irony that could have converted argument into dialectic. For all his fascination with the past of South Carolina and the nation, he could not view history as something that was happening to him.

When it was over, his once-imposing plantation gutted and his library burned, his slaves freed, his wife dead, and his community's cause blasted beyond imagining, he sought to resume his literary vocation. It was all he had left. The plantation dream of the Old South had vanished into smoke. In late 1865 he prepared to go to New York in a forlorn attempt to restore his professional ties. To his friend Evert Duyckinck, his onetime ally in the exciting literary wars of Young America, he wrote as follows:

> After four, nearly five, dreadful years, it will give me the greatest pleasure to meet with you again. But say as little as possible to me about the war, and my miserable Country.[13]

Notes

¹[William Gilmore Simms], "Advertisement," *The Charleston Book: A Miscellany In Prose and Verse* (Charleston, S.C.: Samuel Hart, Sen., 1845), pp. 3–4.

²Simms's biographer William Peterfield Trent relates the story of how George William Frederick Howard, Lord Morpeth, visiting Charleston, wanted to know Simms's whereabouts and was informed that the novelist was not considered such a great man in Charleston. "'Simms not a great man!'" replied the astonished visitor; "then for God's sake, who is your great man?" See William P. Trent, *William Gilmore Simms* (Boston and New York: Houghton, Mifflin and Company, 1892), p. 129.

³That this spirit still thrives, more than century after Simms's death, is amply demonstrated by the recent publication of a book, *Intellectual Life in Antebellum Charleston*, eds. Michael O'Brien and David Moltke-Hansen (Knoxville: University of Tennessee Press, 1986).

⁴Richard J. Calhoun's excellent essay, "The Ante-Bellum Twilight: *Russell's Magazine*," *Southern Literary Journal*, III, 1 (Fall 1970), pp. 89–110, handily places *Russell's* in the context of pre-secession Charleston.

⁵Grayson's "What Is Poetry?" first appeared in *Russell's*, I (July 1857), pp. 327–37. Timrod's rejoinder, likewise entitled "What Is Poetry?", is published in 2 (October 1857), 52–58. Both essays are available to the modern reader in *The Essays of Henry Timrod*, edited with an Introduction by Edd Winfield Parks (Athens: University of Georgia Press, 1942).

⁶"Literature in the South," *The Essays of Henry Timrod*, p. 91. The essay appeared first in *Russell's*, V (August 1859), pp. 385–395.

⁷Jon Wakelyn's *The Politics of a Literary Man* (Westport, Conn.: Greenwood Press, 1973), pp. 170–171.

⁸Simms, letter to James Henry Hammond, July 15, 1847, in *The Letters of William Gilmore Simms*, eds. Mary C. Simms Oliphant, Alfred Taylor Odell, and T. C. Duncan Eaves (Columbia: University of South Carolina Press, 1952–1956), II, 332. This five-volume work, together with a recent supplement, edited by Oliphant and Eaves and published as Volume VI in 1982, is an indispensable work for anyone dealing in the literary history of the Old South.

⁹Hammond, letter to Marcellus C. M. Hammond, August 25, 1858, in *The Hammonds of Redcliffe*, ed. Carol Bleser (New York and Oxford: Oxford University Press, 1981), p. 7.

[10] Lewis P. Simpson's *The Dispossessed Garden: Pastoral and History in Southern Literature* (Athens: University of Georgia Press, 1975), No. 16 of the Mercer University Lamar Memorial Lectures, deals with Simms in the second lecture, "Slavery and the Culture of Alienation," pp. 34–64.

[11] "Ante-Bellum Charleston," *Southern Bivouac*, n.s. I (November 1885), pp. 257–268. An abridged version may be found in *The Literature of the South*, rev. ed., eds. Thomas Daniel Young, Floyd C. Watkins, and Richmond C. Beatty (Indianapolis, Ind.: The Bobbs, Merrill Company, 1968), pp. 321–347.

[12] Simms quotes it as "Quos" rather than "Quem" in a letter to James Lawton, November 13, [1860], in *Letters,* IV, 265.

[13] Letter to Evert Duyckinck, October 1, 1865, in *Letters,* IV, 523.

Appendices and Notes

T. C. DUNCAN EAVES ON THE OCCASION OF
HIS WINNING THE DISTINGUISHED FACULTY AWARD
COURTESY OF JULIET CARUANA EAVES

Thomas Cary Duncan Eaves:
A Biographical Sketch

LEIGHTON RUDOLPH

Thomas Cary Duncan Eaves, Duncan to his many friends, was born in Union, South Carolina, in 1918, the only child of Donald Matheson and Louisa Duncan Eaves. Of English and Scottish ancestry, he had a sense of family that led him to become acquainted with his English relatives and to enroll his three daughters in the Matheson clan. His pride in his native state, his grandfathers' participation in the Civil War, and his home in Union were an essential part of his personality.

As a boy he studied art with a teacher in Union and later in Tahlequah, Oklahoma, and Woodstock, New York. Although he painted well enough to give a one-man show in his early teens, he later abandoned painting to concentrate on other interests—among them collecting antiques, miniatures, rugs, and books. As a boy he was fascinated by the movies: he was an indefatigable movie-goer and never forgot a film or its cast nor lost his delight in them.

After attending public schools in Union, in 1935 he entered The Citadel, the military college of South Carolina in Charleston. Finding the military education not to his liking, he transferred to the University of North Carolina in 1936 and found both the social and academic aspects of Chapel Hill more to his taste. Along with a very active social life that included joining a fraternity and becoming an expert bridge player, he found sufficient intellectual stimulus to win election to Phi Beta Kappa and to be graduated A.B. with honors in 1939. After a year at the University of Cincinnati, where he took a master's degree in 1940, he transferred to Harvard, where he was a teaching fellow and tutor while taking an M.A. in 1943 and a Ph.D. in 1944. While at Harvard he worked with and became a close friend of Professor Hyder E. Rollins and Professor George W. Sherburn, the latter directing his doctoral dissertation on the illustrations of the principal English novels of the eighteenth century. In the summer of 1943 he had an ACLS (American Council of Learned Societies) grant and did research on his dissertation at the Huntington Library, where he met and became a friend of Professor Samuel Chew of Bryn Mawr.

Having been barred from military service by faulty vision, in 1944 he accepted an instructorship at Rutgers, which for two years offered proximity to the attractions of New York. After spending 1946–1947 as an assistant professor at the College of William and Mary, he left the academic world for an advertising job in New York which he held until forced to resign due to an illness. In the fall of 1949 he came to the University of Arkansas as an assistant professor and was promoted to associate professor in 1952, professor in 1957, and University Professor in 1984. Among the academic awards he received were a Guggenheim grant for research in England in 1957–1958, a Fulbright visiting professorship to the University of Florence in 1960–1961, a grant from the ACLS and from the Arkansas Research Reserve Fund for research on Richardson in England in the summer of 1967, and the University of Arkansas Alumni Award for Research in 1969.

As a teacher he inspired and charmed his students as he made the Restoration and eighteenth century come to life: he easily persuaded his students to memorize "The Rape of the Lock" and to read the unabridged *Clarissa*. Although his lectures were charged with wit, humor, and anecdote that intrigued his students but never obscured the intellectual content of his carefully planned but seemingly *ex tempore* lectures, the immediate result of his lectures was a following of students for whom he was almost a cult figure; more permanent were the many dissertations he directed and the scholarly articles conceived in his seminars.

Eaves's first major scholarly project was almost a case of serendipity: while he was convalescing from a long illness at home in Union in 1948, he was asked by Mary C. Simms Oliphant to assist in collecting and editing the letters of her grandfather, the novelist William Gilmore Simms, for an edition by the University of South Carolina Press. She had begun collecting Simms's letters in 1937 in collaboration with Alfred Taylor Odell of Furman University, but Odell's sudden death in 1947 brought the project to a halt. Eaves agreed to join her and began at once an undertaking which was finished only in 1982 when the sixth and final volume of letters was published.

His first step was to complete as far as possible the collection of letters by further checking and soliciting both old and new sources, whereby more than two hundred additional letters were collected. Then, with the advice of Professor Hyder E. Rollins of Harvard University, textual principles concerning verbatim transcription of the text, emendations, and annotations were established. The great number of letters dashed off by Simms forced his editors to omit from the edition the long public letters, which were really essays, in order to publish the personal letters, only a few of which had been published. The most laborious part of the editorial chore was the annotation of the letters to eighty-six correspondents which spanned almost four decades and treated literature, politics, social issues, and personal interests to correspondents not confined to South Carolina but spread all over the country. The inclusion of Donald Davidson's introduction summarizing Simms's place in American literature and of Alexander S. Salley's biographical sketch of Simms went far to fill the gap caused by the absence then and now of a satisfactory biography and critical evaluation of the author.

Although the other problems were by no means minor, the annotations were the most difficult problem and required both an encyclopedic knowledge of the eighty-two volumes of fiction, verse, history, criticism, and miscellaneous works that Simms had dashed off as well as an intimacy with the history and family of every South Carolinian in public life in the generation before the Civil War. No detail was too insignificant for diligent pursuit, whether a detail of publication, the identity of an obscure correspondent, or a long forgotten character or work of a minor author. At times, as if to relieve the tedium of what might seem trivial, he interjected humorous anecdotes, such as the one concerning the time Isaac Nimmons, Simms's body servant, was upset when Mrs. William Cullen Bryant pulled up the skirts of the maids at Woodlands to see that they were provided with the proper undergarments.

The first five volumes of letters published between 1952 and 1956 and a sixth volume in 1982 of more than two hundred additional letters which Eaves had collected since the publication of the fifth volume, were a masterpiece of scholarly editing. Furthermore, as the task progressed, errata and addenda were carefully noted in order to keep the entire work as current and correct as possible. It was typical of his generosity that he agreed with Mrs. Oliphant to retain Professor Odell's name as one of the editors of all of the first five volumes of the letters. Although as editor Eaves cannot take credit for the content of the letters, he did make available in a definitive edition a body of letters which records almost the entire American literary and political scene as observed by the most important writer in the South in the decades between the Nullification Crisis and the Civil War.

After the presumed completion of the edition of the Simms letters in 1956, Eaves asked Ben Drew Kimpel, a fellow student at the University of North Carolina and a colleague at the University of Arkansas since 1952, who had long been helping him transcribe the Simms letters, to join him in writing a biography of the English novelist Samuel Richardson, a project suggested to Eaves by his friend and advisor at Harvard, Professor George W. Sherburn. Since Kimpel had helped him greatly with the transcriptions of four of the first five volumes of Simms letters and the two had published a translation of Goethe's *Torquato Tasso* in 1956, thereby demonstrating scholarly compatibility, the suggestion was accepted, and the collaboration begun in 1956 produced *Samuel Richardson* in 1972 and had almost finished a study of Pound's *Cantos* when Kimpel died in 1983.

The publication of *Samuel Richardson* by the Clarendon Press in 1972 marked the end of a major project which had been accompanied by Eaves's direction of more than twenty doctoral dissertations and the joint Eaves-Kimpel publication of thirty-six articles on Richardson and related topics. The choice of the particular biographical topic and period grew out of Eaves's interest in the subject of his doctoral dissertation, the illustrations of Richardson's novels. Here, however, he and Kimpel combined the talents of the literary critic of eighteenth-century fiction, the social historian of Augustan England, and the careful but dispassionate biographer in order to publish a genuinely definitive life of the novelist. In the biography we find in great detail accounts of his ancestry, immediate family, domestic affairs, and friends of all social classes as well as discussions of his business affairs, literary activities, and what there was of a public life. For fear that the biography would be over-burdened by detail, Eaves tried to publish as many of the less important details as possible prior to the publication of the biography, and much of such information that he had collected in two separate annual leaves spent in England appeared in scholarly notes and articles. Perhaps the excellence of the biography, like the excellence of his teaching, lay in his spirited infusion of his joy of living into Richardson's accounts of his having his portrait painted by Highmore, advising Lady Bradshaigh on matters of diet and exercise, or creating the most memorable serving girl in English fiction.

The critical reception of *Samuel Richardson* was an exercise in superlatives: among the reviews, one finds that it is "a magnificent and long-awaited study that will remain the standard account of Richardson for many years to come"; "it can be read from beginning to end with interest and pleasure"; and "their splendid summary chapters—are vigorous and lucid. . . . But their most minute biographical finds are sometimes the most interesting, because they have come to light in the pursuit of important questions."

After the publication of Samuel Richardson the Eaves-

Kimpel team immediately chose another major project, a line-by-line explication of Ezra Pound's *Cantos*, the choice of Kimpel this time. It was a fortuitous selection since Kimpel had a good command of all the languages Pound used and Eaves enjoyed the literary sleuthing required by Pound's extensive and exotic—if not erratic—reading and ideographic method. For over a decade the two worked on Pound at Eaves's home during the term and spent vacations in the United States and abroad tracing Pound's sources. They met late every evening to review the day's work and discuss their plans for the immediate future and the presentation of their findings. These discussions were followed by Kimpel's roughing out a draft which was put into a more nearly final form by Eaves before a joint final draft was settled upon. Shortly before his death in April, 1983, Kimpel remarked that he expected to have a rough draft completed and ready for Eaves's polishing by the beginning of the fall term. After Kimpel's death Eaves continued the work until almost incapacitated by paralysis, and the work at present remains unfinished. The nature of their work, however, is plainly evident in the twenty-three articles, many of them major, they did publish. Eaves continued the research with the help of a graduate assistant until his death on April 4, 1986, which left unfinished a project that had already won high praise from Pound scholars.

Although the function of a *festschrift* is to recognize and pay tribute to the scholarly achievement of a lifetime, in the case of Duncan Eaves it is impossible to separate into discrete categories his personal life, his teaching, and his scholarly publications because the same qualities characterize them all. The brilliant and inquiring mind, the energetic pursuit of knowledge, the meticulous weighing of evidence, and a polished prose style were complemented by a broad sense of humor, a love of and gift for storytelling, and a delight in the contemplation of all aspects of human nature.

Bibliography of the Works of T. C. Duncan Eaves
(In Chronological Order)

Books

Editor (with Mary C. Simms Oliphant and Alfred Taylor Odell), *The Letters of William Gilmore Simms*. Vol. I. Columbia: University of South Carolina Press, 1952.

Editor (with Mary C. Simms Oliphant), *The Letters of William Gilmore Simms*. Vol. II. Columbia: University of South Carolina Press, 1953.

Editor (with Mary C. Simms Oliphant), *The Letters of William Gilmore Simms*. Vol. III. Columbia: University of South Carolina Press, 1954.

Editor (with Mary C. Simms Oliphant), *The Letters of William Gilmore Simms*. Vol. IV. Columbia: University of South Carolina Press, 1955.

Editor (with Ben D. Kimpel), *The Informal Reader*. New York: Appleton-Century-Crofts, 1955.

Editor (with Mary C. Simms Oliphant), *The Letters of William Gilmore Simms*. Vol. V. Columbia: University of South Carolina Press, 1956.

Translator (with Ben D. Kimpel), Goethe's *Torquato Tasso*. Fayetteville: The University of Arkansas Press, 1956.

Editor (with Cesare G. Cecioni), *Anglia*. Firenze: Valmartina, 1964.

Editor (with Ben D. Kimpel), Samuel Richardson's *Pamela*, Riverside Edition. Boston: Houghton Mifflin, 1971.

Author (with Ben D. Kimpel), *Samuel Richardson: A Biography*. Oxford: The Clarendon Press, 1971.
Editor (with Mary C. Simms Oliphant), *The Letters of William Gilmore Simms*. Vol. VI. Columbia: University of South Carolina Press, 1982.

Articles

An asterisk (*) denotes works written in collaboration with Ben D. Kimpel.

" 'The Marlowe Family' by Joseph Highmore: A Note on the Illustration of Richardson's *Clarissa*," *Huntington Library Quarterly,* 7 (November 1943), 89–96.

"George Romney: His Tristram Shandy Paintings and Trip to Lancaster," *Huntington Library Quarterly,* 7 (May 1944), 321–326.

"The Publication of the First Translation of Fielding's *Tom Jones*," *The Library,* 4th s., 26 (September-December 1945), 189–190.

"Joseph Highmore's Portrait of the Reverend Edward Young," *Studies in Philology,* 43 (October 1946), 668–674.

"A Note on Lord Byron's *Select Works,* 1823," *The Library,* 5th S., 1 (June 1947), 70–72.

"Edward Burney's Illustrations to Evelina," *PMLA,* 62 (December 1947), 995–999.

"The Second Edition of Thomas Gray's Ode on the Death of a Favourite Cat," *Philological Quarterly,* 30 (January 1951), 91–94.

"An Unrecorded Children's Book Illustrated by Thomas Bewick," *The Library,* 5th S., 5 (March 1951), 272–273.

"Graphic Illustration of the Novels of Samuel Richardson, 1740–1810," *Huntington Library Quarterly,* 14 (August 1951), 349–383.

"An Early Admirer of Keats," *PMLA,* 67 (September 1952), 895–898.

"Poe's Last Visit to Philadelphia," *American Literature,* 26 (March 1954), 44–51.

"Fielding's *Shamela Andrews*," *The Major In English* (Pub-

244

lished by Arkansas Experiment in Teacher Education, a Project Sponsored by the Fund for the Advancement of Education, 1956), 23–32.

*"The Geography and History in *Nostromo*," *Modern Philology*, 56 (August 1958), 45–54.

*"The Publisher of *Pamela* and Its First Audience," *Bulletin of the New York Public Library*, 64 (March 1960), 143–146.

"Dr. Johnson's Letters to Richardson," *PMLA*, 75 (September 1960), 377–381.

*"Richardsoniana," *Studies in Bibliography*, 14 (1961), 232–234.

⁺"Samuel Richardson's London Houses," *Studies in Bibliography*, 15 (1962), 135–148.

*"Samuel Richardson and His Family Circle: The Wildes," *Notes and Queries*, n.s. 11 (July 1964), 264–270.

*"Samuel Richardson and His Family Circle: The Leakes," *Notes and Queries*, n.s. 11 (July 1964), 264–70.

*"Samuel Richardson and His Family Circle: Richardson's Will," *Notes and Queries*, n.s. 11 (August 1964), 300–304.

*"Samuel Richardson and His Family Circle: Richardson's Ancestry," *Notes and Queries*, n.s. 11 (September 1964), 343–347.

*"Samuel Richardson and His Family Circle: Richardson's Immediate Family," *Notes and Queries*, n.s. 11 (October 1964), 362–371.

*"Samuel Richardson and His Family Circle: William Richardson," *Notes and Queries*, n.s. 11 (November 1964), 402–406.

ⁱⁱ"Samuel Richardson and His Family Circle: Benjamin Richardson," *Notes and Queries*, n.s. 11 (December 1964), 467–469.

*"Cowper's 'An Ode on Reading Mr. Richardson's "History of Sir Charles Grandison,"'" *Papers on Language and Literature*, 2 (Winter 1966), 74–75.

*"Richardson's Helper in Creating the Character of Elias Brand," *Notes and Queries*, n.s. 14 (November 1967), 414–415.

*"The Fight for Barbara on Stage," *D. H. Lawrence Review*, 1 (Spring 1968), 72–74.

*"Henry Fielding's Son By His First Wife," *Notes and Queries*, n.s. 15 (June 1968), 212.

*"Richardson's Connection with Sir William Harrington," *Pa-

pers on Language and Literature, 4 (Summer 1968), 276–287.
*"The Composition of *Clarissa* and Its Revision before Publication," *PMLA,* 83 (September 1968), 416–428.
*"Samuel Richardson and His Family Circle," *Notes and Queries,* n.s. 15 (December 1968), 448–450.
*"Edward Young's Comment on Colley Cibber," *Notes and Queries,* n.s. 21 (July 1974), 256–257.
*"Two Names in Joseph Andrews," *Modern Philology* (May 1975), 408–409.
*"The Text of Congreve's Love For Love," *The Library,* 30 (December 1975), 334–336.
*"A Chesterfield Anecdote," *Notes and Queries,* n.s. 23 (November 1976), 494–495.
*"An Uncollected Letter by Alexander Pope," *Notes and Queries,* n.s. 24 (May-June 1977), 238.
"Amelia and Clarissa" in *A Provision of Human Nature: Essays on Fielding and Others, in Honor of Marian Austin Locke,* Ed. Donald Kay. University of Alabama: University of Alabama Press, 1977, pp. 95–110.
*"The Sources of Cantos XLII and XLIII," *Paideuma,* 6 (Winter 1977), 333–358.
*"The Sources of the Leopoldine Cantos," *Paideuma,* 7 (Spring and Fall 1978), 249–277.
*"The Source of Canto L," *Paideuma,* 8 (Spring 1979), 81–93.
*"Pound's 'Ideogrammic Method' as Illustrated in Canto XCIX," *American Literature,* 51 (May 1979), 513–518.
*"Pound's Use of Sienese Manuscripts for Cantos XLII and XLIII," *Paideuma,* 8 (Winter 1979), 513–518.
*"Without Saying 'O'," *American Notes and Queries,* 18 (1980), 142–143.
*"Note on 'e li mestiers Ecoutes,'" *Paideuma,* 9 (Fall 1980), 311–312.
*"A Note to Ezra Pound's Canto LXXXV and 'Pound and Pumpelly,'" *English Language Notes,* 17 (June 1980), 292–294.
*"American History in *Rock Drill* and *Thrones,*" *Paideuma,* 9 (Winter 1980), 417–439.
*"Herbert Hoover and the London Judge," *Paideuma,* 9 (Winter 1980), 505–507.

*"Two Notes on Ezra Pound's *Cantos*," *Modern Philology*, 78 (February 1981), 285–288.
*"'Tremaine at Two in the Morning' and Other Little Mysteries," *Paideuma*, 10 (Fall 1981), 307–310.
*"Pound's Pisan Cantos," *Explicator*, 40 (Fall 1981), 43.
*"More on Pound's Prison Experience," *American Literature*, 53 (November 1981), 469–476.
*"Ezra Pound's Use of Sources as Illustrated in His Use of Nineteenth-Century French History," *Modern Philology*, 80 (August 1982), 35–52.
*"How the Medici Went Bust," *Paideuma*, 11 (Fall 1982), 282.
*"Ezra Pound's Anti-Semitism," *South Atlantic Quarterly*, 81 (Winter 1982), 56–69.
*"Pound's Research for the Malatesta Cantos," *Paideuma*, 11 (Winter 1982), 406–419.
*"Messire Uzzano in 1442," *Paideuma*, 11 (Winter 1982), 449–450.
*"Ezra Pound on Hitler's Economic Policies," *American Literature*, 55 (March 1983), 48–54.
*"The Birth of a Nation: A Note on Pound's Canto XIX," *Philological Quarterly*, 62 (Summer 1983), 417–418.
*Review of *Samuel Richardson: A Man of Letters* by Carol Houlihan Flynn, in *Journal of English and Germanic Philology*, 82 (July 1983), 451–453.
*"Some Curious 'Facts' in Ezra Pound's *Cantos*," *ELH*, 50 (Fall 1983), 627–635.
*"The Intentional Fallacy-Fallacy and Related Contemporary Orthodoxies," *South Atlantic Quarterly*, 83 (Winter 1984), 103–113.
*"An Unpublished Pamphlet by Samuel Richardson," *Philological Quarterly*, 63 (Summer 1984), 401–409.
"In Memoriam: Ben Drew Kimpel (1915–1983)," *Paideuma*, 12 (Fall & Winter 1983), 495–497.
Review of *The Roots of Treason* by E. Fuller Torrey. *American Literature*, 56 (October 1984), 447–449.
*"'Major Forms' in Pound's *Cantos*," *Iowa Review*, 15 (Spring-Summer 1985), 51–66.

Doctoral Dissertations Written under the Direction of Thomas Cary Duncan Eaves

Slattery, William Carlin. "The Correspondence Between Samuel Richardson and Johannes Stinstra, the Dutch Translator of *Clarissa*." 1961.

Dill, Stephen Horton. "An Analysis of Some Aspects of Daniel Defoe's Prose Style." 1965.

Pierson, Robert Craig. "A Study of the Text of Richardson's *Sir Charles Grandison*." 1965.

Skinner, James Lister. "William Cowper's Use of the Heroic Couplet." 1965.

Montgomery, Lyna Lee. "The Prosodic Techniques of Edward Young and John Keats in Heroic Couplets and Blank Verse." 1967.

Talburt, Nancy Ellen Brown. "The Use of Family Relationships for Dramatic Effect in the Novels of Samuel Richardson." 1967.

Coleman, Viralene Johnson. "The Dramatic Adaptations of Richardson's *Pamela* in the 1740s." 1969.

Temple, E. R. A. "The Somber World of *Clarissa*." 1969.

Warde, William Booth. "Revisions in the Published Texts of *Clarissa*." 1969.

Tebbetts, Terrell Louis. "A Critical Study of Blake's *America*." 1971.

Humphrey, Theodore Carl. "Henry Fielding: An Annotated Bibliography of Studies and Editions. 1895–1970." 1972.

Peterson, Carrol David. "The Development of William Godwin's Thought After 1793." 1972.

Stamper, Donald Rexford. "Success and Openness in English Fiction from Richardson Through Jane Austen." 1973.

Boudreaux, David E. "An Annotated Bibliography of the Criticism and Editions of Samuel Richardson (1895–1974)." 1975.

Peterson, Jane E. "Metric and Syntactic Experimentation in Blake's Prophecies of 1788–1794." 1975.

Tulley, Anita. "Innocence and Experience as Comic Values in Restoration and Eighteenth-Century Drama." 1975.

Wood, John August. "The Reflection of Mass Culture in Restoration and Eighteenth-Century Drama." 1977.

Eastham, Leah Raye. "Charlotte Ramsay Lennox: A Critical Study of Her Novels." 1977.

Elliott, Patricia D. "A Critical Variorum Edition of William Blake's *The Book of Urizen*." 1977.

Bruton, John Whitley. "Colley Cibber's *The Double Gallant: Or, The Sick Lady's Cure* A Critical, Old-Spelling Edition." 1978.

Coy, Julius Garbett. "William Wycherly as a Poet: A Study of His *Miscellany Poems*." 1978.

Duke, Kathleen Mary. "Women's Education in the Eighteenth-Century British Novel." 1980.

Musa, Mohammed Ali. "The Subterranean Caverns: The East and Its Progeny in Eighteenth-Century English and French Literature." 1981.

Lawson, Tom O. "Samuel Richardson's *Sir Charles Grandison* and Its Influence on Jane Austen's *Persuasion* and George Eliot's *The Mill on the Floss*." 1983.

Scott, John Walter. "Swift and the Grotesque: To Vex Rather Than Divert." 1985.

Van Laningham, Kathy L. Mandrell. "The Memoirs of Count de Gramont: A New Translation and Annotation." 1986.

Notes on Contributors

James B. Meriwether received his undergraduate degree from the University of South Carolina and his graduate degrees from Princeton. Now McClintock Professor of Southern Letters at the University of South Carolina, he has written extensively upon Faulkner, Simms, and other Southern writers.

Anne M. Blythe, managing editor of Seajay Press, received her undergraduate and graduate degrees from the University of South Carolina. Most of her work has been devoted to Southern women writers, and her essay in this volume is her first publication upon a male writer.

Linda Elkins McDaniel has published articles on Simms, Poe, Styron, and Faulkner. Now at the University of Southern Mississippi, she teaches Literature of the South and American Literature and is currently writing Annotations to William Faulkner's *Flags in the Dust* for Garland Press.

Nicholas G. Meriwether graduated in 1987 with a degree in history from Princeton University. His senior thesis was an analysis of Simms's critical philosophy, which included an early version of his essay for this book.

James E. Kibler, Jr., is Professor of English at the University of Georgia. Books on Simms under his authorship or editorship include *The Pseudonymous Publications of William Gilmore Simms* (1976), *The Poetry of William Gilmore*

Simms: An Introduction and Bibliography (1979), and *William Gilmore Simms: A Reference Guide* (1980). David Moltke-Hansen, like Simms, studied at the College of Charleston and did his graduate work in history at the University of South Carolina. Author of numerous essays on South Carolina cultural history, Moltke-Hansen co-edited and contributed to *Intellectual Life in Antebellum Charleston.* He is director of the South Carolina Historical Society.

Mary Ann Wimsatt is Associate Professor of English at Southwest Texas State University, where she serves as managing editor of *Studies in American Humor.* The author of articles on Simms and other Southern writers, she served as associate editor of *The History of Southern Literature.* Her book on Simms will be published by Louisiana State University Press in 1988.

Rayburn S. Moore is Professor of English, University of Georgia. He is the author of a book (1972) and many articles on Hayne and of several essays on Simms, the editor of Hayne's letters (1982), and a senior editor of *The History of Southern Literature* (1985).

Miriam J. Shillingsburg, Professor of English at Mississippi State University, has held an NEH Fellowship and a Fulbright lectureship in Australia. She is the author of numerous articles on Simms and other nineteenth-century American authors as well as an editor of Washington Irving.

John McCardell is Professor of History and Dean of Academic Development and Planning at Middlebury College. The author of, among other works, *The Idea of a Southern Nation* (1979), which received the Allan Nevins Prize of the Society of American Historians, he is now at work on a general history of the Old South and a biography of William Gilmore Simms.

Louis D. Rubin, Jr., University Distinguished Professor of English at the University of North Carolina at Chapel Hill, is completing a book-length study of Simms, Poe, Timrod and the literary situation of the Old South. He is a native of Charleston, South Carolina.

Leighton Rudolph took his undergraduate degree at the University of Arkansas and his graduate degrees at Harvard. Since 1947 he has taught American literature at the University of Arkansas. He was a colleague and friend of Duncan Eaves for almost four decades.